Emotions and Sociology

A selection of previous *Sociological Review* Monographs

Life and Work History Analyses[†]
ed. Shirley Dex

The Sociology of Monsters[†]
ed. John Law

Sport, Leisure and Social Relations[†]
eds John Horne, David Jary and Alan Tomlinson

Gender and Bureaucracy[*]
eds Mike Savage and Anne Witz

The Sociology of Death: theory, culture, practice[*]
ed. David Clark

The Cultures of Computing
ed. Susan Leigh Star

Theorizing Museums[*]
ed. Sharon Macdonald and Gordon Fyfe

Consumption Matters[*]
eds Stephen Edgell, Kevin Hetherington and Alan Warde

Ideas of Difference[*]
eds Kevin Hetherington and Rolland Munro

The Laws of the Markets[*]
ed. Michael Callon

Actor Network Theory and After[*]
eds John Law and John Hassard

Whose Europe? The turn towards democracy[*]
eds Dennis Smith and Sue Wright

Renewing Class Analysis[*]
eds Rosemary Cromptom, Fiona Devine, Mike Savage and John Scott

Reading Bourdieu on Society and Culture
ed. Bridget Fowler

The Consumption of Mass
ed. Nick Lee and Rolland Munro

The Age of Anxiety: Conspiracy Theory and the Human Sciences
eds Jane Parish and Martin Parker

Utopia and Organization
ed. Martin Parker

[†]Available from The Sociological Review Office, Keele University, Keele, Staffs ST5 5BG.
[*]Available from Marston Book Services, PO Box 270, Abingdon, Oxon OX14 4YW.

The Sociological Review Monographs

Since 1958 *The Sociological Review* has established a tradition of publishing Monographs on issues of general sociological interest. The Monograph is an edited book length collection of research papers which is published and distributed in association with Blackwell Publishing. We are keen to receive innovative collections of work in sociology and related disciplines with a particular emphasis on exploring empirical materials and theoretical frameworks which are currently under-developed. If you wish to discuss ideas for a Monograph then please contact the Monographs Editor, Rolland Munro, at *The Sociological Review*, Keele University, Newcastie-under-Lyme, North Staffordshire, ST5 5BG.

Emotions and Sociology

Edited by Jack Barbalet

Blackwell Publishing/The Sociological Review

First published in 2002

Blackwell Publishing
108 Cowley Road, Oxford, OX4 1JF, UK

and
350 Main Street
Malden, MA 02148, USA

British Library Cataloguing in Publication Data

A CIP catalogue record for this book is available from the British Library

Library of Congress Cataloging-in-Publication Data applied for

ISBN 1-4051-0557-7

Printed and bound by Page Brothers, Norwich.

This book is printed on acid-free paper.

Contents

Contents

Introduction: why emotions are crucial

Jack Barbalet

Introduction

The word 'emotion' carries a lot of weight: indeed, it is overburdened with meaning. Its widest application is probably as a term of pejorative evaluation. When it is used here, though, emotion simply indicates what might be called an experience of involvement. A person may be negatively or positively involved with something, profoundly involved or only slightly involved, but however or to what degree they are involved with an event, condition or person it necessarily matters to them, proportionately. That it matters, that a person cares about something, registers in their physical and dispositional being. It is this experience that is emotion, not the subject's thoughts about their experience, or the language of self-explanation arising from the experience, but that immediate contact with the world the self has through involvement.

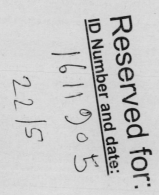

...motion and reason typically leads ...gard it as an inappropriate category ...ological and behavioural pathology, ...ominate. Indeed, there is a tradition ...ndividual social actors derives from ... executing them, under the aegis ...tracting impulses and emotions. ... Max Weber, *The Protestant Ethic* ...it is by no means confined to this

...is the fact that all actions, and ...ilitating emotions if successful ...ow could a person deal compe- ...emotion of confidence in their ...ons of enabling others, without ...ncourage success, without the ...rests, and so on. Reason, too,

Blackwell Publishing,
, MA 02148, USA.

requires its back-ground emotions, without which there is no reason; these include feelings of calmness, security, confidence, and so on. This is not an argument against reason, only against the inflation of reason at the expense of emotion. Without the appropriate emotions underpinning and supporting reason, reason turns to its opposite.

A well-developed appreciation of emotions is absolutely essential for sociology because no action can occur in a society without emotional involvement. By society I mean an interactive system. The smallest society in this sense, then, is a single human person choosing between alternatives, for such a choice requires an internal dialogue. And choice itself must include the choice to do nothing. Everything, then, in the human universe, requires emotional involvement. Consider the issue of social order, for example, arguably a key concern in sociology.

Emotion and social explanation

Conventional accounts explain the inclination of people in society to conform, more or less, to an established order of practices in terms of external constraints, especially the constraints of force or of a system of norms. These alternatives are often thought to be exhaustive of all possibilities, giving rise respectively to what are known as the 'coercion' and 'integration' theories of society. An entire industry has arisen through attempts to reconcile these opposed, partial and flawed approaches, but it is an industry that adds little to the currency of sociological thought.

Social order and stable conformity cannot be explained by coercive force, because the likely outcome of coercive force is resistance, either organized and therefore conflictual, or frictional resistance, productive of not order but the disorder of apathy, indifference and alienation. Similarly, social order cannot be explained by a system of social norms because in any unequal society, which is to say in *any* society, there is an absence of a general agreement concerning norms. Instead, we find that social groups tend to adhere to norms and values that reflect their position in the unequal pattern of the distribution of resources.

More recently there has arisen another account of social conformity that shares with an emotions approach the idea of 'internal' rather than 'external' constraint. But instead of operating in terms of an emotion, say shame, following Elias (1939), for instance, or Scheff (1988), or any emotion at all, this account operates in terms of internal calculation. Rational choice theory holds that individuals conform to a social order because it is expedient to do so, on the basis of a calculation regarding the costs of not conforming weighed against the benefits of conforming. It is doubtful that this account offers much. First, people seldom have information regarding the actual costs and actual rewards of a particular choice of action, and therefore do not have the means to make a real calculation. Second, actions in society occur in a flow, and there is seldom a timeframe available that would be required to make the necessary calculations.

The situation is in fact even more difficult than these considerations suggest: the costs and befits of most actions cannot be known until after the action is concluded, therefore there is never relevant information for a decision based on a calculation to act. The 'expedient calculator' of rational choice theory is therefore simply a metaphor; it points to a linguistic turn consistent with prevailing cultural symbols but does not accurately represent the events to which it refers.

As a matter of fact, one function of emotion is precisely to solve the problems that a reliance on calculation would create. Our emotional reactions to events include those feelings that indicate whether an experience is likely to lead to pleasure or pain, to be favourable or unfavourable. That is to say that emotions point to problems a person faces, and they delimit a set of likely solutions. And they do this practically instantaneously. Not only do emotions provide instant evaluation of circumstance, they also influence the disposition of the person for a response to those circumstances. It is for these reasons that it is possible to say that *emotions link structure and agency*. This is an absolutely crucial proposition for sociology, seldom stated and under-appreciated, demonstrably true and heuristically invaluable.

The structured differentiation of emotions

Emotions are not simply in individual acts of conformity but in social interactions more broadly. A general theory of emotions based on this idea is in Kemper, *A Social Interactional Theory of Emotions* (1978). There are three basic steps in Kemper's argument: first, all social interactions can be characterized in terms of two formal dimensions of social relations, namely power and status, or what might be called involuntary and voluntary compliance, for instance, or constraint and regard, and so on. Power and status can be scaled in terms of whether they are in excess of what is required in the relationship, adequate for it, or insufficient. Agency—who might be responsible for too much or not enough power, say—can similarly be differentiated, as 'self' or 'other'. The second step holds that specific physiological processes are stimulated by specific experiences of power and status. This idea is well known: there is a direct relationship, for instance, between social stress and myocardial infarction. Finally, Kemper shows that particular emotions are physiologically specific. For instance, anxiety is associated with secretion of the hormone epinephrine; anger is associated with secretion of the hormone noradrenaline. The physiological processes in Kemper's account are thus the mechanisms that translate the structure of interactions into the emotions of the actors.

This is such a beautiful model because it links biology and sociology in an entirely non-reductive way. But that part of the argument need not detain us here, as the physiological processes can be conceived as constituting an inter-

ry variable and our methods textbooks tell us to pay attention only to the independent and dependent variables; in this case, the social structure and the emotions. We are then left with the very compelling idea that the particular emotions that people experience arise out of the structure of the relations of power and status in which they are implicated.

So, if you have insufficient power in a relationship it is likely that you will experience fear, if you have excess power it is likely you will experience guilt. If you have excess status it is likely that you will experience shame, if insufficient status, depression, and so on. In this treatment Kemper gives formal representation to what novelists, for instance, have always relied upon. Novelist can produce in their readers an awareness of a character's emotional state by merely indicating the situation and relationships they are in, because the situation or relationships provide the eliciting conditions for the emotions that persons experience. This is the crucial point: emotion experienced in my body as subjective feeling is part of a transaction between myself and another. The emotion is *in* the social relationship. This last point needs to be amplified.

Emotion *is* in the social relationship, certainly. But what part of the social relationship is emotion? It is that part of the relationship in which the subject of the relationship, the person in the relationship, is in some way changed, and, in being so changed, is disposed to change the relationship itself. Here is the very dynamism of social interaction and social relationships, in the emotion. I interact with another whose status is in excess of what is required to adequately execute the interaction, and that precipitates my anger. I experience the anger as a transformation of my disposition, from accepting the other to remonstrating with the other to cease being haughty or interfering with the way I do things. Depending on how my anger is understood by the other, she will have a commensurate emotional reaction to it, with subsequent changes in her behaviour. And so it will go on.

To say again what was said earlier: emotion is a necessary link between social structure and social actor. The connection is never mechanical because emotions are normally not compelling but inclining. But without the emotions category, accounts of situated actions would be fragmentary and incomplete. Emotion is provoked by circumstance and is experienced as transformation of dispositions to act. It is through the subject's active exchange with others that emotional experience is both stimulated in the actor and orientating of their conduct. Emotion is directly implicated in the actors' transformation of their circumstances, as well as the circumstances' transformation of the actors' disposition to act.

Collective emotions

Kemper's model raises the question of theorizing collective emotions because it imputes structural factors in the etiology of emotional experience. Thus persons sharing common structural circumstances might experience common emotions, without recourse to contagion (Hatfield, Cacioppo and Rapson, 1994), for instance, or other factors. And yet, such aggregations of emotional experience are not group emotions. What I call here group emotions, as opposed to aggregative emotions, arise not because of merely common structural causes but because of relations between members of a group. J.L. Monero's (1951; 1953) work in sociometry is one approach that indicated the reality and significance of group emotions: attractions and repulsions are experienced at the individual level but necessarily underlie the formation, direction and persistence of groups as indivisible entities. There are other sources to this general idea (see Smith and Crandell, 1984). A relevant concept in this regard is that of emotional climate (see Barbalet, 1998, pp. 158–60; de Rivera, 1992).

An emotional climate does not require that every person subject to it experience the same emotion. As emotional climates are group phenomenon and as different people occupy different positions within groups, perform different roles and have different capacities, it is indeed likely that individuals will differ from each other in their emotional experiences. Yet in their relationships they will each contribute to the feelings of the group *qua* group, to its emotional formation or climate. Collective emotions are discussed in various ways in a number of the papers below.

The social significance of emotion is registered by a consideration of particular social processes or institutions. Consider the phenomenon of unemployment, for instance. Before dealing with the emotional dimensions of unemployment it is necessary to say something about unemployment in general. First, the link that employment provides, between the individual and a meaningful relationship with the larger community, is lost in unemployment (Lane, 1991, pp. 260–1), so that unemployment is not merely loss of employment but of a range of associations and capacities, some of which are ostensibly unconnected with employment. Indeed, Karl Mannheim describes how unemployment destroys an individual's 'life plan', and in doing so is much more likely to create 'apathy rather than rebellion in the minds of its victims' (1940, p. 181). Second, the sources of advantage in labour markets may translate to aggravated disadvantage in unemployment. For instance, technologically skilled workers who suffer structural rather than cyclical unemployment may face longer periods of unemployment than less skilled and therefore more mobile workers. These and similar fundamental experiences necessarily contain compelling emotional dimensions. In summary, those who fail in labour markets, according to Robert Lane, following Marie Jahoda, 'learn externality, passivity, helplessness, the importance of luck, chance, and fate . . . [and] many will learn self blame, demoralization, and depression' (Lane, 1991, p. 170).

Thinking of those emotions explained in the simple Kemperian model, it can be predicted that unemployment will typically generate fear, through an insufficiency of one's own power in labour market relations; shame, through an excess of status in terms of the ratio of market relevant qualities to market performance; depression, through an insufficiency of status in terms of the ratio of past standing to present standing; and anger, through an excess of the status of other's standing in labour markets, be they employers, managers, employed workers, or whoever. This is a simple and minimal set of probabilities, to which others must be added. Differential time frames impact on emotional experience, especially around the emotion of hopelessness (see Kurt Lewin, 1948). Resentment has been identified as a key emotion among declining groups in trade cycle movements (Bensman and Vidich, 1962, pp. 37–9). The likelihood of experience of moral indignation in those who are disadvantaged by a distributional system they regard as legitimate can also be mentioned in this context (Barbalet, 2002). Another emotion also typical of the condition of unemployment is boredom (Barbalet, 1999).

No matter what the social phenomenon, its processes and outcome can always be better understood when its emotional dimensions are identified. That is because the emotional dimensions of a thing determine its social significance and course.

Contributions to emotions research

At the present time, research in the sociology of emotions is no longer novel and untried. Since the mid-1970s there has been a growing number of important publications that self-consciously set out to expand the horizons of sociological writing by focussing upon emotions. Indeed, even before the advent of the term, sociology of emotions, sociological writers had demonstrated the centrality of emotions to social processes and sociological explanation. Some of these are well known still, including C. Wright Mills, George Homans, Richard Sennett, Peter Blau, Alvin Gouldner, among others, even if they are not remembered for their discussion of emotions. Others are almost entirely forgotten, such as Sven Ranulf (1933, 1934, 1938), even though their work is arguably pathbreaking (see Barbalet, 2002).

The chapters in the present volume continue, then, the work of a tradition or sub-discipline of sociology that has a strong and vigorous history. Indeed, they demonstrate that a sociological appreciation of emotions should not be construed as a mere sub-specialism of the discipline, focussed only on emotions management and social psychological in its orientation. The chapters below bring a concern with emotions to core themes of sociological inquiry. They not only contribute to our sociological understanding of emotions, they also make important contributions to the substantive fields they address—and there are a number of these.

In the first chapter below, Chris Shilling shows that we can understand the history of sociology itself, and developments within it, through the ways in which the concept of emotions has served as an organizing principle in research and explanation. The very last chapter, by Ian Burkitt, explores emotional experiences in terms of social and cultural processes. Burkitt shows how speech genres, bodily activity, and social relationship articulate together in the production of specific emotions. These two chapters demonstrate how examination of emotions enhances both social theory and sociological research.

The chapters by Mabel Berezin and Theodore Kemper each d[
of political processes in terms of emotions. Berezin explores the
emotions for political processes and institutions. The idea that
emotional is not new, of course. But Berezin's treatment of the re
them leads us to rethink how we understand not just politics but
Emotions are not episodic disruptors of but essential to politics: they sustain
political processes, underlie political action and mobilization, and are embedded in political institutions. Berezin concludes with an elaboration of the key
conceptual issues a political sociology of emotions might address.

Complementing Berezin's broad approach, Kemper's chapter focuses on the
emotions generated by a single event, namely the attacks on New York and
Washington of September 11, 2001. By distinguishing ten different publics,
Kemper demonstrates the force of his interactional theory of emotions, which
predicts the emotional content of reactions to September 11 in each of them.
Like Berezin, Kemper is also interested in the distinction between individual
level and group level emotions, and especially the different types of coping
responses that emerge for individuals on the one hand and groups on the
other. Kemper's account of the structural conditions of coping strategies, the
character of group emotional experience, and the type of coping responses
that form out of them, offers significant insights into political processes in
general.

Economics, both as financial processes and organization, is the focus of the
following two chapters, by Jocelyn Pixley and Helena Flam. Pixley shows that
while economists typically ignore emotions, core concepts of economic discourse, including interest and expectation, are inherently and profoundly emotional. She goes on to show how economic decision-making, for example, can
be best understood as a process in which emotions are not only necessary but
can be conceptualized to enhance explanatory purchase. The chapter concludes
with the significance of an emotions approach to economic practices including
economic policy. The emotional component of persons, as managers and
employees, is shown by Flam to be crucial for an understanding of economic
organizations. The sociology of organizations has long been aware of the importance of emotional display in management and the emotional costs of employment. Flam's contribution is to show that these issues do not exhaust the
relevance of emotions in organizations. Indeed, Flam moves beyond the
narrow perspective of an exclusive orientation to emotional labour and shows
how an appreciation of the role of emotions need not be confined to economic
organization but also disorganization, not merely employment but also
unemployment.

A third set of chapters, by Charlotte Bloch and Jack Barbalet, consider emotions in science and research. Bloch's chapter reports an empirical study of
academic researchers and the structural conditions of research activity. The
interactional elements of research, she shows, are competition and recognition.
Within this framework the social relationships of research require participants
to manage a number of key emotions, including those of uncertainty, shame,

.er, and pride. Bloch's account not only develops our understanding of emotions and emotional culture, but enriches the sociology of research organizations and their environments. Barbalet examines the changing and uneven
relationship between emotion and science. In doing so he outlines an approach
to the sociology of science that gives priority to the emotional engagements of
scientists, not only in terms of their motivation, but in the core activities of
scientific discovery and validation. In doing so Barbalet points to resources
neglected by conventional sociologists of science. His paper concludes by suggesting the benefits of an examination of science to a sociology of emotions,
and to a sociology of science that appreciates the constructive role of emotions.

Together, then, the chapters constituting this *Sociological Review Monograph*
achieve at least three things: first, they provide a clear statement of the significance of emotions for sociological research; second, they report on the contributions of previous sociologists who have enriched our understanding of both
emotions and the substantive fields under discussion; and finally, each chapter
that follows makes a significant contribution of its own both to the sociological study of emotions and to each of the key areas of sociology they address.
Here is the state of the art and the prospects of an exciting future for sociology.

References

Barbalet, J.M. (1998) *Emotion, Social Structure and Social Theory: A Macrosociological Approach.*
Cambridge: Cambridge University Press.
Barbalet, J.M. (1999) 'Boredom and social meaning'. *British Journal of Sociology* 50(4): 631–
46.
Barbalet, J.M. (2002) 'Moral indignation, class inequality and justice', *Theoretical Criminology.* 6(3):
279–97.
Bensman, Joseph and Arthur Vidich (1962) 'Business cycles, class, and personality'. *Psychoanalysis
and Psychoanalytic Review.* 49: 30–52.
Elias, Norbert (1939) [1978] *The History of Manners.* Oxford: Basil Blackwell.
Hatfield, Elaine, John T. Cacioppo, and Richard L. Rapson (1994) *Emotional Contagion.* Cam-
bridge: Cambridge University Press.
Kemper, Theodore D. (1978) *A Social Interactional Theory of Emotions.* New York: Wiley.
Lane, Robert (1991) *The Market Experience.* Cambridge: Cambridge University Press.
Lewin, Kurt (1948) [1973] 'Time perspective and morale'. Pp. 103–24, in his *Resolving Social
Conflicts,* edited by Gertrud Weiss Lewin. London: Souvenir Press.
Mannheim, Karl (1940) *Man and Society in an Age of Reconstruction: Studies in Modern Social
Structure.* New York: Harcourt, Brace and World.
Monero, J.L. (1951) *Sociomety, Experimental Method and the Science of Society: An Approach to a
New Political Orientation.* New York: Beacon House.
Monero, J.L. (1953) *Who Shall Survive? Foundations of Sociomety, Group Psychotherapy and Socio-
drama.* New York: Beacon House.
Ranulf, Svend (1933) *The Jealousy of the Gods and Criminal Law at Athens: A Contribution to the
Sociology of Moral Indignation. Volume 1.* Copenhagen: Levin and Munksgaard.
Ranulf, Svend (1934) *The Jealousy of the Gods and Criminal Law at Athens: A Contribution to the
Sociology of Moral Indignation. Volume 2.* Copenhagen: Levin and Munksgaard.
Ranulf, Svend (1938) *Moral Indignation and Middle Class Psychology: A Sociological Study.* Copen-
hagen: Levin and Munksgaard.

de Rivera, Joseph (1992) 'Emotional climate: social structure and emotional dynamics'. Pp. 197–218 in *International Review of Studies on Emotion,* edited by K.T. Strongman. New York: John Wiley & Sons.

Scheff, Thomas S. (1988) 'Shame and conformity: the deference-emotion system'. *American Sociological Review.* 53: 395–406.

Smith, Kenwyn K. and Stuart D. Crandell (1984) 'Exploring collective emotions'. *American Behavioral Scientist.* 27(6) 1984: 813–28.

The two traditions in the sociology of emotions

Chris Shilling

Abstract

The sociology of emotions is an established specialism within the discipline and its products have become increasingly visible parts of the sociological landscape since the late 1970s. This specialism has also demonstrated, at least to its own satisfaction, the importance of emotions for social action and order, and for those related moral issues concerned with self-determined and other-oriented action. Paradoxically, however, the relationship between the sociology of emotions and mainstream sociology remains relatively cool. Emotional issues are still portrayed in many general accounts of the discipline as a luxurious curiosity that properly resides on the outer reaches of the sociological imagination. Just as unfortunately, certain sociologists of emotions have accused the foundations of the discipline of neglecting emotional issues, and have sometimes excluded classical theorists from their discussions.

This chapter argues that emotional phenomena occupy an important place in sociology's heritage which has yet to be explicated fully by the sub-discipline. The subject of emotions, like the closely related subject of the body, may fade from various classical writings. Nevertheless, the major traditions of sociological theory developed particular orientations towards the social and moral dimensions of emotional phenomena. I begin by examining the relevance of emotions to the context out of which the discipline emerged, and then focus on how the major theorists of order (Comte and Durkheim) and (inter)action (Simmel and Weber) conceptualized emotional phenomena. The chapter concludes with a brief assessment of Parsons's contribution, and suggests that his analysis of the religious foundations of instrumental activism provides a provocative account of the relationship between values, emotions and personality that can usefully be built on.

Introduction

The sociology of emotions is now an established specialism within the discipline. Its products have become increasingly visible parts of the sociological landscape since the late 1970s and include a growing number of original and review articles (eg, Shott, 1979; Gordon, 1981; Thoits, 1989; Burkitt, 1997), and the recovery of a 'hidden history' of intellectual resources concerned with the social consequences of emotions (eg, Collins, 1975, 1987; Hammond, 1983; Shilling,

1997; Barbalet, 1998). These have been accompanied by the development of major theoretical perspectives on emotions and social life (eg, Kemper, 1978; Hochschild, 1983; Denzin, 1984; Smith, 1992), the consolidation of a 'figurational' approach concerned with the relationship between the emotional habitus of individuals and large-scale historical transformations (eg, Elias, 1939 [2000]; 1987), and the establishment of gendered and feminist perspectives on emotions that have sought to transcend what they identify as the 'malestream' bias of traditional theories (eg, Hochschild, 1975; Jaggar, 1989; Seidler, 1998). Perhaps the clearest indication of the arrival of this new sub-disciplinary area, however, has been the establishment since the mid-1980s of emotion sections within various national sociological associations, and the publication of a growing number of edited collections and texts designed to consolidate the emotions as a viable area of study (eg, Franks and McCarthy, 1989; Kemper 1990; Wentworth and Ryan, 1994; Bendelow and Williams, 1998; Williams, 2001).[1]

The sociology of emotions has also demonstrated, at least to its own satisfaction, the importance of emotions for the key sociological issues of social order and action, and the closely related moral questions of whether individuals are able to engage in self-determined action and whether they possess the will to act in the interests of others. This is evident in analyses of the effects of emotional energy, pride and shame on the binding and unbinding of social relationships (Collins, 1988; Lindholm, 1990; Scheff, 1994), the significance of emotion in structural processes (Barbalet, 1998), the importance of 'feeling rules' in obstructing self-determined actions (Hochschild, 1983), and the effects that 'technologies for the production of bystanders' exert in encouraging people to become *blasé* when witnessing the suffering of others (Tester, 1998).

If the subject of emotions is now recognized as crucial to a comprehensive understanding of key sociological questions, it would appear that the sub-discipline has come of age. Paradoxically, however, the relationship between the sociology of emotions and mainstream sociology remains relatively cool. Emotional issues are still portrayed in many general accounts of the discipline as a luxurious curiosity to be classified alongside the 'bizarre' subjects that periodically interest the outer reaches of the sociological imagination. Just as unfortunately, certain sociologists of emotions have accused the foundations of the discipline of neglecting emotional issues, and have sometimes excluded classical theorists from their discussions (eg, Thoits, 1989).

In this chapter I argue that emotional phenomena occupy an important place in sociology's heritage which has yet to be explicated fully by the sub-discipline. The subject of emotions, like the closely related subject of the body, may fade from various classical writings. Nevertheless, it is often forgotten that the major traditions of sociological theory developed particular orientations towards the social and moral dimensions of emotional phenomena. This amnesia has developed for two major reasons. First, the subject of emotions was dealt with *via* an array of disparate concepts within classical sociology, not always self-evidently relevant to the form in which contemporary analysts have examined emotional issues. Second, common interpretations of Parsons's (1937: 768) agenda, setting the definition of sociology as the science of 'common value integration', did much to erode the disciplinary status of emotions and give contemporary analysts of emotions reason to believe that classical theory is marginal to their concerns.

Contemporary accounts of the sociological tradition vary widely, yet Dawe's (1970) division of the subject into the sociologies of order and action remains a useful starting point for illuminating the place of emotions within the discipline (Barbalet, 1998). As the other contributions in this volume illustrate, other approaches developed alongside and sometimes in opposition to these traditions, yet the scope and influence of these sociologies of order and action is unrivalled (Shilling and Mellor, 2001). In analysing this heritage, I do not believe it is useful or even possible to provide a precise definition of emotions. The term itself was often marginalized within, or even missing from, the discipline's various concerns with effervescent attachments, moral sentiments, vitalistic energies, affectual actions, 'pre-social' contents, psychic responses, passions and related phenomena which might now be classified under the umbrella term 'emotions'. Nevertheless, classical sociology's analyses of these phenomena was concerned with how embodied subjects experienced and expressed their contact with the social and natural worlds (eg, Shilling, 2001). It examined the various ways in which social actors were propelled towards, cemented within or separated from these worlds, and shares many of the concerns which characterize the contemporary interest in emotions and social life.

I begin by examining the relevance of emotional issues to the social and intellectual context out of which the discipline emerged, and then focus on how the major theorists of order (Comte and Durkheim) and (inter)action (Simmel and Weber) conceptualized emotional phenomena. The chapter concludes with a brief assessment of the contribution of Talcott Parsons. Parsons has been seen as preparing the ground for the 'cognitivist' approach towards sociology which dominated the discipline from the late 1930s to the 1970s (Barbalet, 1998), yet his analysis of the religious foundations of instrumental activism provides a provocative account of the relationship between values, emotions and personality that has yet to be utilized by sociologists of emotions.

Divine order, emotions and the rise of sociology

Sociology and the modern social sciences emerged in a context shaped by the changes that occurred in the West during the centuries succeeding the medieval era, and the responses to these changes in the Enlightenment and Counter-Enlightenment. The medieval era, it has been suggested, was characterized by an affectual intensity, volatility and unpredictability far greater than is common to contemporary life. Huizinga (1924 [1955: 10]), for example, notes that experience was based around 'violent contrasts' involving a 'perpetual oscillation between despair and distracted joy, between cruelty and pious tenderness.' Elias (1939 [2000]) reaches related conclusions and associates the medieval era with an emotional *habitus* which disposed individuals to escalate arguments into deadly fights, and to take pleasure from torturing enemies. These intense emotional responses were not, however, unregulated. The medieval view of divine order held that emotional experience was integrated into a sacred moral community (a community which included this-worldly political authorities), by God's representative on earth, the Catholic Church. The incorporation of violence into legal processes through the 'trial by ordeal', for example, was often overseen by a priest. More generally, the Church sought to inspire blissful anticipation and terror through visions of salvation and damnation, and used these to bolster its authority (Camporesi, 1988). This was exemplified by the Eucharist; a ritual that was understood to involve the highly charged, literal incorporation of Christ as food into the body of the individual, and the incorporation of the individual into the Body of Christ (the Church). In short, these 'violent' and 'vascillating' passions were harnessed to rituals and forms which prevented them from making 'havoc of life' (Huizinga, 1924 [1955: 50]).

If intense experience and expression was an accepted part of daily life, political concerns about the 'emotional frenzy of the crowd' grew during the late medieval era. Displays of overindulgence in carnival celebrations, for example, often exceeded the intent of religious and civic authorities (Bakhtin, 1965 [1984]), while emotional expression flowed, 'like an oil slick', over the religious rituals that sought to order them (Durkheim, 1912 [1995: 328]). As the notion of divine order faded, subsequent attempts to answer the question of where emotions figure within human attempts to construct social and moral orders proved increasingly problematic.

The religious conflicts associated with the Reformation were of particular importance to changing attitudes towards emotions. Humanists like Montaigne held that 'part of our humanity is to accept responsibility for our bodies, our feelings . . . even if we cannot always keep these things under complete control', and sought to limit the truth claims of abstract thought (Toulmin, 1990: 40). The religious wars of the 17th century, however, created a context in which the later protagonists of modern philosophy faced political intolerance and the dogmatic claims of rival theologians. In this context, a 'Quest for Certainty' became increasingly popular among philosophers as a path to establishing truths which were ubiquitous, universal, timeless and independent of the vagaries of the emotions. This quest was based on the rational, non-partisan powers of the *mind*, and was exemplified by Descartes. Descartes claimed that the essence of our humanity subsisted in our ability to think, while our emotions were things done to us by our bodies, and turned this distinction 'into a practical contrast between (good) rationality and (bad) sentiment or impulsiveness' (Toulmin, 1990: 134–5).

Descartes exerted a major influence on the dominant western philosophical approach towards emotions, but it was Hobbes's analysis of the relationship between the passionate nature of individuals and the problem of social order that exerted an even greater effect on the foundations of sociology. Writing in the aftermath of civil war in England, Hobbes was concerned with the moral consequences of the break from medieval traditions and the rise of modern individualism (Hobbes, 1651 [1914]). This concern is associated with his conception of individuals as passionate subjects. The individual constitutes 'a 'body in motion', and the 'essential natural feature' of humans is not their potential for nobility, justice or rationality, but 'the appetites and aversions that motivate their actions' and which sustain thought and determine intellectual and moral character (Hobbes, 1650 [1962]; Gardiner, Metcalf and Beebe-Center, 1937: 184; Levine, 1995: 272).

These passions, which determined human nature, also formed the basis of civil society for Hobbes. This was not because they immediately inclined people towards contractual arrangements, but because the war to which they led stimulated in individuals appetites and aversions which subsequently inclined them to peace. Thus, individual passions include a strong desire for power and fear of death, and a propensity for 'rapacity and cruelty' which surpassed that of animals (Hobbes, 1658 [1991]: 40). Human existence was characterized by ceaseless competition, 'griefe' rather than 'pleasure', and a universal 'desire and will to hurt' (Hobbes, 1651 [1914]: 64–7; 1658 [1991]: 40, 114). Life was characterized by a 'Warre of every one against every one' in which 'every man has a Right to every things; even to another's body' (Hobbes, 1651 [1914]: 67). If passions had led people into this instinctual hell, however, they subsequently inclined people to transfer their power to an absolute sovereign; an 'artifical body which provides the framework in which the real bodies of men can find security and peace' (Turner, 1984: 88). The advantage of this single ruler, Hobbes held, was that it was 'less subject to passion than the multitude' (Gardiner, Metcalf and Beebe-Center, 1937: 185).

If Hobbes proved so influential to the development of sociology, it was because his writings addressed a concern of enduring social importance. This became especially prominent during the Enlightenment and Counter-Enlightenment. These political and intellectual movements possessed opposed views on the ability of human reason to provide the means for a society based on the moral principles of liberty, equality and fraternity. Politically, the Enlightenment supported rational orders conducive to social progress, and tended to condemn the Church's concern with emotional order as irrational, superstitious and associated with corrupt clerical authority. Intellectually, there was considerable diversity within the Enlightenment *philosophes*. Adam Smith (1776 [1950]), for example, drew a parallel between emotion and reason, and viewed sympathy and self-love as providing the possibility of a self-equillibriating market economy. Nonetheless, the dominant strand within Enlightenment thought viewed individuals as rational authors of their own actions (Cassirer, 1951; Hamilton, 1992). The Counter-Enlightenment, in contrast, opposed the primacy of reason as a means for organizing society. De Maistre's understanding of the Terror of the French Revolution as the descent of humanity into the chaos of a Godless, anarchic existence, expresses how many thinkers came to despair of the moral consequences of the Enlightenment and emphasizes the importance of emotional attachment to tradition (Nisbet, 1966: 57).

The Enlightenment and Counter-Enlightenment formed important parts of the context out of which sociology emerged, and their contrasting approaches towards emotions help us understand the place of this subject within the discipline. On the one hand, it has been suggested that sociology is a continuation of the 'critical rationalism' characteristic of Enlightenment (Hamilton, 1992). This rejects a significant place for emotions within the discipline, and justifies this with reference to the potentially nationalistic overtones of Romanticism—which reacted against the rationalism of the Enlightenment and espoused value relativism and emotion as the basis of action and community. On the other hand, commentators like Nisbet (1966) suggest that the discipline's concern with social and moral order makes it an extension of the Counter-Enlightenment's philosophically conservative concern with community, and with the emotional dimensions of meaning and order. The association of atomized, rationalized individualism with social dissolution, for example, was common in nineteenth century French thought (Lukes, 1973: 196). This perspective suggests that human emotions are an essential part of identity and order, and should be central to sociology.

It is misleading, however, to present the status of emotions in sociology as a simple derivation from Enlightenment *or* Counter-Enlightenment thought. First, historians have noted that many Enlightenment philosophers examined the power of emotions in relation to problems of social order (James, 1997). Second, it has been suggested that the Enlightenment's concern with reason and the 'faculties of the head' could not have taken shape without the parallel development of 'a previously unexplored language of the heart' (DeJean, 1997: 79). Third, while the French Revolution may be associated with the ending of an 'other-wordly' approach towards human life, its passionate promotion of reason as a human substitute blurred distinctions between 'secular rationality' and 'sacred emotion' (Durkheim, 1912 [1995]). Finally, sociology developed on the basis of different *national traditions* of philosophy as much as it did through a dialogue with Enlightenment and Counter Enlightenment thought. If we are to understand more fully the significance sociology attributed to emotions, it is to these traditions we must turn.

Two traditions in the sociology of emotions

The writings of Comte and Durkheim, and Simmel and Weber, are most prominently associated with laying and developing the discipline's concerns with order and action. The role and status accorded to emotions in their writings is related to the wider French and German traditions of social thought to which they belong.

Order and emotions

French thought, from Montesquieu onwards, generally identifies society as a supra-individual phenomenon which possesses the capacity to generate emotional orientations in individuals that are supportive of social and moral order. Society is the source of those moral sentiments and thoughts instilled into individuals through such institutions as the family and education. The embodied individual, in contrast, is marked by a duality consisting of asocial impulses and social capacities; capacities that need to be stimulated and harnessed if people are to join together into a moral order.

These assumptions informed the works of major French philosophers irrespective of their political allegiances. The writings of Rousseau and de Maistre, for example, were associated respectively with the Enlightenment and Counter-Enlightenment. Rousseau idealized the human condition in the 'state of nature', providing a stark contrast to Hobbes's view. Nevertheless, Rousseau's 'natural man' is motivated by instinct and impulse: it is only in civil society that such 'animalistic' traits are transformed into a moral sense of justice and duty. Although private property corrupts human's natural instincts, the ultimate emergence of the 'general will' would provide an emotional, intellectual and moral foundation for good government. If Rousseau ultimately attributes precedence to the capacities of the social whole over the instincts of the 'natural individual', so too does de Maistre (Levine, 1995: 154–5, 174–5). De Maistre focused on common authority, and on the need for society to structure the emotions. Individuals are governed by 'dark instincts' he argued, yet social order could draw strength from people's emotional attachments to superstition, obscure saints and rituals (Berlin, 1979: 22–3).

This is the context in which the French 'inventor' of sociology, Comte, and his successor, Durkheim, took as their starting point already existing 'society'; a category that possessed the status of a moral absolute in their writings. Critical of theories suggesting society was an aggregate of individuals, they viewed the social whole as an organism, as possessing parts that fulfilled needs in relation to the 'health' of the whole, and as able to stimulate morally positive emotions in individuals. Both theorists recognized the importance of emotions for social action, then, but emphasized the capacity of the *collectivity* to stimulate and direct these emotions in a manner supportive of moral order.

Comte: the positive polity and emotional fetishism

Comte conceived of positivism as a theoretical approach and a combination of methods designed to gain scientifically valid data *and* increase the moral content of society. Positivism was not simply a means for investigating society in terms of what Durkheim later called 'social facts', but sought to portray and contribute to society as a transcendent moral entity that embraced the emotional and intellectual capacities of people as they developed during human evolution. This is evident in his assessment of the Enlightenment. Comte welcomed the Enlightenment liberation of human thought from traditional knowledge and suspicion, yet believed that Enlightenment secularism, individuality and rationality were associated with an egoism and materialism that eroded the social emotions and moral values underpinning social cohesion (Comte, 1853, Vol. II:

37; Nisbet, 1966: 228; Pickering, 1993: 263, 693). Instead of constituting a culminating moment in history, the Enlightenment was just one episode in the evolution of humankind. Intellectual development and the stimulation of collective emotions progress *together* through the civilizing process envisaged by Comte; a process which resulted in his utopian notion of the 'positive polity' (Comte, 1853, Vol. II: 157).

Comte's conception of the positive polity reflects two major related features of his work. First, it was developed through organismic analogizing in which society was conceived of as a social organism equal to the individual organism in biology (Pickering, 1993: 208). Second, it incorporated a view of morality which culminated in an evolutionary sophisticated 'religion of humanity' possessed of the capacity to stimulate emotions that bind individuals into a sense of unity encompassing past and present generations (Comte, 1853, Vol. II: 555–6; Pickering, 1997: 31–2). This religion answers a permanent emotional need in individuals, the need to love something greater than the self (Aron, 1965: 103).

Comte's concern with the importance of emotion is embedded within his view of human nature. Comte referred to human nature as the *tableau cerebral* and suggested that it might be regarded as twofold (consisting of the heart and mind), or threefold (consisting of two dimensions of the heart—sentiment/affection and action/will—together with the mind). Comte also argued that the impulse to act comes from the heart rather than the intelligence, which only guides or seeks to control this emotional impulse to act (Aron, 1965: 88). Human action of any sort possesses a relationship to emotional impulses, but these impulses could be channelled or shaped in different ways in different epochs, and could be used to motivate that moral action (action prompted by feelings and ideas of empathy, altruism and self-sacrifice) essential to social order (Comte, 1853, Vol. I: 150). The positive polity provided the most effective context in which this moral action could be motivated, however, and constituted Comte's ultimate solution to the problem of order. Once established, Comte suggested that it could transform the emotional energies of its members, imbuing them with moral propensities congruent with a religion of humanity, even though they would still be subject to the pressure of biological appetites and egoistic strivings (Comte, 1853, Vol. II: 350–2; Levine, 1995).

The organismic analogizing central to Comte's analysis of the positive polity was validated by subsequent scholars who transformed it into an explicit form of functionalism (Turner and Maryanski, 1998: 110–111). His conception of a religion of humanity, and his associated analysis of fetishism, however, has been referred to as 'positivist wine poured into medieval bottles' and prompted people to describe him as a 'mad religious reformer' (Nisbet, 1966: 58).[2] This helps explain why Comte's concerns with the emotional foundations of humanity have rarely been taken seriously by sociologists. Nevertheless, his analysis of religous fetishism is worth examining here as it displays a concern with emotional transcendence that became central to sociology.

Fetishism occurs when people invest objects with values and powers that actually stem from human actions and social relationships. It is generally associated with Marx's analysis of how commodity circulation alienates people from their essential humanity. Comte did not want to abolish fetishism, though, but saw in it something enduring within human nature. In the early stages of the civilizing process, fetishism was an 'empire of the passions' that endowed all types of phenomena with energy and god-like qualities (Comte, 1853, Vol. II: 190), yet it could also stimulate moral action by taking people *beyond* themselves and promoting in them a sense of affinity between the universe and humanity (Comte, 1853, Vol. II: 190). It may be difficult for modern minds to empathize with the primitive world of fetishism, but the emotional impetus that gave it life remains powerful (Comte, 1853, Vol. II: 190). Comte (1853, Vol. II: 190) argued that our 'high intellectual culture' cannot prevent us from being placed into a state of 'radical fetishism' by overwhelming hope or fear, and hoped sociology could stimulate a new fetishism that would centre on the celebration of humanity (Pickering, 1993: 698–9).

Comte's vision of positive sociology culminates in an organically and morally integrated positive polity that is analogous to a perfectly functioning human body. A major problem with his work for many critics, however, involves their view that his analysis of emotion was driven by religious considerations. This view has predominated, yet Comte's consideration of emotions as a medium through which moral action and social order are reproduced was developed by his successor, Emile Durkheim.

Durkheim: symbols and social sentiments

Durkheim's writings on social solidarity are centrally concerned with collective effervescence; a notion designed to capture the idea of social force at its birth. Collective effervescence induces changes in individuals's emotional experience and expression, and in their mental apprehensions of the social world. It spreads 'contagiously' between individuals, is expressed through shared patterns of bodily marking, gesture and action, and is able to substitute the world immediately available to our perceptions for another, moral world in which people interact on the basis of a shared system of symbolic representations (Durkheim, 1912 [1995]; 1914 [1973]). This effervescence is initiated by human gatherings, which generate 'a sort of electricity' that launches individuals 'to an extraordinary height of exaltation', and is mediated by socially sanctioned rituals (Durkheim, 1912 [1995: 217]). The pervasiveness of this stimulation is such that there 'is virtually no instant of our living in which a certain rush of energy fails to come to us from outside ourselves' (Durkheim, 1912 [1995: 213]).

How does this analysis of emotional energy fit with Durkheim's definition of sociology as the study of 'social facts', things that are 'above, beyond and out of reach' of individuals (Durkheim, 1895 [1982])? 'Social facts' may not appear to accord emotions much significance, but refers to a continuum of phenomena ranging from major institutional structures to types of *feeling* promoted by collective gatherings. Furthermore, while Durkheim's (1895 [1982]) early writings regard social facts as a collective *constraint* on individuals, his later work empha-

18

sizes how they represent the common symbolic and emotional processes which *positively integrate* individuals into social and moral orders (Lukes, 1982: 5). It is this concern with the integrative functions of social facts that helps explain why emotions became central to his theory of society (Shilling, 2003).

Durkheim portrayed society as expressed through a symbolic order; a collective representations of signs, myths, ideas and beliefs common to both the consciousness and the conscience of individuals within a social group. These symbols constituted the forms through which 'individuals imagine the society of which they are members and the obscure yet intimate relations they have with it' (Durkheim, 1912 [1995: 227]). They do not stand alone, however, nor do they only constrain thought. Instead, collective symbols represent the outcome of the ritual processes through which collective effervescence becomes conscious of itself (Durkheim, 1912 [1995: 227, 238]). These processes occur when emotions are structured through various rites to 'fix' themselves to those symbols that are central to people's identity and understanding. This transfer of energy helps a group become conscious of itself as a moral community, binds people together, and structures the *inner lives* of individuals in accordance with collective symbols (Durkheim, 1912 [1995: 221–3], 239; Gane, 1983: 4).

The emotional power of these ritual processes has been illustrated with reference to Durkheim's account of the piacular rite of mourning (Barbalet, 1994), yet is also evident in 'heroic' actions. In the case of self-sacrifice, for example, Durkheim looks to the soldier struggling to defend the country's flag on the battlefield and suggests that 'the soldier who dies for his flag dies for his country'. This sacrifice of life for the sake of the symbol can only be explained because the flag has become charged with the emotional power of the collective life of the country (Durkheim, 1912 [1995: 222]).

Why does the symbolic order of society exert such a profound emotional effect on individuals? For Durkheim, this is because the symbolic order is built around representations of what is *sacred* to group life; things 'set apart and forbidden' from the profane, mundane world of daily life. Consequently, it is able to stimulate an intense emotional effervescence in those who experience its contents. This effervescence is so powerful, indeed, that Durkheim (1912 [1995]: 44) argues that there can be no society without a sense of the sacred: the sacred energizes the symbolic order of society and motivates people to act in relation to the moral norms of that order.

Durkheim's writings have been criticized for being functionalist, yet while the collective emotional experience of the sacred can reinforce social order, it can also stimulate social change and revolution. The sacred can be benevolent, life-giving and associated with order, love and gratitude, or can be violent, death-bringing and associated with disorder, fear and horror (Durkheim, 1912 [1995: 412–6]). Durkheim's writings on the French Revolution of 1798, for example, were part of a broader concern with the effervescence that characterizes creative and revolutionary epochs in which social change revitalizes society. The Revolution involved a stimulation of emotional energies that produced both superhuman heroism and bloody barbarism, as ordinary individuals became transformed into new, more extreme beings (Durkheim, 1912 [1995: 213]). Nevertheless, along with this violent transformation of individuals, effervescent actions transformed a range of profane phenomena into sacred things which *strengthened* revolutionary society. Despite the avowedly anti-religious character of the Revolution, notions of Fatherland, Liberty and Reason assumed a sacred quality which exerted an emotionally solidifying impact on the new society (Durkheim, 1912 [1995: 216]).

Durkheim, like Comte, not only accorded a prominent role to the collective stimulation of emotions in the constitution of social life, but addressed the question of what it is about individuals that allows them to be affected in this manner. Durkheim (1914 [1973]) held that individuals possess a *homo duplex* nature, being internally divided between individual, egoistic, asocial impulses and social capacities for collective thought and emotion. These opposed features of human being mean that the incorporation of individuals into a social order is never guaranteed, but also ensures that individuals are emotionally and cognitively receptive to collective existence (Durkheim, 1912 [1995: 209, 221, 239, 274]). This tension between the social and asocial pole of humans provides a foundation for social revitalization and conflict, yet also a basis for social decay. As Durkheim's (1897 [1952]) study of suicide suggests, without the sacred forces of collective effervescence the power of society as an integrative force can fade, and individuals can even lose their thirst for life.

Durkheim places great importance on the relationship between the symbolic and moral order of society, and emotionally effervescent action. The effervescent 'stimulating action of society' should not be seen simply in terms of social order or change, however, but as an *economy of energy* which prompts different modes of action resulting in different social outcomes. Durkheim argued that sacred forces have an intensely virulent energy that are 'always on the point of escaping the places they occupy and invading all that passes within their reach' (Durkheim, 1912 [1995: 322]). In a society full of collective vitality, for example, 'surplus' energy frequently finds expression in the production of works of art and new ideals and forms of action (Pickering, 1984: 529–30). Durkheim's suggestion (1912 [1995: 353]) here is that the collective effervescence experience of the sacred *strengthens* individual minds and actions; individuals are revitalized by the heightening of emotion. This energy needs regular replenishing, however, if it is not to fade, if individuals are not to retreat into their egoistic impulses, and if society is not to fall into moral decay (Durkheim, 1912 [1995: 342, 385]).

Action and emotions

If Comte and Durkheim belong to a French tradition of thought that started from the social whole, the German tradition began from the creative and ethical capacities of the *individual* and invested this figure with the responsibility for rising above their natural impulses and affects and constructing their own social and moral environment (Levine, 1995). In this context, it developed two dominant views towards emotions. On the one hand, the likes of Kant (1797 [1985])

20

viewed emotions as an impediment to self-determining actions. People's moral orientations derived from the inherent human capacity to *transcend* emotions and desires and comply with the universal 'categorical imperative'. On the other hand, a clear distinction was made by Nietzsche and others between the natural affects that reflected human immanence, and those emotionally wilful capacities that enabled people to transcend their limitations and become their true selves. Herder (1784–91 [1968]), for example, extolled sentiment as the basis on which individuals achieved transcendence, believing that people craved for spiritual self-determination, for moral independence and moral salvation. He drew culturally and morally relativistic conclusions from his analysis, yet shared with Kant a concern with 'nature-transcending and self-determining subjects' (Levine, 1995: 187–8).

This priority accorded to the self-transcending individual profoundly influenced Simmel and Weber. Nevertheless, they were also sensitive to how individual acts could produce irrational outcomes which *constrained* their subsequent capacity for emotional experience and freely chosen action.

Simmel: Interaction and the emotional degradation of the 'moral soul'

Simmel's analyses of the rationalizing effects of modernity on personality, and the prominence of the *blasé* attitude as a means of coping with the sensory stimuli of the metropolis, have provided a rich resource for analysts of emotions (Gerhards, 1986 [1994]). It is Simmel's concept of the 'moral soul', however, that is key to his concern with this subject. Simmel (1914 [1997]) views the soul as an individual possession: it stimulates the need to develop a unique personality (which integrates our emotions and intellect around a coherent identity), and helps resolve internal conflicts between our pre-social and individualized emotions and abilities and our social capacities which may obstruct this development (Simmel, 1904 [1997: 43]; 1908a [1971: 252]). If the soul encourages the development of an integrated personality, however, the realization of this goal remains problematic. The soul can be developed only through interaction, yet the forms through which interaction occurs ultimately ossify and blunt this development, leaving a gap between an individual's vital, emotional being and their ability to express what is essential to their life.

Simmel argues that interactions are initiated and framed as a result of what he views as 'primary emotions' or pre-social contents (eg, erotic, religious or aggressive impulses) that propel individuals towards others, and the mental forms individuals employ in orientating themselves to others (Simmel, 1908b [1971]: 23; 1908c [1971]; Levine, 1971: xxxvii; Gerhards, 1986 [1994]).[3] Interaction *develops*, however, via the creation of reciprocal mental orientations and 'secondary', social emotions that derive from the exchanges and sacrifices integral to human associations (Simmel, 1907 [1990: 82]; Simmel, 1908c [1971]). 'Gratitude' and 'faithfulness', for example, are central to the maintenance of interactional forms and the development of personality. Gratitude is an internalized, emotionally experienced 'moral memory of mankind' which originates when an individual receives in interaction any sacrificial good such as a complement (Simmel, 1950: 388). Gratitude can prompt new interactions, and 'ties together different elements of society via microscopic but infinitely tough threads' (Simmel, 1950: 395, 392). Faithfulness also derives from the sacrificial character of interaction. Irrespective of the motives for establishing a relationship, its development may stimulate a deep inner feeling of faithfulness, binding interactants together after the motive that initiated that relationship has gone (Simmel, 1950: 379–87). Society, indeed, 'could simply not exist, as it does, for any length of time', without the existence of faithfulness to supplement and bind together the impulses, passions and interests of individuals (Simmel, 1912 [1997: 170]; 1950: 379).

Social emotions allow the soul to express itself by providing a foundation for the personality to development through stable relationships that resist the whims of passing impulses. Nevertheless, there remains a fundamental tension for Simmel between those forms that actually exist, and those that allow for the ongoing development of personality. Forms arise from and allow for the expression of life's vital contents, yet acquire 'a logic and lawfulness of their own' which alienates them from the dynamic responsible for their creation (Simmel, 1918 [1971: 375]). People may develop a faithfulness towards particular interactional forms, yet these forms soon become distanced from the individualities of their participants and no longer provide them with a means of expressing their individuality. This solidification of forms is exemplified in Simmel's writings on the transformation of emotions in modernity.

Simmel associates the metropolis and the money economy with a qualitative change in emotional life. While pre-modern times were characterized by emotionally saturated relationships that encompassed the individual, modernity possesses an intellectualist character based on psychological foundations that confront the 'swift and continuous shift of external and internal stimuli' (Simmel, 1907 [1990: 444]; Simmel, 1903 [1971: 325]). With every day lived in the city, the individual confronts a velocity of sensory contrasts that make 'the slower, more habitual, more smoothly flowing rhythm of the sensory-mental phase of small town and rural existence' impossible to maintain (Simmel, 1903 [1971: 325]). The money economy intensifies this situation by treating *everything* in terms of exchange value (Simmel, 1907 [1990: 444]). This promotes the domination of means over ends and promotes a moral relativism in which money becomes a universal evaluator of worth. People become drained of emotional vitality, distanced from stable emotional relationships, and develop an 'emotional screen' against intense affects (Simmel, 1907 [1990: 255, 429–30, 491, 512]).

This defensive screen or 'psychic response' to modernity has at its centre cynicism and the *blasé* attitude. The *cynical attitude* revels in demonstrating that moral ideals are available to anyone able to buy them. Respect and admiration are offered to those with money, and denied to those without it, irrespective of their moral character (Simmel, 1907 [1990: 255]). In becoming *blasé*, the individual adjusts their nerves to city life, nerves which have become exhausted by overstimulation, by minimizing their response to them (Simmel, 1903 [1971: 329–30]). This promotes a devaluation of one's own and other people's worth through 'an alienated emotion of distance, remoteness, and indifference' (Barbalet, 1998: 55). Gratitude and faithfulness disappear and are replaced by a 'rationally calculated economic egoism' (Simmel, 1903 [1971]: 327).

Cynicism and the *blasé* attitude offer protection against modernity, but signify a gulf and conflict between the emotional capacities of individuals and modern forms. People cannot engage with the increasing mass of cultural forms in a manner that would develop their personality, nor can they express their individuality within the ossified and levelling interactional forms characteristic of modernity (Simmel, 1898 [1997: 119]; 1911 [1968: 43]). Instead, individuals are fragmented into their 'particular energies' and are left with a 'lack of something definite at the centre of the soul', impelling 'a search for momentary satisfaction in ever-new stimulations' (Simmel, 1907 [1990: 454, 467, 484]). For Simmel, there is no collective effervesence which enables individuals to 'complete' their personalities by merging with a collective conscience. The soul is doomed to frustration as individuals confront emotional sterility and face the almost impossible task of becoming all that they could be.

Weber: the heroic individual and emotional control

Weber's analysis of the rationalized environs of modernity has at its centre the self-determining human subject struggling to impart life with meaning, to avoid action motivated exclusively by affects, and to forge their personalities in line with freely chosen yet passionately held values. This struggle is especially acute as a result of the disenchantment of social life. Mechanized capitalism operates independently of moral norms, while individuals rarely encounter charismatic authorities able to enthuse and emotionally connect them to 'ultimate values'.

Emotions occupy an ambivalent role in Weber's analysis. They are normatively devalued as an exclusive motivator for action, and eroded by a rationalized social system. Indeed, Weber's (1968) typology of social action posits affectual action as opposite to, and undermining of, that freely chosen, goal-directed rational action that defines us as human (Weber, 1968: 25; 1905 [1975: 178]). Weber's writings on politics, science and personality, however, express a concern about individuals who make decisions in the *absence* of a passionate commitment to rational action (Barbalet, 2000). This is not an endorsement of emotion as a *motivator* of action, but suggests individuals should harness the core of their emotional selves to freely-chosen rational actions. Such action has become increasingly difficult in the modern age.

Rationally organized 'for a vocational, workaday life', the modern age promotes calculability over sentiment, robs people of emotional warmth, and promotes 'the world dominion of unbrotherliness' (Weber 1915 [1948]: 357). This is typified by the rational bureaucratic form which reorganizes 'everything it comes into contact with according to strictly "instrumentally-rational" principles' (Mommsen, 1974: 63–4), and 'develops the more perfectly, the more it is "dehumanized," the more completely it succeeds in eliminating from official business love, hatred, and all . . . irrational, and emotional elements which escape calculation. This is appraised as its special virtue by capitalism' (Weber, 1968: 975).

This rationalized system provides people with a massive increase in their knowledge of *how* to pursue scientific and technical goals, but cannot assist them in arbitrating between these goals (Weber, 1919a: [1948: 147–8]; 1919b [1948: 123]). This is associated with the devastating effects rationalization has on that emotionally saturated form of experience, charisma, that Weber holds has the power to inject meaning into social life. Charisma represents an intense 'other wordly' experience: it is a vehicle for human creativity, and can ignite social change (Weber, 1968: 432–3). While charisma traditionally swept 'through the great communities like a firebrand, welding them together', it recedes 'before the powers . . . of rational association after it has entered the permanent structures of social action' and now echoes only in 'the smallest and intimate . . . personal human situations' (Weber, 1919a [1948: 155]). The devitalization of charisma may not affect the 'mechanical foundations' of capitalism, but blunts the possibility of *creative* social change, indicates the diminishing importance of individual action, and threatens the ability of individuals to pursue meaningful lives (Weber, 1968: 1148–9; Eisenstadt, 1968; Collins, 1986).

These developments are associated with various factors, but Weber identifies the protestant ethic as one of the more important 'carriers' of rationalizing processes. Protestantism placed unprecedented demands on its followers to discipline their emotions and bodies. Nevertheless, Weber (1904–05 [1991: 102–3]) suggests that the followers of Calvinism would have felt devastated by the doctrine of predestination and experienced 'feeling[s] of unprecedented loneliness' as well as the agonies of self-doubt in the fear of damnation. Instead of opposing emotions, then, Calvinism tended to dislocate forms of positive emotional experience from a religious meaning system: it was left to the pastoral mediation of this doctrine to rescue the affects as a valued human capacity.

If Weber's analysis of Protestantism and rational capitalism is characterized by a deep pessimism, he identified aspects of human life capable of escaping rationalization. The 'boundless giving of oneself' in love 'is as radical as possible in its opposition to all functionality, rationality, and generality'(Weber, 1915 [1948: 342, 347]). Eroticism can appear 'like a gate into the most irrational and thereby real kernal of life, as compared with the mechanisms of rationalization' (Weber, 1915 [1948: 345]). Weber (1968) also sought to reinstate hope for the future by suggesting that charismatic breakthroughs, possessed of the potential to reverse the ossification of society, may occur in the future. However, while Weber suggests that charismatic leaders may emerge during periods of social crises, his analysis of capitalism does not contain the self-destructive tendencies characteristic of Marx's work, and identifies no stratum in Western society able to reinject vital emotions or fundamental values into the world (Weber, 1919a [1948]; Kalberg, 1980).

Despite this vision of modernity, Weber sought to reconcile at the individual level the exercise of free rational action with a passionate commitment to 'righteous action'. He suggested that individuals should create a personality which harnesses their inner emotional selves to freely chosen goals. This 'ethic of personality' imposes arduous demands on the individual: it is 'only through vigilent awareness and active exertion can the individual progress from . . . a life governed by the chaotic impulses of . . . given nature to one governed by the coherent values and meanings of . . . consciously formed personality' (Brubacker, 1984: 97). Nevertheless, the heroic personality possesses the potential to *combine* emotional commitment to an action with the careful mental weighing of the consequences of that action.

Emotions in action, emotions in order

The status of emotions in the sociologies of order and action differ in two major ways. The first involves the location of emotions, and the extent to which they possess an independent causal significance or are usually stimulated by other social factors. In Comte's and Durkheim's organic models of collective life, societies possess the capacity to stimulate in individuals emotional qualities which bind people into a moral community. Once stimulated, however, they can be expressed by individuals in a manner which infects others, leading to new ideas and to actions which may be destructive of extant social authorities. The writings of Simmel and Weber, in contrast, focus on the emotions of individuals. For both writers, the transcendence of natural emotions constitutes an important variable in the individual exercise of self-determination; affecting whether individuals are able to construct their own moral standards. It is worth noting, however, that *each* of these theorists operates with something of a *homo duplex* model of the individual in which the essence of truly human existence involves transcending the natural self. Transcendence from the natural components of self results for Comte and Durkheim in the harnessesing of individuals to a collectivity. For Simmel, it results in the supplementation of pre-social emotions and individual frames by social emotions and reciprocal mental orientations. For Weber, it involves a supercession of affectual or habitual action and a passionate pursuit of rational action.

The second major characteristic that distinguishes these sociologies concerns their conclusions about the social consequences of emotions. Comte's approach to the evolution and development of emotions was shaped by his belief in the emergence of a Religion of Humanity, while Durkheim's expectation that new periods of collective effervescence would revitalize modern societies mitigated his fears about threats to social and moral order. The work of Simmel and Weber, in contrast, was marked by pessimism. Each valued self-determined action, yet understood such action to be increasingly frustrated in modernity. For Weber, this necessitated an heroic stance in the face of the amoral rationalizations of modernity. For Simmel, the fate of individuals in modernity is a tragic one: the soul requires interactional forms that allow for the expression of its deepest inner desire for a coherent personality, yet individuals are surrounded by a world of unassimilable objects that make the pursuit of meaning and authenticity increasingly hopeless (Coser, 1971: 192). Ironically, these sociologists of action appear to recognize the ultimate causal primacy of the social whole (Dawe, 1979).

The expulsion of emotions from sociology?

If emotional issues were important to the founders of sociology, why did these concerns appear new to the new sub-discipline which emerged in the late 1970s? Parsons's enormously influential conception of sociology as a coherent disciplinary enterprise concerned with normative action and order does much to answer this question.

In responding to the Hobbesian 'problem of order', Parsons (1937) rejected the idea that passions were central to the issue of social cohesion, and held that the 'founding fathers' of sociology converged in realizing that adherence to the basic moral *values* of a society was a precondition of consensual order. Sociology, according to Parsons, viewed social action as motivated primarily by *normative* considerations that supported a social system's core value system, rather than by passionate affects or rational self-interest. Thus, despite Durkheim's concern with the effervescent features of group life, and the *homo duplex* nature of humans, Parsons (1937: 449; 1978: 225) argued that he remained 'Cartesian to the end', emphasizing 'the cognitive component' of social action. Similarly, Parsons's (1978) reading of Weber glossed his suggestion that the absence of irrefutable values in the modern world could result in unbearable existential angst, and suggested instead that his work demonstrated the ubiquity of normative consideration. Those sociologists who could not be interpreted in this manner, such as Simmel, were ultimately excluded from his 'convergence thesis'.

Parsons undoubtedly helped marginalize the significance of emotions by substituting the discipline's interest in the subject for a concern with the normative nature of social action. His analysis of the importance of 'affective neutrality' to the operation of institutions, for example, appeared to relegate emotions to the spheres of friendship and family relationships, and associate their public expression as a manifestation of social strains which needed to be dissipated (Barbalet, 1998: 16–18; O'Neill, 1985: 18). Nonetheless, Parsons's critics may have overlooked what he can contribute to our understanding of the contemporary relationship between culture and emotions. In particular, his analysis of the religious foundations of 'worldly instrumental activism' can be interpreted as an analysis of the emotional foundations of modernity.

Disagreeing emphatically with the contention that 'the Protestant Ethic is dead' Parsons analyses Christian values as informing the cultural value system of modern America, and as providing a 'pre-contractual' foundation for apparently secular orders of modern life (Parsons, 1978: 168, 240). This foundation contains a significantly emotional element which underpins the instrumental orientation of modern life. Protestantism imbued people with 'a strong sense of responsibility for achievements in this-worldly callings, the obverse of which was the ambition to "succeed"' (Parsons, 1978: 202–3). This pursuit of success did not support 'anarchic individualism' but *institutionalised individualism* which encouraged people to contribute 'to the building of the holy community' on Earth' and which has resulted in the production of modern personalities who achieve '*high levels of gratification*' from full participation in a social system (Parsons, 1970: 860; emphasis added).

What we have here is not an eradication of emotional considerations, but an argument which suggests that human passions and impulses become ordered, *via* socialization, into a human personality supportive of a 'worldly instrumental activism' dedicated to improving the capacity and productivity of the social system (Parsons, 1970: 860; 1991: 53). Modern emotional responses are thus patterned, rather than obliterated, by these cultural values. For Parsons, emotions are 'necessarily integrated with cognitive patterns; for without them there could be no coordination of action in a coherently structured social system' (Parsons, 1964: 209). The grief engendered by 'early' deaths involving the tenuation of a promising career, for example, is directly related to the religious concern of a 'calling' cut short (Parsons, 1978). In a related vein, the 'bias in favour of operating' that characterizes medical practice is associated with the emotional basis of instrumentalism in which '[a] decision to operate' is usually welcomed as a sign that '"something is being done"'. (Parsons 1951: 466–7).

Parsons may not always use a conceptual language which highlights the emotions, but this should not be taken to suggest that they are missing from his analysis. Indeed, he draws directly on Durkheim's definition of religion as belonging to 'the serious life' (a sector of life informed by *the* most intense emotional experiences) when discussing the apparent exclusion of 'emotional reactions' from medics acting in the face of death (Parsons, 1978: 280, 299). This 'emotional screen' against emotions can be usefully contrasted with Simmel's more pessimistic analysis of the development of the *blasé* attitude, and provides us with an intriguing basis on which we may analyse the development of personality within the modern world.

Conclusion

The scope of this chapter has been deliberately restricted to classical sociology, a period of the discipline and a form of writing that, arguably, ended with Parsons. If classical resources have yet to be utilized fully, however, I want to conclude by suggesting that two of the most important contributions they can make to our concern with emotions are a sensitivity to social and historical *context*, and a concern with the significance of emotions for social and moral *wholes*.

Comte, Durkheim, Simmel and Weber each recognized that the experience, expression and naming of particular emotions changed through time, and that *different* social structures had *distinctive* effects upon the emotional dimensions of human experience. Durkheim was worried that the effervescence that characterized premodern societies was waning in the modern era and could be replaced by an increase in anomie, for example, while Simmel expressed a concern that the emotional vitalism characteristic of human life was being blunted by *blasé* attitude. Even Parsons, who has been accused of temporarily eradicating the subject from the sociological imagination, was clearly concerned with the regulation and harnessing of emotions to modern value systems. In the context of this variety and diversity, there is much to be said for maintaining this broad concern with emotions, and not restricting ourselves by stipulating exclusive, final definitions of the subject (cf. Thoits, 1989).

Classical sociology also displayed a concern with the consequences of emotions for social and moral *wholes*, and this focus can usefully guard against an extension of those writings which are preoccupied with validating the emotional experiences of different groups or with the emotional components of the reflexive self in the late modern age. These examples of 'emotivism', of rejecting the general moral standards that have concerned the discipline and of reducing them to matters of individual feelings and group preferences, would seriously damage the longterm prospects of the sociological study of emotions (MacIntyre, 1985). Classical sociologists were concerned with the effects of emotions on the moral content of social orders and on the ability of individuals to act morally. To lose this concern would be to lose an essential part of the discipline.

Acknowledgement

This paper draws on and develops some of the themes that I investigated with Philip A. Mellor in *The Sociological Ambition* (Sage, 2001).

Notes

1 A sociology of emotions section was established in the American Sociological Association in 1986, while the British Sociological Association established a study group for the sociology of emotions in 1989, and the Annual Conference of the Australian Sociological Association has had a sociology of emotions panel since 1992.
2 Comte's work is usually characterized as being marked by a gulf between his 'scientifically-focused' *Cours de philosophie positive* and the later arguments for a new religion proposed in the *Système de politique positive*. These later writings have been largely rejected by contemporary sociologists, but this rejection does not allow us to appreciate the general importance he attributed to emotions in the binding of social relationships (Shilling and Mellor, 2001).
3 This notion is adapted from Kant's view that a priori categories of cognition exist, enabling humans to impose order on the natural world, but differs in three main ways. Simmel's forms impose conscious order on *all* human life and its contents and not just on cognitive understanding. Instead of being fixed and immutable, they emerge and develop over time as a result of the inherent creativity of individuals. Instead of being located purely in the mind of the knowing individual, they are stabilized by recurring patterns of interaction.

References

Aron, R. (1965) *Main Currents in Sociological Thought 1*. London: Weidenfeld & Nicolson.

Bakhtin, M. (1965 [1984]) *Rabelais and His World*. Bloomington: Indiana University Press.

Barbalet, J. (1994) 'Ritual emotion and body work: A note on the uses of Durkheim', in W. Wentworth and J. Ryan (eds), *Social Perspectives on Emotion, Vol. 2*. Greenwich, Connecticut.: JAI Press.

Barbalet, J. (1998) *Emotion, Social Theory and Social Structure. A Macrosociological Approach*. Cambridge: Cambridge University Press.

Barbalet, J. (2000) 'Beruf, rationality and emotion in Max Weber's sociology', *European Journal of Sociology*, 41(2): 329–51.

Bendelow, G. and Williams, S. (1998) (eds) *Emotions in Social Life. Critical Themes and Contemporary Issues*. London: Routledge.

Berlin, I. (1979) *Against the Current. Essays in the History of Ideas*. London: Hogarth Press.

Brubacker, R. (1984) *The Limits of Rationality. An Essay on the Social and Moral Thought of Max Weber*. London: George Allen and Unwin.

Burkitt, I. (1997) 'Social relationships and emotions' *Sociology*, 31(1): 37–55.

Burkitt, I. (1999) *Bodies of Thought*. London: Sage.

Camporesi, P. (1988) *The Incorruptible Flesh*. Cambridge: Cambridge University Press.

Cassirer, E. (1951) *The Philosophy of the Enlightenment*. Princeton: Princeton University Press.

Collins, R. (1975) *Conflict Sociology*. New York: Academic Press.

Collins, R. (1986) *Weberian Sociological Theory*. Cambridge: Cambridge University Press.

Collins, R. (1988) 'Theoretical Continuities in Goffman's Work', in P. Drew and A. Wootton (eds), *Erving Goffman. Exploring the Interaction Order*. Cambridge: Polity

Comte, A. (1853) *The Positive Philosophy of Auguste Comte. Vols. I & II*. Translated by Harriet Martineau, London: John Chapman.

Coser, L. (1971) *Masters of Sociological Thought. Ideas in Historical and Social Context*. New York: Harcourt Brace Jovanovich.

Dawe, A. (1970) 'The two sociologies', *British Journal of Sociology*, 21: 207–218.

Dawe, A. (1979) 'Theories of social action', in T. Bottomore and R. Nisbet (eds), *A History of Sociological Analysis*. London: Heinemann.

DeJean, J. (1997) *Ancients against Moderns*. Chicago: University of Chicago Press.

Denzin, N. (1984) *On Understanding Emotion*. San Francisco: Josey Bass.

Durkheim, E. (1895 [1982]). *The Rules of Sociological Method*. Edited by S. Lukes, translated by W.D. Halls. London: MacMillan.

Durkheim, E. (1897 [1952]) *Suicide*. London: Routledge.

Durkheim, E. (1912 [1995]). *The Elementary Forms of Religious Life*. Translated by Karen E. Fields. New York: Free Press.

Durkheim, E. (1914 [1973]) ' The dualism of human nature and its social conditions'. In R.N. Bellah (ed.), *Emile Durkheim on Morality and Society*. Chicago: University of Chicago Press.

Eisenstadt, S.N. (1968) *Max Weber on Charisma and Institution Building*. Chicago: Chicago University Press.

Ekman, P. (1984) *Approaches to Emotion*. Hillsdale, NJ: Lawrence Erlbaum.

Elias, N. (1939 [2000]) *The Civilising Process*. Cambridge: Blackwell.

Elias, N. (1987) 'Human beings and their emotions: a process-sociological essay', *Theory, Culture & Society*, 4: 339–361.

Franks, D. and McCarthy, E.D. (1989) (eds) *The Sociology of Emotions: Original Essays and Research Papers*. Greenwich, CT: JAI Press.

Gane, M. (1983) 'Durkheim: the sacred language', *Economy and Society*, 12, 1: 1–47.

Gardiner, H., Metcalf, R., and Beebe-Center, J. (1937) *Feeling and Emotion. A History of Theories*. New York: American Book Company.

Gerhards, J. (1986 [1994]) 'Georg Simmel's contribution to a theory of emotions', in D. Frisby (ed.), *Georg Simmel. Critical Assessments, 3. Vols*. London: Routledge.

Gordon, S. (1981) 'The sociology of sentiments and emotions', in M. Rosenberg and R. Turner (eds), *Social Psychology. Sociological Perspectives*. New York: Basic Books.

Hamilton, P. (1992) 'The Enlightenment and the birth of social science', in S. Hall and B. Gieben. (eds), *Formations of Modernity*. Cambridge: Polity.

Hammond, M. (1983) 'The sociology of emotions and the history of social differentiation', in Collins, R. (ed.), *Sociological Theory*. San Francisco: Jossey-Bass.

Herder, J. (1784–91 [1968]) *Reflections on the Philosophy of the History of Mankind*. Chicago: University of Chicago Press.

Hobbes, T. (1650 [1962]) 'Human nature or the fundamental elements of policy' in T. Hobbes *Body, Man and Citizen*. Edited and with an introduction by R.S. Peters. New York: Collier Books.

Hobbes, T. (1651 [1914]) *Leviathan*. Introduction by A. Linday. London: J.M. Dent & Sons.

Hobbes, T. (1658 [1972]) 'On Man', in *Man and Citizen*. ed. B. Gert. Garden City, NY: Doubleday.

Hochschild, A. (1975) 'The sociology of feeling and emotion: selected possibilities', in M. Millman and R. Kanter (eds), *Another Voice: Feminist Perspectives on Social Life and Social Science*. New York: Anchor.

Hochschild, A. (1983) *The Managed Heart. Commercialization of Human Feeling*. Berkeley: University of California Press.

Huizinga, J. (1924 [1955]) *The Waning of the Middle Ages*. Harmondsworth: Penguin.

Jaggar, A. (1989) 'Love and knowledge: emotion in feminist epistemology', in S. Bordo and A. Jaggar (eds), *Gender/Body/Knowledge: Feminist Reconstructions of Being and Knowing*. New Brunswick, NJ: Rutgers University Press.

James, S. (1997) *Passion and Action. The Emotions in Seventeenth Century Philosophy*. Oxford: Clarendon Press.

Kalberg, S. (1980) 'Max Weber's types of rationality: cornerstones for the analysis of rationalizing processes in history', *American Journal of Sociology*, 85(5): 1145–1179.

Kant, I. (1797 [1985]) *Foundations of the Physics of Morals*. London: Macmillan.

Kemper, T. (1978) *A Social Interactional Theory of Emotions*. New York: John Wiley.

Kemper, T. (1990) (ed.) *Research Agendas in the Sociology of Emotions*. New York: State University of New York Press.

Levine, D. (1971) 'Introduction', in *Georg Simmel On Individuality and Social Forms*. Chicago: University of Chicago Press.

Levine, D. (1995) *Visions of the Sociological Tradition*. Chicago: University of Chicago Press.

Lindholm, C. (1990) *Charisma*. Oxford: Blackwell.

Lukes, S. (1973) *Emile Durkheim*. London: Penguin.

Lukes, S. (1982) 'Introduction' to S. Lukes (ed.), *The Rules of Sociological Method and Selected Texts on Sociology and Its Method*. Houndmills: Macmillan.

MacIntyre, A. (1985) *After Virtue*. 2nd Edition. London: Duckworth.

Mommsen, W. (1974) *The Age of Bureaucracy, Perspectives on the Political Sociology of Max Weber*. New York: The University Library.

Nisbet, R. (1966 [1993 2nd edition]) *The Sociological Tradition*. New Brunswick, New Jersey: Transaction.

O'Neil, J. (1985) *Five Bodies: the Human Shape of Modern Society*. Ithaca, NY: Cornell University Press.

Parsons, T. (1937 [1968]) *The Structure of Social Action*. New York: Free Press.

Parsons, T. (1951) *The Social System*. London: Routledge.

Parsons, T. (1964) *Essays in Sociological Theory. Revised Edition*. New York: The Free Press.

Parsons, T. (1970) 'On building social system theory: A personal history', *Daedalus*, 99(4): 826–881.

Parsons, T. (1978) *Action Theory and the Human Condition*. New York: The Free Press.

Pickering, M. (1993) *Auguste Comte: An Intellectual Biography, Vol. I*. Cambridge: Cambridge University Press.

Pickering, M. (1997) 'A New Look at Auguste Comte', in *Reclaiming the Sociological Classics*, edited by Charles Camic. Oxford: Blackwell.

Pickering, W.S.F. (1984) *Durkheim's Sociology of Religion*. London: RKP.

Scheff, T. (1994) *Bloody Revenge. Emotions, Nationalism and War*. Boulder: Westview Press.

Seidler, V. (1998) 'Masculinity, violence and emotional life', in G. Bendelow and S. Williams (1998) (eds), *Emotions in Social Life. Critical Themes and Contemporary Issues*. London: Routledge.

Shilling, C. (1997) 'Embodiment, emotions and the sensation of society', *The Sociological Review*, 45(2): 195–219.

Shilling, C. (2001) 'Embodiment, experience and theory. In defence of the sociological tradition', *The Sociological Review*, 49(3): 327–344.

Shilling, C. (2003) 'Embodiment, emotions and the foundations of social order: Durkheim's enduring contribution', in J.C. Alexander and P. Smith (eds), *The Cambridge Companion to Durkheim*. Cambridge: Cambridge University Press.

Shilling, C. and Mellor, P.A. (2001) *The Sociological Ambition. Elementary Forms of Social and Moral Life*. London: Sage.

Shott, S. (1979) 'Emotions and social life: a symbolic interactionist analysis', *American Journal of Sociology*, 84(6): 1317–1334.

Simmel, G. (1898 [1997]) 'A contribution to the sociology of religion', in J. Helle (ed.), *Essays on Religion*. New Haven: Yale University Press.

Simmel, G. (1903 [1971]) 'The Metropolis' in D. Levine (ed.), *Georg Simmel On Individuality and Social Forms*. Chicago University of Chicago Press.

Simmel, G. (1904. [1997]) 'Religion and the contradictions of life', in H.J. Helle (ed.), *G. Simmel. Essays on Religion*. New Haven: Yale University Press.

Simmel, G. (1907 [1990]) *The Philosophy of Money*. Edited and with an introduction by Tom Bottomore and D. Frisby. London Routledge.

Simmel, G. (1908a [1971]) 'Group expansion and the development of individuality', in D. Levine (ed.), *Georg Simmel On Individuality and Social Forms*. Chicago University of Chicago Press.

Simmel, G. (1908b [1971]) 'The problem of sociology', in D. Levine (ed.), *Georg Simmel On Individuality and Social Forms*. Chicago University of Chicago Press.

Simmel, G. (1908c [1971]) 'How is society possible?' in D. Levine (ed.), *Georg Simmel On Individuality and Social Forms*. Chicago University of Chicago Press.

Simmel, G. (1911 [1968]) 'On the concept and the tragedy of culture', in G. Simmel *The Conflict in Modern Culture and Other Essays*. (trans. P. Etzkorn). New York.

Simmel, G. (1912 [1997]) 'Religion', in J. Helle (ed.), *Essays on Religion*. New Haven: Yale University Press.

Simmel, G. (1914 [1997]) 'Rembrandt's religious art', in H.J. Helle (ed.), *G. Simmel. Essays on Religion*. New Haven: Yale University Press.

Simmel, G. (1918 [1971]) 'The conflict in modern culture', in in D. Levine (ed.), *Georg Simmel On Individuality and Social Forms*. Chicago University of Chicago Press.

Simmel, G. (1950) *The Sociology of Georg Simmel*. Glencoe, Ill: Free Press.

Smith, A. (1776 [1950]) *An Inquiry into the Nature and Causes of the Wealth of Nations*. London: Methuen.

Smith, T.S. (1992) *Strong Interaction*. Chicago: The University of Chicago Press.

Tester, K. (1998) ' "Bored and blasé": television, the emotions and Georg Simmel', in G. Bendelow. and S. Williams. (1998) (eds), *Emotions in Social Life. Critical Themes and Contemporary Issues*. London: Routledge.

Thoits, P. (1989) 'The sociology of emotions', *Annual Review of Sociology*, 15: 317–342.

Toulmin, S. (1990) *Cosmopolis. The Hidden Agenda of Modernity*. Chicago: University of Chicago Press.

Turner, B.S. (1984) *The Body and Society*. Cambridge: Blackwell.

Turner, J.H. and Maryanski, A.R. (1988) 'Is "neofunctionalism" really functional?', *Sociological Theory*, 6: 110–121.

Weber, M. (1904–05 [1991]) *The Protestant Ethic and the Spirit of Capitalism*. London: Harper Collins.

Weber, M. (1905 [1975]). 'Knies and the problem of irrationality', in *Roscher and Knies: The Logical Problem of Historical Economics*. trans. Guy Oakes. NY: Free Press.

Weber, M. (1915 [1948]) 'Religious rejections of the world and their rejections', in H.H. Gerth and C.W. Mills (eds), *From Max Weber: Essays in Sociology*. London: Routledge and Kegan Paul.

Weber, M. (1919a [1948]) 'Politics as a Vocation', in H.H. Gerth and C. Wright Mills (eds), *From Max Weber*. London: Routledge.
Weber, M. (1919b [1948]) 'Science as a Vocation', in H.H. Gerth and C. Wright Mills (eds), *From Max Weber*. London: Routledge.
Weber, M. (1968) *Economy and Society, 2 Vols*. Berkeley: University of California Press.
Wentworth, W. and Ryan, J. (1994) *Social Perspectives on Emotion*. Greenwich: JAI Press.
Williams, S. (2001) *Emotions and Social Theory*. London: Sage.

Secure states: towards a political sociology of emotion

Mabel Berezin

Abstract

Emotion and politics is the study of the non-cognitive core of politics. Emotion and politics presents its own special set of difficulties. First, emotions are experienced individually but politics is by definition a collective phenomena. This means that the social analyst has to attempt to understand how an individual micro-level instinct, an emotion, contributes to collective macro-level processes and outcomes. Second, emotions are ontologically in the moment. Emotions and sound have similar properties. Music or noise either soothes or jars the central nervous system. Emotions too affect the central nervous system and even social scientists have begun to acknowledge the relevance of neurobiology to their studies. The physicality of emotion suggests that a robust analysis of emotion demands a multi-disciplinary approach, and not that emotions are outside of the purview of the social sciences. This chapter begins from the position that much theoretical, analytic and empirical work remains to be done in the study of politics and emotions. It represents a first attempt to explore, from multiple angles, how emotions matter to politics. The chapter proceeds on four levels: first, it develops the concepts *secure state* and *community of feeling* as analytic frames that unite politics and emotion; second, it explores how emotions are embedded in political institutions; third, it takes up the issue of emotion and collective action; and lastly, it suggests the conceptual issues that a political sociology of emotions might address.

Politics and emotion

Sociologists have begun to recognize that emotions are as constitutive of macro-level social processes as they are of individual psychology (for example, Barbalet, 1998, Berezin, 1997a, 1999c; Goodwin, Jasper and Polletta, 2001; Massey, 2002; Turner, 2000). Sociologists are not alone in their recent attention to emotion. Between 1999 and 2001, major works on emotions have appeared in political science (Elster, 1999; Braud, 1996), history (Reddy, 2001), moral philosophy (Nussbaum, 2001) and neuroscience (Damasio, 1999). The recent outpouring of cross-disciplinary scholarship on emotions makes arguing for their importance *jejeune*. Emotions clearly matter—but how?

This chapter discusses emotions in the political sphere. Certain assumptions govern a macro-sociological approach to emotions whether the particular focus is politics, economics or culture. Stability, institutionalization, routinization, as social theorists from Weber to Parsons have emphasized are the core social processes of modern society—that is, post-1789 Europe. In the *The Birth of Tragedy* (1872), Friedrich Nietzsche distinguished between the Apollonian and the Dionysian—the rational and the expressive. Nietzsche viewed the rational as the Achilles heel of what some analysts label western Eurocentric society. Nietzsche is pointing to the central tension of modernity—the tension between emotion and its expression (laughter, tears, rage) and rationality, or as Weber ([1920] 1976) elaborated in his discussion of the Protestant ethic—the passionless, methodical, and relentless pursuit of order through work.[1]

Modernity's commitment to routinization, or as Weber articulated it, legal authority, relegated emotions to the shadows of both theory and history. The market and the nation-state, the twin public institutions that embed the economic and the political in modern social life were a-emotional, in theory, if not in practice, from inception. The private sphere was the legitimate social space for emotion. Beginning in the 18th century and continuing into the 19th, cadres of intellectuals (novelists, essayists, letter writers) buried emotions in an ideology of sentimentalism located in the private sphere of the family and bourgeois courtship rituals (Reddy, 2001; Watt, [1957] 2001; Habermas, [1962] 1989, pp. 43–51). When not being sentimentalized, emotions were demonized or neutralized. Civilization, as Freud ([1930] 1961) argued, requires the suppression of collective emotion. Durkheim ([1915] 1965) recognized the emotional dimension of social life when he described the rites and rituals of aboriginal tribes; yet emotions receded when he formalized his approach to social categorization and knowledge. Durkheim's ([1897] 1966) approach to suicide as a social, and not a psychological, phenomenon gave birth to the modern social science of deviance.

Social analysts who study the political, whether they are sociologists or political scientists, view emotions as extrinsic to the study of politics. The issues that engage these social scientists, the nation-state, the law, voting behavior, and political parties are predicated on a conception of rationality. Emotions, if considered at all in socio-political analysis, take the form of deviant behavior patterns—authoritarian personalities (Lipset, 1960) or backward peasants who cannot adjust to modernity (Banfield, 1967).[2] Emotion has lurked in the interstices of classical political sociology and carried more positive valences than contemporary analyses would suggest. Scholars, who study the modern nation-state, whether from a culturalist or institutionalist perspective, have overlooked Weber's argument that a 'political community' derives its force as well as its legitimacy from its 'emotional foundations' (Weber, 1978, p. 903). Students of democracy have given short shrift to the fact that John Stuart Mill did not see much hope for the 'free institutions' of representative democracy without a significant degree of 'fellow-feeling' among co-nationals.[3] Ironically, it is rational choice theorists puzzling over issues of risk and trust, as frequently exemplified in studies of political violence, who have made the initial contributions to a political sociology of emotions.

This chapter begins from the position that much theoretical, analytic and empirical work remains to be done in the study of politics and emotions. It represents a first attempt to explore, from multiple angles, *how* emotions matter to politics. The chapter proceeds on four levels: first, it develops the concepts *secure state* and *community of feeling* as analytic frames that unite politics and emotion; second, it explores how emotions are embedded in political institutions; third, it takes up the issue of emotion and collective action; and lastly, it suggests the conceptual issues that a political sociology of emotions might address.

Parsing political emotion

The study of emotion and politics is the study of the non-cognitive core of politics. Emotion and politics presents its own special set of difficulties. First, emotions are experienced individually but politics is by definition a collective phenomena. This means that the social analyst has to attempt to understand how an individual micro-level instinct, an emotion, contributes to collective macro-level processes and outcomes. Second, emotions are ontologically in the moment. Emotions and sound have similar properties. Music or noise cither soothes or jars the central nervous system. Emotions too affect the central nervous system and even social scientists have begun to acknowledge the relevance of neurobiology to their studies (eg, Turner, 2001). However, this simply means that a robust analysis of emotion demands a multi-disciplinary approach, and not that emotions are outside of the purview of the social sciences.

Aesthetic philosopher Suzanne Langer (1951) drew the connection between music and emotion when she described music as a 'morphology of feeling' and argued: '. . . the forms of human feeling are much more congruent with musical forms than with the forms of language, music can *reveal* the nature of feelings with a detail and truth that language cannot approach' (p. 199). Codifying, managing, mobilizing emotions transforms them into culturally accepted behaviours, situates them in time and space and, depending upon the context, adds a political dimension to the emotion. A person or a group in a fit of joy, fear, anger, overcome by laughing, weeping or fighting is not simultaneously mobilizing, managing or codifying. Emotion as immediately experienced is socially ineffective, destabilizing and a-political. We have only to think of the difference between a riot and a revolution.

Elster (1999) persuasively demonstrates that to understand the relation between emotion and social life requires the dis-entangling of cause and effect. For example in the case of civil wars, there is always a question as to whether escalating violence based on longstanding hatred is the cause *or* the effect of present conflicts. In Italy during the period between the fall of Mussolini's fascist regime and the end of the Second World War, members of fascist and communist squads engaged in large-scale vigilante murders of each other (Pavone,

1991). Justification for murder varied depending upon which side you were on, ie, you were saving Italy either from fascism or from communism. Civil wars also provide an opportunity for persons or groups who did not like each other much to begin with to get even with each other in the name of the cause. The moral high ground is quickly lost; and more importantly, the relation between collective cause and collective effect is virtually impossible to pull apart. Do I hate you because you are a fascist or do I hate you because I have always hated you and now have an opportunity to kill you without censure? Or to take a slightly more positive example, do I pay my taxes because I love my country and want to see distributive justice for all its citizens; or do I pay my taxes because if I do not, I will be fined and pay even more? The preceding counterfactuals suggest that in the political realm effects or manifestations, ie, emotions expressed in actions, provide a more fruitful avenue of analysis than triggering instances—which may, but only may, represent the official public narrative.

If there is any point of agreement in the new study of emotions, it is that they are so constitutive of social, and by extension, political life that they cannot be ignored. To borrow from Weber, emotions govern non-rational but not irrational action. To the extent that action is oriented toward others, it is social; to the extent that action is oriented toward institutions, it is both social *and* political. What is required is that we develop a working definition of emotion as a process that places in bold relief the capacity of emotions to infuse both the social and the political spheres.

Emotions, whether positive or negative, are physical *and* expressive responses to some sort of destabilization. One of the earliest definitions of emotions comes from Aristotle's *Rhetoric* (1991) that describes emotions as, '. . . those things by the alteration of which men differ with regard to those judgments which pain and pleasure accompany, such as anger pity, fear and all other such and their opposites' (p. 141). Aristotle's definition is worth citing, because it shows that one of the earliest social analysts who thought about emotion incorporated the concept of de-stabilization and difference, ie, 'alteration.' Emotions are a response to threat, ie, the fight or flight mechanisms that biologists frequently emphasize. Threats can also be positive. The rhetoric of sexual love in various languages highlights de-stabilization. In English, we fall in love; in both French and Italian, love is a thunderbolt—*coup de foudre* or *culpo di fulmine*, respectively. Social beings do not live continually either on the precipice or in social stasis. Marriage institutionalizes sexual love. Social actors do not live completely without affect, which is what a case of perfect stability would be, nor in a state of perpetual affect. Individuals experience social life somewhere in between the predictable comfort of routine (stability) and the discomfort that contingent events (instability) pose.[4]

Recent work in neuroscience supports an action approach to emotion. Damasio (1999) argues that emotions are neurological phenomena that to some degree are always more or less present—whether the individual is aware of them or not. Emotions in this sense generate feelings of which an individual is more or less conscious (Damasio, 1999, pp. 37; 50–53). What Damasio describes as 'feeling made conscious' is what social scientists tend to focus upon in their discussion of emotions. While Damasio recognizes that 'learning and culture' give emotion meaning, context, location in time and space, is not his primary interest as a neuroscientist. Nevertheless, it is ours as social scientists. Neuroscience verifies for social science that emotion represents a material state of human nature, an extension of the body that is necessary to consider. Emotion even from the purely biological perspective is relatively uninteresting until it manifests itself in the 'conscious' recognition of feeling. From a sociological perspective, as opposed to psychological or psychoanalytic perspective, we may argue that emotions are unproblematic until they result in social or collective action. What is interesting from a social science perspective is *not* that we have emotions but the mechanisms that transpose these emotions into some sort of action or institutional arrangement—that is the moments in which we do and do not act emotionally. If we focus on action, rather than emotion *per se*, we direct our attention to the *when*, the temporal dimension of emotional display that is central to all social life but particularly crucial for understanding the relation between politics and emotion.

Recasting emotion in political terms: the secure state and the community of feeling

An even cursory glance at the emerging literature on emotions makes it clear that scholars have a difficult time coming to terms with precisely what an emotion is (Lutz and White, 1986; Thoits, 1989). Kemper (1987) lists four primary emotions that he combines to come up with twenty-three secondary emotions. Turner (2001, p. 74) arrays the manifestations of four primary emotions on scale that ranges from low to high intensity. Jasper (1998, pp. 406–407), whose primary interest is in social movements, distinguishes between affective emotions such as love and hate and reactive emotions such as outrage and grief. He adds a third category that he labels 'moods' that includes defiance, enthusiasm and envy. The abundance of available literature that catalogues emotions suggests that naming emotions is perhaps not the most fruitful analytic task.

A political sociology of emotions should avoid cataloguing—but not completely. Some emotions are more relevant to politics than others are. Alternatively, if emotions are a response to instability then some emotions are more likely then others to emerge in the political sphere and have discernible political consequences. In his *Rhetoric*, Aristotle (1991) argues that the moral persona of the speaker is as important a part of the rhetorical power to persuade as any intrinsic worth of the argument offered. Persuasion is ultimately about the distribution of individual and collective resources. The constraint and deployment of emotions is an essential component of rhetoric and by extension politics. Aristotle identifies ten emotions that he considers fundamental to human nature and thus fair game in the rhetorical repertoire. Of these ten, anger, calm, friendship and enmity, fear and confidence, pity and indignation, may be recalibrated in terms that apply to modern political organization. The remaining four, shame, favour, envy and jealousy are more applicable to discussions of feudal or tribal forms of political organization.[5]

Anger, enmity, fear and indignation are different forms of reaction to threat; whereas, calm, friendship, confidence, and pity are responses to security. The first group articulates with the feeling of pain; the second with the feeling of pleasure. Or to put another way, the first group may excite hate; the second may excite love—in the sense of *caritas* rather than *eros*. To be analytically useful, these emotions must be systematically recast in terms that aggregate their potential political effects. This article develops the ideal types of the *secure state* and the *community of feeling* as analytic prisms that refract specific historical events and movements in terms that render emotions politically meaningful.[6]

The secure state

Political scientists regard the Treaty of Westphalia, signed in 1648, as the beginning point of modern international relations and the sovereign territorial state. The Treaty arguably marks the beginning of security as a political concept—but security signifies much more than the merely political. Security with its attendant feelings of confidence and comfort is the emotional template of the major form of modern political organization—the democratic nation-state. The territorially bounded state inspires confidence and loyalty in its members, citizens, by providing internal (police) and external (military) security. In exchange, citizens develop an emotional bond that makes them willing to defend the security of the state under threat and to forfeit income to taxes. Patriotism and civic nationalism are the positive descriptors of this feeling of attachment (Viroli, 1995; the collected essays in Nussbaum, 1996). The *secure state*, in theory if not in practice, generates a feeling of social compassion that permits communal empathy, and generosity (Nussbaum, 2001, pp. 401–440). In market societies, voluntary associations fill the emotional space of social compassion; in societies committed to redistribution, the state provides social welfare.[7]

The opposite of the secure state is the insecure state. The paradigmatic *secure state* is the modern nation-state; in contrast, the *insecure state* is a polity that may assume many forms. For example, an *insecure state* may be a state in dissolution *or* in formation. A contemporary example is the former Eastern Europe that has experienced a range of emotions from the benign to the malignant in the period of transition. Fear and lack of confidence are the hallmarks of political insecurity. The cause could be an internal threat as residents of established nation-states respond to the influx of immigrants from Africa, the Middle East and Eastern Europe; it may also be a response to a real or perceived external threat. At the analytic level, violence from the purely symbolic to the physical is the effect of the collective experience of the emotion of insecurity. Aggression from war to ethnic cleansing is a manifestation of fear of external threats; xenophobia, resentment and discrimination are manifestations of threats to internal security.

The *secure state* and its opposite the *insecure state* is an ideal type that situates virtues and vices that usually occupy political theorists and moral philosophers within a set of political institutions. This analytic approach explores emotion as a latent structure of affect within a macro political structure—the state.

Communities of feeling

In contrast to the *secure state*, *communities of feeling* are a-structural. The *secure state* channels emotional energy within the polity; *communities of feeling* generate emotional energy in support of or against the polity. Scheler (1992, p. 54) uses the term to signify emotional connection. Shared private grief is his example. Scheler's view of *community of feeling* has two weaknesses: first, it assumes participants understand the emotions that they are sharing, or the objects about which they are becoming emotional; and second, it does not fully appreciate the collective nature of emotion. In previous work (Berezin, 1997b; 2001), I have argued that *communities of feeling*, whether staged or spontaneous, serve to intensify emotional identification with the polity and derive emotional power from their transience. They bring individuals together in a bounded, usually public, space for a discrete time period to express emotional energy. *Communities of feeling* borrows from Raymond Williams' (1977, pp. 132–3) concept, 'structure of feeling' that he describes as a 'social experiences in solution.' Williams contrasts 'feeling' to discursive elements such as 'world-view' and 'ideology' which are linguistic and textual. 'Structure of feeling' underscores the indeterminacy of emotion: 'we [Williams] are concerned with meanings and values as they are actively lived and felt, and the relations between these and formal or systematic beliefs are in practice variable (including historically variable), over a range from formal assent with private dissent to the more nuanced interaction between selected and interpreted beliefs and acted and justified experiences.'

The indeterminancy of emotion is particularly salient in the political realm. Nation-states use parades, holiday, public rituals, and rallies to generate *communities of feeling*. In the mid-1930s in Italy, the fascist regime staged a series of large rallies in Rome—for the sole purpose of creating emotional energy (Berezin, 2001, pp. 90–92). The absolute political effects of such rallies are completely indeterminate. *Communities of feeling* as a political strategy may be a bankrupt endeavour. The emotional energy produced may be negative as well as positive. Yet, no matter what the outcome, political spectacle is as old as politics itself—suggesting that political élites believe in the emotional energy that spectacle generates.

If the emotional effects of staged *communities of feeling* are indeterminate; the effects of spontaneous *communities of feeling* are even more so. Effective emotional politics appropriates rather than generates emotional energy. Examples of appropriation abound. Kertzer (1980) described how the Italian Communist Party fed off the ritual energy of the Catholic Church to recruit party members and to sustain commitment among them. More recently, British Prime Minister Tony Blair attempted to feed off the emotional energy generated by the thousands who flocked to London when the Princess Diana died. He was quick to label her the 'People's Princess'—no doubt hoping to infuse his Labour Party with Diana's charisma. The Socialist Prime Minister and the Conservative President vied for public space as they quickly appropriated the spontaneous outpouring of exuberance in Paris on Bastille Day 1998 when the French celebrated their victory in the World Cup (Berezin, 1999c).

In the fall of 2001, in response to the terrorist attacks on the World Trade Centre, a group of American Senators stood united on the steps of the Capitol building in Washington and spontaneously broke into a chorus of *God Bless America*. In contrast to Europe, where politicians appropriate free-floating emotional energy, in America the market appropriated the emotional energy around the song and recordings were suddenly bestsellers. *God Bless America* has a history *vis à vis* emotion and politics. It is not an American political anthem. Irving Berlin composed the song for a Broadway play staged in the 1930s. Kate Smith, a popular singer, sang it at the end of War Bond Rallies during the Second World War to mobilize citizens to invest in the war.[8] In his study of mass persuasion that focused on the War Bond Drive, Merton (1946) found that people bought the Bonds because they found both the singer, and by extension, the song—comforting and maternal. Security embodied in maternal affect is a form of emotional energy that in the War Bond Drive created a politically effective *community of feeling*—effective because people bought the Bonds.

Embedding emotion in political institutions

The modern nation-state is the historical analogue of the *secure state*. Territorial sovereignty and membership criteria gave rise to unique legal institutions that bound individuals to the modern nation-state. The political institutions of the modern nation-state inscribe emotion in the polity and the rights and duties of citizenship channel collective emotional energy towards its maintenance.

The process of state formation began, some scholars argue, as early as the 16th century depending upon the part of Europe one considers. Elias (1994) in his history of the development of social control in Europe, *The Civilizing Process*, began in the 17th century with an analysis of etiquette books. Elias excavated the development of a rising bourgeois class for whom the containment of emotion, or what he calls the 'economy of affects,' was crucial for achieving social power and status (p. 27). Elias documented the first stage of a process that aimed to suppress overt display emotion. However, the development of the modern nation-state with emotion firmly embedded in diverse institutions did not begin to occur until the 19th century and in some instances took until the 20th to complete. Laws governing nationality were first enacted in the 19th century as part of European civil codes (Hansen and Weil, 2001).

The nation-state is better thought of as a project rather than a fixed entity. 'Project' denotes ongoing actions where collective actors institutionalize new norms, values, and procedures (Berezin, 1997). Nation-state projects are historically specific forms of political organization that wed bureaucratic rationality (the infrastructure of the state) to the particularism of peoples and cultures (the nation as community). Modern nation-states are vehicles of political emotion. Citizenship defines legal membership in modern nation-states. Conceptually, citizenship has evolved from a conception of rights attached to persons (Marshall, 1964) to a discussion of rules of inclusion (Brubaker, 1992) and relational processes (Somers, 1993). Focusing upon citizenship as a boundary-making device attenuates its affective dimensions. Citizenship is more than simply a juridical relationship. It is also signals an emotional bond that arouses feelings of national loyalty and belonging in a politically bounded geographical space (Berezin, 1999a).

The institutions of the nation-states move the epistemological—citizenship as category—towards the emotional—citizenship as felt identity. Berezin (1997) argues that competition and necessity intertwine identity with institutions. The success or strength of the nation-state as an identity project depends upon first, the other identities with which it must compete; and second, the strength of the competing institutions that buttress those identities. A central paradox underlies nation-state projects. Without loyal members, ie, citizens who identify with the project, a state will be at a comparative disadvantage in international relations and competition. On the other hand, a state cannot create new identities from whole cloth. The existing identities from which it borrows or appropriates its cultural and emotional claims can, unless eliminated, at any moment re-emerge to undermine the nation-state project.

Political sociologists customarily turn to Weber's writings on legitimation and domination when they wish to write about the modern nation-state. However, Weber's writings on political community are far more useful when one wishes to elaborate the relation between the nation-state and emotion. Weber ([1922] 1978, pp. 901–926) defines political community as a form of association that governs social actions among 'inhabitants of the territory' who share culture and bonds of solidarity. The political and the territorial are fungible— necessary, but not sufficient for creating a 'political community.' Political community is not reducible to either economics (ie, market activity) or politics (ie, territorial control). Weber argues that 'joint memories' shape ties that run deeper than the 'merely cultural, linguistic or ethnic.' Without a shared history, we have politics but not community. Following the logic of Weber's argument, we may add that time is an essential dimension of political community. Time is as necessary as space to the formation of political community—or the emotional dimension of attachment and shared experience.

Discussions of nationalism have subsumed the emotional dimensions of political community. The literature on nationalism is voluminous and growing. In the late 19th century, students of nationalism such as Renan saw the nation as a biological entity—a community of attachment among groups with fictive bloodline. Much of the scholarship in recent years has focused on putting this primordial conception to rest. However, in denying the blood connection, scholars have gone excessively over to the constructed view of nationalism. Revisionist scholarship has de-emotionalized political community. Constructivism has as difficult a time accounting for the recent resurgence of ethnic nationalism as primordialism had in accounting for the multi-ethnic nation-state.

This is not to say that the territorial narratives that national and local cultural entrepreneurs fabricate are unimportant. To borrow Benedict Anderson's now familiar formulation (1991, p. 7), the modern nation-state is an 'imagined community' that creates a spirit of 'fraternity' that creates a feeling of 'attachment' to the state in the form of 'love for the nation' (Anderson, 1991, pp. 141; 143). Nation-state is a two-pronged institutional and conceptual entity. The state is in the 'business of rule' and focuses upon bureaucratic efficiency and territorial claims; the nation is in the business of creating emotional attachment to the state. 'Imagined' community was a novel concept when it first appeared in 1983. Its principal battle has been won and scholars generally accept to some degree the constructed dimension of 'nation-ness.' However, scholars have either glossed over or simply assumed 'political love' without delving into what sociologist Robert W. Connell (1990, p. 526) has described as the 'structure of cathexis' or the 'patterning of emotional attachments' to the polity.

Calhoun's (1997) account of nationalism that connects kinship to the institution of the nation-state bypasses some of the analytic and empirical difficulties of the essentialist versus the constructivist position. He argues that nationalism borrows its rhetorical frames from the language of kinship. Biology dictates that everyone participates to some degree in kinship relations. Because kinship is nearly universal, family metaphors resonate emotionally and lend themselves to building a shared national identity (Berezin, 1999b). The physicality of territory, from the family home to the neighbourhood to the nation-state, underscores propinquity in space and duration in time. Propinquity and duration generate familiarity or comfort and create a form of cultural and emotional attachment to and identification with the place that an individual or group inhabits.[9] Viewed from the prospective of comfort, emotional attachment to place, what the Germans call *Heimat* is not irrational particularism but an ingrained emotional response to temporally durable environmental factors. Jusdanis (2001) makes a similar observation when he argues for a 'necessary nation.'

Hunt (1992, p. 196) in her analysis of the 'family romance' of the French Revolution suggests that the emotional metaphor of family is vacuous if not situated in a specific cultural and historical context. Historical and theoretical accounts demonstrate that 19th century nation-states did not just come together due to the elective affinity of compatriots but were forged from wars as well as the suppression of local and regional cultures and institutions. Eugen Weber's now classic study of nation-state making in 19th century France, *Peasants Into Frenchmen* (1976), described this process of successful institution building in detail.

Nation-state projects require two kinds of activities to create emotional attachment and identity. The first sort of activity is the compulsory participation in institutions that affect all citizens. These activities typically are the military, the schools and the national language. For this reason, the suppression of regional language and dialect is usually the first item on the nation-state building agenda. Fighting, learning, speaking, as collective actions create a shared culture of participation. The second activity is consumption—the consumption of national images, words and symbols in newspapers, art, literature, theater. National languages, literatures and education systems as well as museums, monuments and music serve to keep the spirit of national belonging alive (for example, Mukerji, 1997; Corse, 1997). Production and consumption serve to imprint the nation cognitively and emotionally upon the identities of its citizens. If France is the archetypal successful 19th century nation-state project, one has only to cross the Alps to Italy where the Fascist regime tried to complete the failed work of 19th century institution building (Berezin, 1999b).

Emotion and collective action: ritual, social movements and violence

The modern nation-state contains emotions within political institutions. Emotions of membership are rarely transparent except under conditions of threat from internal or external forces. A reservoir of national emotional energy, as well as military conscription, helps to convince citizens to fight for their country during war time. A perceived internal enemy makes some citizens rise to defend their turf. For example, the standard explanation for the electoral success of right wing parties in contemporary Europe is the increase in the number of resident immigrants (see Eatwell, 2000). The political emotions so far described are *intra-institutional* responses constitutive of the *secure state*.

A range of political emotions exists that are *extra-institutional*. *Communities of feeling* are emotional responses to events that lie outside institutionalized politics. In contrast to the *secure state*, where the form is invariant and the content is historically specific, ie, the modern nation-state, the *community of feeling* displays variation as to form and content. Whereas the *secure state* and the modern nation-state speak to the issues of law and emotion; the *community of feeling* speaks to the issue of collective action and emotion. Rituals, social movements and mass violence are the three forms of collective action most germane to issues of political emotion.

Emotion is the pivot upon which political ritual turns. As Geertz (1973, p. 449) argues in his discussion of the Balinese cockfight, ritual display serves as a kind of 'sentimental education' in its use of 'emotion' for 'cognitive ends'. Ritual is performative as well as representational and we attenuate its political significance if we restrict its impact to the cognitive. Discursive ritual knowledge is ultimately indeterminate. Public political ritual is performance; and performance, whether it occurs in the tightly bounded world of the theater or the more permeable social space of a public piazza, is a highly elusive entity because its effects are experiential. The experiential, or performative, nature of ritual points us in the direction of action.

In Kertzer's (1988) monograph on ritual and politics, ritual is defined as 'symbolic behavior that is socially standardized and repetitive. . . . Ritual action has a formal quality to it. It follows highly structured, standardized sequences and is often enacted at certain places and times that are themselves endowed with special symbolic meaning. Ritual action is repetitive and, therefore, often redundant, but these very factors serve as important means of *channeling emotions* [emphasis added], guiding cognition, and organizing social groups' (p. 9). By taking an action approach to political ritual, Kertzer suggests that rituals are formalized manifestations of emotion. He does not distinguish between rituals that occur with state sponsorship and those that occur in opposition to the state.

State-sponsored rituals are temporary moments of exit from ordinary life that dramatize emotional commitment to the standard institutions of the polity. National holiday, festivals, parades, commemorations are periodic attempts to fan the flames of institutionalized political passions and commitments. These types of ritual events are part of the woof and weave of modern political institutions and they occur in nation-states independently of the ideology of the regime in power. Studies of public political ritual range widely in time and space. Examples include: the 'theatre state' of 18th century Bali (Geertz, 1980); the festivals of the French Revolution (Ozouf, 1988); the rallies of Weimar Germany (Mosse, 1991); the myths of state socialism (Verdery, 1999); strategies of patriotism in 19th century America (Bodnar, 1992); commemoration rituals in America (Spillman, 1997); public rituals in Fascist Italy (Berezin, 1997).[10]

In my study of twenty years of Italian fascist public ritual, I identified five components of ritual activity that combined and re-combined forming a ritual repertoire aimed at intensifying emotional identity with the fascist regime. These components were: first, the *myth of the founding event*; second, the *forging of enemies and heroes*; third, *the appropriation of the commonplace*; fourth, the *merging of sacred and secular*; and fifth, the using of *categories of persons as symbolic icons*. These ritual actions are commonplace in the modern polity. Nation-states have founding myths from the storming of the Bastille to the signing of the Declaration of Independence. Enemies and heroes forge bonds of solidarity and intensify feelings of community—us against them. The American politician who regularly shakes hands with the crowds appropriates the everyday. Even nation-states such as the United States that are committed to the separation of Church and state have references to the deity in their political rituals. The American president takes the oath of office with his hand on the Bible. Modern monarchs with their schedule of public activities are recurrent examples of public individuals who are institutionalized national symbols.[11]

Public political rituals are *communities of feeling* that serve as arenas of emotion, bounded spaces, where citizens enact and vicariously experience collective national selfhood. Ritual action communicates familiarity with form and this familiarity may be as simple as the recognition that one is required to be present at an event. Familiarity and identity are co-terminus. The repeated experience of ritual participation produces a feeling of solidarity—'we are all here together, we must share something;' and lastly, it produces collective memory—'we were all there together.' What is experienced and what is remembered is the act of participating in the ritual event in the name of the polity.

Ritual eliminates indeterminacy in social space, the carefully staged crowding of bodies in public spaces, but this does not presume that ritual eliminates indeterminacy as to meaning. Ritual by acting out emotion includes indeterminacy. Public political ritual creates an open interpretive space. Solidarities and memories—the identities of subjects who have gathered under similar circumstances—may be extremely fluid. Emotion may obliterate the old self but there is no guarantee as to what form the new self or identity might assume.

Collective actors with grievances against the state may easily appropriate the same repertoire of ritual actions learned from state sponsored events to use against the state. It simply requires the channeling of emotional energy in a new direction. Social movements scholars have taken the lead in emphasizing the importance of emotions to political sociology (Aminzade and McAdam, 2001). Goodwin, Jasper and Polletta (2000) remind us that the sociological study of social movements, originally the purview of social psychology, began with emotions. Beginning in the 1970s, structuralist approaches to social movements that emphasized organization and opportunity overshadowed and finally eliminated social psychology (for an analysis, see Tarrow, 1998). When psychology crept into collective action studies, it did so under the rubric of rational choice. Olson's *The Logic of Collective Action* (1965) is the classic analytic work that looks at collective action from a rational choice perspective.

The collection of essays in *Passionate Politics* (2001), underscore the importance of bringing emotions to bear on the study of social protest. Focusing on laughter, shame, anger, fear and emotional narratives of various stripes, the contributors individually and collectively argue for the importance of emotions to the analysis of social and political mobilization. The concluding essay of the volume (Amenta and Polletta, 2001) is a plea for methodological and conceptual rigour and a warning that it is far too easy to slip into description in the study of emotion and social movements. Goodwin's (1997) study of the Huk mobilization in Thailand analyzes how movement leaders exploited 'affective' or 'libidinal' ties between movement members to strengthen the organization. Goodwin's study is important because it is a first step towards theorizing the mechanisms through which politics and emotions combine in social movements. By pointing to ties deep within the group, ie, within couples, Goodwin identifies personal commitment as a form of dyadic solidarity that has an emotional spillover effect to the political project at hand.

While social movements scholars are on the tracks of emotions, students of violence have had a head start. What could be more emotional than hatred and fear of so intense a nature that it leads to forms of mass violence from genocide to ethnic cleansing to group executions? Yet, emotions are not the dominant frame in studies of violence (for a review of this literature see Brubaker and Laitin, 1998). Among the scholars who concern themselves with violence, those who take a formal analytic approach, ie, those that concern themselves principally with rationality, have made the most headway. This is in part because violence appears to be emotional and not rational and consequently requires explanation.

Many studies in this genre such as Gambetta's study of the Sicilian mafia (1993) and Gould's studies (1999; 2000) of blood feuds in Corsica focus on honour societies in which shame is to be avoided at all costs and revenge is a normal articulation of justice. These societies have a pre-modern form of social organization that avoids the legal institutions of the modern nation-state. Justice in 20th century Sicily and 19th century Corsica was meted out alongside of, and in opposition to, the national legal system. Family honour is central in these types of societies—but the seeking of revenge, if it is to be effective, cannot be a simply individual act. As Gould (2000) argues, an eye for an eye is a problem of collective action. Gould argues that the amount of violence Corsican vendettas produce depends upon the strength or weakness of intra-group solidarity. Gould (1999) finds that the more fragile group solidarity is, the more likely the group is to respond with violence in order to instill fear and protect the group from further threat. Conversely, groups with a reputation for solidarity do not resort to violence as frequently—presumably because they are less likely to be attacked and the cost of revenge is high. Intensely solidaristic groups engage in 'contingent collectivism' or to put it more colloquially they choose their vendettas carefully (Gould, 2000).

Although on the surface, it appears that Gould has de-emotionalized revenge, probing more deeply suggests that his studies re-enforce the issue of emotion. The general assumption is that emotion in vendetta is a product of hate and anger, but a closer analysis of the cases that Gould presents suggests that the dominant emotion revolves around the threat to group security. If security were not at issue, there would be no need for 'contingent' revenge. Similarly, if security were not at issue, every act of aggression against the individual would be viewed as an insult to the family and action would immediately follow. What Gould's studies suggest is that is not only the honor but also the security of the family that is at stake. In the public sphere, even the relatively pre-modern and rural public sphere, security and confidence in continuity and stability located in the emotional sphere of the family takes precedence to free-floating anger.

Laitin's (1995) study of nationalist violence in the Basque region of Spain presents findings that can be re-interpreted in a similar vein. Laitin asks why a high level of nationalist violence characterizes the Basque region in contrast to Catalonia which has a low level of violence but an equally strong sub-national culture. Catalonian culture was assimilated into the national political culture through strong trade union organizations that also happened to preserve the Catalonian language and culture. The Basque region, on the other hand, had a more rural form of social organization characterized by high levels of youth association. At the appropriate moment, nationalist activists could draw on loyalties forged in formal and informal youth associations to support outbursts of nationalist violence, which tended when they occurred to be of a spectacular nature. Associational life in the Basque region was solidaristic, whereas associational life in Catalonia was interest driven. The Basque region was not more violent than Catalonia because it was organizationally more suited to it (the rational analysis) but arguably because friendship bonds that the rural society fostered produced an emotional spillover, not unlike the 'libidinal ties' that Goodwin described, to the political arena. The Gould and Laitin studies are examples drawn from a range of similar studies that are occupy rational choice theorists. These studies can be re-interpreted to suggest that emotion is a component of violent activity. The emotion, however, is not hatred but the emotion of solidarity that prior emotional ties provide.

Secure spaces: towards a political sociology of emotions

In an essay on 'Patriotism,' Roberto Michels (1965, p. 157) observes that, 'Variety is strange to most persons.' What Michels is discussing under the rubric of 'patriotism,' scholars today would discuss under the rubric of nationalism or national identity. He discusses the need to create a 'homeland', a secure space, to overcome the multiple differences that separated every little European village and town from each other. His observation on 'variety,' is germane to the evolving discussion of emotion and politics within this chapter. Michels was writing during the 1930s when totalitarian regimes in Russia and Europe appeared to be eliminating variety energetically. If, however, one abstracts from the historical moment that engaged Michels, he is underscoring a point that was not lost on 19th century nation making élites—constructed similarity produces security, stability and loyalty.

The observation that security and stability are related is not a defense of the *status quo*. Rather, it is a fact of human psychology that has implications for the relation between politics and emotions. As argued at the beginning of this chapter, emotion and its manifestations are linked to the proportion of stability versus instability one experiences. This holds from the micro level of human interaction to the macro level of political activity. In a sense, emotions operate as protective physiological cues that warn us individually or collectively that something is in flux. What this points to is that there is a relation between trust, risk and emotion. Without risk, or the threat of de-stabilization, emotions lie dormant. The American philosopher, William James (1956) held that rationality was a sentiment—or an emotion. He argued that familiarity with objects and events produced a feeling that they were rational. James argued that all humans need a sense of a 'relation of a thing to its future consequences.' The need, as James put it, to have 'expectancy defined' is the core of the 'sentiment of rationality.' Coleman's (1990) conception of 'trust' that incorporates the idea of futurity resonates with James' conception of rational sentiment. Coleman (1990, p. 99) argues that trust is essentially a bet on the future. As Coleman is a rational choice theorist, he is interested in how individual actors assess risk—that is, how they place those bets—or how they make rational choices. However, no matter what one's tolerance for risk is, whether one is proven correct in the risk that one takes is something that in most social interaction—only time will tell. Thus, all trust has a temporal dimension to it. However, it also has a cultural and emotional dimension to it. The individual and collective experience of trust and risk is a matter of degree and not absolutes.

Familiarity is a better guide to individual and collective action then a calculus of rationality. Recent work on prejudice by Sniderman and his collaborators (2000) underscores this point. Sniderman was interested in what makes groups so dislike other groups that they are willing to act against them. His hypothesis was that the colour of skin would be the dominant source of prejudice in societies that were predominantly white. Using the United States as his model, Sniderman conducted a controlled experiment in Italy, which had recently experienced an influx of white immigrants from the former Eastern Europe and black immigrants from Africa. To Sniderman's surprise, he found that Italians disliked Eastern Europeans more than they disliked Africans—or, that skin colour with its attendant emotions of fear and race hatred was not an isolatable source of prejudice. Pushing his data further, Sniderman examined the voting behavior of his sample, particularly their support of parties with anti-immigrant platforms. There has recently been an increase in the electoral success of right-wing parties in Italy as in the rest of Europe. Sniderman found that at the political extremes of left and right—a small proportion of his sample as well as the population at large—race hatred on the right and radical egalitarianism on the left influenced political behaviour. But, extremism on either end was not driving elections in contemporary Europe. His startling finding was that individuals in the majority supported order, stability and continuity independently of where they placed themselves with respect to political ideology. In other words, it was a general commitment to the familiar coupled with a fear of instability, and not a generalized feeling of hatred, that predicted prejudice in sentiment and action. Emotions played a part in anti-immigrant politics but, as in the case of the earlier discussion of the vendettas, not the emotions one would expect.

Sniderman's research re-enforces the idea that security and insecurity are important political emotions because the fear that insecurity generates that is the interaction between trust and risk actually lead collectivities to act on their emotions. But how can we extrapolate from this finding to the larger political arena? In the modern political sphere, the institutions of the nation-state, the *secure state*, adjudicate risk. Institutions provide a framework of expectations or 'futurity.' Parsons (1954) articulated this when he argued that institutions are, 'patterns governing behavior and social relationships which have become interwoven with a system of common moral sentiments which in turn define what one has a "right to expect" of a person [or group, or corporate body] in a certain position' (p. 143). The law, the police and the military keep the territory of the state secure; enforced common language and schooling protect the national culture. Citizenship, membership over time, produces feelings of belonging, loyalty and trust; citizenship law specifies who will participate in the national *community of feeling*.

The fundamentally sociological question of a mechanism remains. Under what conditions will political emotion from patriotic fervour to ethnic violence erupt? The short answer is that when the institutions that govern the polity are threatened, change or dissolve—political emotion will manifest itself in some sort of action. This is a claim that requires systematic and comparative empirical investigation. We can briefly speculate for the remainder of this chapter. Threat includes the obvious of war or external attack. As the recent events on September 11 in the United States demonstrated, attack has the potential to generate a wellspring of national loyalty. One of the reasons that the *secure state* needs to resort to various *communities of feeling* described is to keep political passion alive in the absence of threat. When the state institutions are weak or have a weak hold in the local social structure, as in the case of the vendetta, political passion follows its own logic. When institutions change, as in contemporary Europe where European union is redefining the nature of the nation-state, emotions may manifest themselves in popular protest. When the institutions of the state collapse completely as they did in the former Eastern Europe, there is no buffer to contain political emotion and violence can ensue.

However, political emotion does not only have negative valence. Just as neuroscience has argued that emotions are physiological and relate to the body, they also relate concretely to those secure spaces ie, the home, the neighbourhood, the nation-state, where emotions of all sorts are experienced. The spatial dimension of politics is one of the reasons that kinship metaphors are so salient in political culture. The *secure state* can also be the *empathetic state*—in which it is possible to live in community and generosity with one's fellow citizens. A developed political sociology of emotions should take as one of its principal tasks the elaboration of the mechanisms that trigger security and its opposites.

Notes

1 For an alternative formulation that focuses on the hidden emotion of rationality, see Barbalet (2000).
2 In contrast to these early studies in political psychology, Eliasoph's (1998) study of political apathy and Herzfeld's (1992) study of indifference and bureaucracy take as their problem the absence of emotion.
3 Cited in Kraus (2000: 143).
4 Sewell (1996) in his discussion of an 'eventful sociology' underscores the importance of contingency for historical explanation. An appreciation of contingency is also important to an understanding of the relation between emotion and politics.
5 Shame implies honor. For a discussion of how rational forms of political organization such as the nation-state incorporate honor in the notion of 'patrie,' see the recent edition of the lectures that Lucien Febvre gave at Collège de France between 1945 and 1947 (Febvre, 1996).
6 In Weberian terms, ideal types are constructs derived from empirical phenomena but not reducible to them.
7 On the comparative development of voluntary associations, see the collection of essays in Wuthnow (1991).
8 Eyerman and Jamison (1998) have recently pointed to the importance of music as a tool of political mobilization.

49

9 For a benign interpretation of this phenomena, see Entrikin (1999); for a critique of the uncritical acceptance of this view, see Calhoun (1999).
10 Kertzer (1988) and Berezin (1997a) provide samples of available studies.
11 Kantorowicz (1957) is the classic study.

References

Aminzade, Ron and Doug McAdam (2001) 'Emotions and Contentious Politics.' Pp. 14–50 in *Silence and Voice in the Study of Contentious Politics*, eds Ronald Aminzade *et al.* New York: Cambridge.
Anderson, Benedict ([1983] 1991) *Imagined Communities: Reflections on the Origin and Spread of Nationalism*. London: Verso.
Aristotle (1991) *The Art of Rhetoric*. London: Penguin Books.
Banfield, Edward (1967) *The Moral Basis of a Backward Society*. New York: The Free Press.
Barbalet, Jack M. (1998) *Emotion, Social Theory, and Social Structure: A Macrosociological Approach*. Cambridge, UK: Cambridge University Press.
Barbalet, Jack M. (2000) 'Beruf, Rationality and Emotion in Max Weber's Sociology.' *Arch. Europ. Sociol* XLI: 329–351.
Berezin, Mabel (1997a) 'Politics and Culture: A Less Fissured Terrain.' *Annual Review of Sociology* 23: 361–383.
Berezin, Mabel (1997b) *Making the Fascist Self: The Political Culture of Inter-war Italy*. Ithaca, New York: Cornell.
Berezin, Mabel (1999a) 'Democracy and Its Others in a Global Polity.' *International Sociology* 14 (September): 227–243.
Berezin, Mabel (1999b) 'Political Belonging: Emotion, Nation and Identity in Fascist Italy.' Pp. 355–377 in *State/Culture*, ed. George Steinmetz. Ithaca: Cornell University Press.
Berezin, Mabel (1999c) 'Emotions Unbound: Feeling Political Incorporation in the New Europe.' Paper presented to the American Sociological Association Meetings, Chicago, Illinois.
Berezin, Mabel (2001) 'Emotion and Political Identity: Mobilizing Affection for the Polity.' Pp. 83–98 in *Passionate Politics: Emotion and Social Movements*, eds Goodwin, Jeff, James M. Jasper, and Francesca Polletta. Chicago: University of Chicago Press.
Bodnar, John (1992) *Remaking America: Public Memory, Commemoration, and Patriotism in the Twentieth Century*. Princeton: Princeton University Press.
Braud, Philippe (1996) *L'Emotion en politique*. Paris: Presses de Sciences Po.
Brubaker, Rogers (1992) *Citizenship and Nationhood in France and Germany*. Cambridge: Harvard University Press.
Brubaker, Rogers and David D. Laitin (1998) 'Ethnic and Nationalist Violence.' *Annual Review of Sociology* 24: 423–452.
Calhoun, Craig (1997) *Nationalism*. Minneapolis: University of Minnesota Press.
Calhoun, Craig (1999) 'Nationalism, Political Community and the Representation of Society: Or, Why Feeling at Home is not a Substitute for Public Space.' *European Journal of Social Theory* 2 (2): 217–231.
Coleman, James (1990) *The Foundations of Social Theory*. Cambridge: Harvard University Press.
Connell, Robert W. (1990) 'The State, Gender and Sexual Politics.' *Theory and Society* 19: 507–543.
Corse, Sarah (1997) *Nationalism and Literature*. Cambridge: Cambridge.
Damasio, Antonio R. (1999) *The Feeling of What Happens: Body and Emotion in the Making of Consciousness*. New York: Harcourt Brace and Co.
Durkheim, Emile ([1915] 1965) *The Elementary Forms of the Religious Life*. Translated by Swain, Joseph Ward. New York: The Free Press.
Eatwell, Roger, ed. (2000) 'Far-Right in Europe: In or Out of the Cold.' Special Edition of *Parliamentary Affairs* 53 (3): 407–531.
Elias, Norbert (1994) *The Civilizing Process*, translated by Edmund Jephcott. Oxford: Blackwell.

Eliasoph, Nina (1998) *Avoiding Politics: How Americans Produce Apathy in Everyday Life.* Cambridge: Cambridge University Press.

Elster, Jon (1999) *Alchemies of the Mind: Rationality and the Emotions.* New York: Cambridge University Press.

Eyerman, Ron and Andrew Jamison (1998) *Music and Social Movements.* Cambridge, UK: Cambridge University Press.

Febvre, Lucien (1996) *Honneur et Patrie*, edited by Therese Charmasson and Brigitte Mazon. Paris: Perrin.

Freud, Sigmund ([1930] 1961) *Civilization and Its Discontents*, translated and edited by James Strachey. New York: W.W. Norton and Co.

Gambetta, Diego (1993) *The Sicilian Mafia.* Cambridge: Harvard University Press.

Geertz, Clifford (1973) 'Deep Play: Notes on the Balinese Cockfight.' Pp. 412–453 in *The Interpretation of Cultures.* New York: Basic.

Geertz, Clifford (1980) *Negara.* Princeton: Princeton University Press.

Goodwin, Jeff, James M. Jasper and Francesca Polletta (2001) 'The Return of the Repressed: The Fall and Rise of Emotions in Social Movement Theory.' *Mobilization* 5: 65–84.

Goodwin, Jeff, James M. Jasper, and Francesca Polletta, eds (2001) *Passionate Politics: Emotions and Social Movements.* Chicago: University of Chicago Press.

Goodwin, Jeff (1997) 'The Libidinal Constitution of a High-Risk Social Movement: Affectual Ties and Solidarity in the Huk Rebellion, 1946 to 1954'. *American Sociological Review* 62: 53–69.

Gould, Roger V. (1999) 'Collective Violence and Group Solidarity in Corsica.' *American Sociological Review* 64: 356–380.

Gould, Roger V. (2000) 'Revenge as Sanction and Solidarity Display: An Analysis of Vendettas in Nineteenth-Century Corsica.' *American Sociological Review* 65: 682–704.

Habermas, Jurgen ([1962] 1989) *The Structural Transformation of the Public Sphere*, Thomas Burger, trans. Cambridge: MIT.

Hansen, Randall and Patrick Weil, eds (2001) *Towards a European Nationality: Citizenship, Immigration and Nationality Law in the European Union.* New York: St. Martin's.

Herzfeld, Michael (1992) *The Social Production of Indifference.* Oxford: Berg.

Hunt, Lynn (1992) *The Family Romance of the French Revolution.* Berkeley: University of California Press.

James, William (1956) 'The Sentiment of Rationality.' Pp. 63–110 in *The Will to Believe and Other Essays in Popular Philosophy.* New York: Dover Publications, Inc.

Jasper, James M. (1998) 'The Emotions of Protest: Affective and Reactive Emotions In and Around Social Movements.' *Sociological Forum* 13: 397–424.

Jusdanis, Gregory (2001) *The Necessary Nation.* Princeton: Princeton University Press.

Kantorowicz, Ernst H. (1957) *The King's Two Bodies.* Princeton: Princeton University Press.

Kemper, Theodore D. (1987) 'How Many Emotions are There? Wedding the Social and the Autonomic Components,' *American Journal of Sociology* 93 (2): 263–289.

Kertzer, David I. (1980) *Comrades and Christians.* Cambridge: Cambridge University Press.

Kertzer, David I. (1988) *Ritual, Politics, and Power.* New Haven: Yale University Press.

Kraus, Peter (2000) 'Political Unity and Linguistic Diversity in Europe.' *European Journal of Sociology* 41 (1): 138–163.

Laitin, David D. (1995) 'National Revivals and Violence.' *Arch. Europ. Sociol.* 36: 3–43.

Langer, Susanne K. (1951) *Philosophy in a New Key.* New York: The New American Library.

Lipset, Seymour Martin (1960) *Political Man: The Social Bases of Politics.* Garden City, New York: Doubleday.

Lutz, Catherine and Geoffrey M. White (1986) 'The Anthropology of Emotions,' *Annual Review of Sociology* 15: 405–436.

Marshall, T.H. (1964) 'Citizenship and Social Class,' in *Class, Citizenship and Social Development: Essays by T.H. Marshall*, 71–134. Chicago: University of Chicago Press.

Massey, Douglas S. (2002) 'A Brief History of Human Society: the Origin and Role of Emotions in Social Life', *American Sociological Review*, 67: 1–29.

Merton, Robert K. ([1946] 1971) *Mass Persuasion: The Social Psychology of a War Bond Drive*. Westport, Connecticut: Greenwood Press Publishers.

Michels, Roberto (1949) 'Patriotism.' Pp. 156–166 in *First Lectures In Political Sociology*, translated by Alfred De Grazia. New York: Harper Torchbooks.

Mosse, George L. ([1975] 1991) *The Nationalization of the Masses*. Ithaca: Cornell.

Mukerji, Chandra (1997) *Territorial Ambitions and the Gardens of Versailles*. Cambridge: Cambridge.

Nussbaum, Martha C. (2001) *Upheavals of Thought: The Intelligence of Emotions*. New York: Cambridge University Press.

Nussbaum, Martha C., ed. (1996) *For Love of Country: Debating the Limits of Patriotism*. Boston: Beacon Press.

Olson, Mancur (1965) *The Logic of Collective Action*. Cambridge: Harvard University Press.

Ozouf, Mona ([1976] 1988) *Festivals and the French Revolution*. Foreword by Lynn Hunt. Translated by Alan Sheridan. Cambridge: Harvard University Press.

Parsons, Talcott (1954) 'Propaganda and Social Control.' Pp. 142–176 in *Essays in Sociological Theory*. Glencoe, Illinois: The Free Press.

Pavone, Claudio (1992) *Una guerra civile*. Turin: Bollati Boringhieri.

Polletta, Francesca and Edwin Amenta (2001) 'Conclusion: Second that Emotion? Lessons from Once-Novel Concepts in Social Movement Research.' Pp. 303–316 in *Passionate Politics: Emotion and Social Movements*, eds Goodwin, Jeff, James M. Jasper, and Francesca Polletta. Chicago: University of Chicago Press.

Reddy, William M. (2001) *The Navigation of Feeling*. New York: Cambridge University Press.

Scheff, Thomas J. (1994) *Bloody Revenge: Emotions, Nationalism and War*. Boulder, CO: Westview Press.

Scheler, Max (1992) *On Feeling, Knowing, and Valuing*, edited by Harold J. Bershady. Chicago: University of Chicago Press.

Sewell, William H., Jr. (1996) 'Three Temporalities: Toward an Eventful Sociology.' Pp. 245–80 in *The Historic Turn in the Human Sciences*, ed. Terence McDonald. Ann Arbor: University of Michigan Press.

Sniderman, Paul M., Pierangelo Peri, Rui J.P. and De Figueiredo, Jr., Thomas Piazza (2000) *The Outsider: Prejudice and Politics in Italy*. Princeton: Princeton University Press.

Somers, Margaret R. (1993) 'Law, Community, and Political Culture in the Transition to Democracy,' *American Sociological Review* 58 (5): 587–620.

Spillman, Lyn (1997) *Nation and Commemoration*. Cambridge: Cambridge.

Tarrow, Sidney (1998) *Power in Movement: Social Movements and Contentious Politics*. 2nd ed. Cambridge: Cambridge University Press.

Thoits, Peggy A. (1989) 'The Sociology of Emotions,' *Annual Review of Sociology* 15: 317–342.

Turner, Jonathan H. (2000) *On the Origins of Human Emotions*. Stanford: Stanford University Press.

Verdery, Katherine (1999) *The Political Lives of Dead Bodies*. New York: Columbia University Press.

Viroli, Maurizio (1995) *For Love of Country: An Essay on Patriotism and Nationalism*. New York: Clarendon Press.

Watt, Ian ([1957] 2001) *The Rise of the Novel*. Berkeley: University of California Press.

Weber, Eugen (1976) *Peasants Into Frenchmen*. Stanford: Stanford.

Weber, Max ([1920] 1976) *The Protestant Ethic and the Spirit of Capitalism*, translated by Talcott Parsons. New York: Charles Scribner's Sons.

Weber, Max (1978) *Economy and Society*, edited by Guenther Roth and Claus Wittich. Vol. II. Berkeley: University of California Press.

Williams, Raymond (1977) *Marxism and Literature*. Oxford: Oxford University Press.

Wuthnow, Robert, ed. (1992) *Between States and Markets: The Voluntary Sector in Comparative Perspective*. Princeton: Princeton University Press.

Predicting emotions in groups: some lessons from September 11

Theodore D. Kemper

Abstract

First, this chapter examines the emotional responses of 10 different publics to the terrorist attacks of September 11, 2001. Through the application of power/status theory (Kemper, 1978), different publics are hypothesized to have different emotions. In all, six emotions—anger, sadness, fear, joy, guilt and shame—are differentially attributed to the ten publics. Second, this chapter inquires into the efficacy of predicting emotions for both individuals and groups. Predictions for individuals may have somewhat greater utility, given that they provide for enlightenment and control, but for both individuals and groups, emotions may be seen as intervening variables of relatively low sociological value. It would be more important sociologically to know the coping responses the emotions lead to. Here theory is relatively scant. Four structural conditions are proposed that may advance understanding of how, under certain conditions, emotions may lead to sociologically relevant coping. Finally, this chapter considers some differences between individual emotions and what may be called 'group' emotions. The principle difference is that individuals, even when emotionally conflicted, experience emotions in their entirety, while groups usually experience a division of labour of the emotion, with different members differentially invested in what can be seen as the dominant emotion of the group. Unlike in individuals, where conflicting emotions are likely to be resolved by a coping response that attempts to accommodate the competing emotions, group coping responses unfold in a social process that is sometimes violent, as different factions compete to establish their emotions and preferred coping responses as conclusive for the entire group.

This chapter is an examination and reflection upon some issues of theory and method raised by a communication I posted in a forum conducted by the International Society for Research on Emotion (ISRE), dealing with the events of September 11, 2001. (The verbatim text of the message is in Appendix 1 below.) I will deal with three issues in particular: (1) predicting emotions; (2) the efficacy and/or utility of predicting emotions; and (3) the difference between emotions as experienced by individuals and as experienced, in some sense, by groups.

Predicting emotions

The *sine qua non* for scientific prediction of any phenomenon, including emotions, is a theory that allows for prediction. It need not be a valid theory, in which case the predictions are likely to be wrong. Also, one can make highly accurate predictions without a theory, but these are not scientific predictions. For example, even very young children develop a quite reliable expectation that when they awake after sleep it will be daylight. They cannot explain why the sun is shining again after a period of darkness—in particular, the rotation of the earth on its axis in a 24-hour time-period—but they are 100 per cent accurate. Nor, to make accurate predictions, need the theory be particularly elegant. The legendarily complex theory of planetary motion offered by Ptolemy does a fairly good job of prediction. But given that Western science prefers its theories to conform to the principle of Occam's razor—that theory is best which supposes the fewest assumptions—Ptolemy's effort succumbed to Copernicus's.

Table 1 in the appendix contains 'predictions' about six emotions (anger, sadness, fear, joy, shame, and guilt) in ten different groups or publics as an aftermath of the terrorism of September 11. To anyone remotely aware of the events and following them in any moderately complete medium, whether television, radio, or newspaper, no theory was necessary to state quite unequivocally what emotions were being felt by which groups. Simple reportage would have been sufficient to establish the distribution of emotions, and prior knowledge about the groups sufficient to have allowed for fairly confident postdiction.

I contend, however, that it was also possible to derive the emotions of the different groups, once one has a sense of their different values and interests, from theory. The theory I used has several elements (full discussion may be found in Kemper, 1978; Kemper and Collins, 1990; Kemper, 1991). The basic proposition of the theory is that *a very large class of emotions results from real, imagined, or recollected outcomes of social interaction.* This definition locates most emotions in the social world, so that, even if the individual is alone, the social impinges to produce emotions. (See Simmel, 1950: 119–120, for discussion of the social dimensions of isolation.)

The critical issue is how to characterize social interaction. Here a body of evidence collected in diverse social science fields including sociology, psychology, anthropology, and social linguistics, has converged on two dimensions of social interaction: *power* and *status* (Kemper and Collins, 1990).

Power, following the definition of Weber (1946), comprises all those actions designed to obtain compliance with one's wishes, desires, and interests over the resistance of an other. If power behaviours are successful, compliance is involuntary. Power includes both threatened and actual physical assault, such as shooting, beating, slapping, pushing, confining, and the like. It also includes the full gamut of noxious verbal assaults, including screaming, denigrating, insulting. It also includes deception and manipulation, such as lying to or lying about. Finally, power includes threatened or actual deprivation of another's wonted or legitimately expected benefits and considerations. When power behaviour is repeatedly successful, a *power structure* emerges, in which the parties in interaction normally expect that one party is more likely to achieve his/her goals and objectives even though the other resists. Once the structure is in place, power behaviours as such are usually unnecessary, since the party with less power is aware of the dire consequences of noncompliance. When two actors engage in continual power acts toward each other, whether offensively or defensively, they are in a state of conflict or, for present purposes, war.

Status, brief for status-accord, includes the roster of behaviours voluntarily bestowed on another that support, enhance, benefit, or otherwise gratify the other. At the ultimate, status-accord is what we would recognize as love. In lesser degrees, we speak of affection, liking, regard, respect, esteem, politeness and so forth. In each of these forms, ignoring here any special differences between them, one actor defers to, honours and gratifies the other in the degree to which the relationship between them specifies (as when a soldier salutes an officer) or supposes (as when friends provide each other emotional support).

In general, a *status structure* emerges, in which actors in a relationship have a stable sense of what is proper and suitable as a mark of the amount of affection, regard, respect, liking, etc., required of and/or deserved from each other. Clearly, the same acts of deference and gratification can be accorded as a result of threat or compulsion (ie, power). This can be seen in the case of the soldier who salutes out of fear of punishment rather than true regard for the higher rank. In any specific case, it is an empirical question as the degree to which compliance is status (voluntary) or power (involuntary) (see Kemper, 1978: 368–389). But it is also the case that a great deal of what is observed as status-accord is authentically such.

Parenthetically, but helping to round out this discussion of the power and status dimensions, it is possible to view *authority* as a relationship in which one actor accepts that another actor has the right to compel him or her to act in ways he or she would prefer not to act, within a defined scope of possible actions. Thus, the army officer has the authority to order an attack on an enemy position, and though the soldier may prefer not to do this, he has earlier accepted that this is a legitimate demand and will, ordinarily, comply with it. Even when authority is formally established in a relationship, there are likely to be many instances where authority is overstepped and compliance is obtained by sheer power.

With power and status concepts in place, we can turn to 'outcomes of social interaction'. Here, we can use a relatively simple heuristic: as the result of an interaction, one's own and/or the other's position in the power structure may have increased or decreased (even if only temporarily), or remained the same. Similarly, one's own and/or the other's status position may have increased, decreased, or remained the same. Given two actors, two dimensions and three possible outcomes, a full depiction of interaction outcomes will entail twelve results, four of which will actually occur. Each of the twelve outcomes is the source of a possible emotion. With both one's own and the other's power and status outcomes in view, each actor can experience up to four emotions.

Considering first what have been called the four primary emotions by many (see Kemper, 1987), *anger* results from a loss of status, *fear* from a loss of power relative to the other, *sadness* from a loss of status that is irremediable, *joy* from a gain of status. These emotions are thus responses to outcomes of interaction in power and status terms. Beyond these primary emotions, *guilt* is understood to be the emotion felt when one understands that one has used excess power on another. *Shame* is understood as the emotion felt when one has acted in a manner that belies the amount of status that one expects another to confer on oneself, that is, one has not acted in a status-worthy manner. (For a full discussion of these emotions, see Kemper, 1978.)

The task now is to examine Table 1 in the appendix to see how the theory generates the predictions. First, the publics or groups under examination. These were chosen because of their frontline or otherwise involved standing with respect to the September 11 attacks. The groups are not mutually exclusive. For example, New Yorkers can include Pacifists/Academic Leftists. Second, the evidence. Clearly the evidence bearing on the predictions came from media reports. They are assumed to be accurate. In any case, they support the predictions. Third, the predictions. These are not predictions in the strictest sense, since they were not offered *a priori*, but only after the attacks. Thus, they must be understood as statements that, given the outcomes of the interaction between these publics and various, relevant others, such and such emotions would have resulted. There is always the danger of shaping the theory, grossly or subtlely, to accommodate the evidence. Fourth, predicting emotions. In general, very little is done by way of predicting emotions, whether in the strong sense of a priori prediction, or even post-diction, as here (see Kemper, 1991, for an instance of *a priori* prediction using the power/status theory). One reason for this is that theorists of emotion have generally refrained from doing so and the data are hard to come by in any case. A further reason is that not many emotions theories are formulated for prediction. In an unusually strong exception, Heise (1989; 1999)[1] presents a very well-developed theory which allows for prediction. Sixth, the emotions. The six emotions considered in Table 1 are conventionally labelled and each label stands for the entire range of feelings that can reasonably be associated with the label. For example, anger is intended to include everything from mild irritation to murderous fury. Thus, some interpolation is required to calibrate the degree to which an emotion is experienced by a particular public.

Let us turn now to some of the specifics of the predictions in Table 1.

The theory predicts that when status is lost *via* action by an other, the emotion most likely to be evoked is anger. Of the ten publics, only New Yorkers/Most Americans are indicated to have felt anger. While this may seem obvious, it must be understood as a differential prediction produced by the theory. More pointedly, given the dominant standing, or status, of the United States in the world community, the September 11 assault can be understood, theoretically, as an immense withdrawal of status by another. Anger is the predicted emotion. None of the other publics had status so markedly withdrawn as did New York and the United States. Therefore, anger is not hypothesized for them.

Sadness is predicted, again differentially, in seven of the ten publics. Since sadness is evoked by irremediable loss, we can see that New Yorkers/Most Americans would be substantially struck. But other publics, whether part of the US population or not, have also some reason to feel sad. It is instructive to partition the groups according to their loss. Such groups as moderate Islamists, Israelis, Authentic US allies, and US Muslims, may all be understood to have suffered a vicarious loss in the terror because of their broad identification or sympathy with the interests of the United States. On the other hand, although Pacifists/Academic Left may share some modest identification with the interests of the United States in the broad sense, I propose that the deeper ground for their sadness can be understood as their having experienced a loss related to an ideological vision of human affairs and the possibility of irenic relations between nations. (Of course, this may be a totally erroneous surmise. It must be considered an hypothesis awaiting test.) Airport Security Agents are yet another distinct group, sharing, it is to be supposed, identification with the United States (although it turns out that substantial numbers of them are not citizens of the US), but also sensing the possibility of job loss as the public abandons air travel and as calls for tighter security focus on the training and competence of the present cadre of security agents.

Fear distinguishes eight of the ten groups, with only fervent Islamists/Radical Left and the Terrorists (which includes the entire Al Qaeda network) omitted from this category. Since fear results from increase in the power of another or loss of one's own power, it should be apparent that the attacks induced considerable fear, most in those (New Yorkers/Most Americans) who had experienced the increase of power of the terrorists. Only Authentic Allies of the US are likely to have felt fear on somewhat the same grounds. Closely identified with the interests of the US, they could also be targeted for terrorist acts. However, other publics are hypothesized to have quite different grounds for fear. Airport Security Agents come under threat of job loss. Pacifists/Academic Left fear that the US retaliation may harm (Afghan) civilians, with whom they identify on ideological grounds. Moderate Islamists fear that the US may strike their country and also that, given the sanction and cover of US reaction to terrorism, Israel too will act more aggressively in response to Palestinian terror attacks. Opportunistic Allies of the US mainly fear that they will themselves become the target of terror attacks if they cooperate too closely with the US. Muslims in the US can be understood to fear that non-Muslims will attack them personally and generally act in a biased fashion toward them.

Joy results from an increase in status. Understandably, the Terrorists and their supporters, namely Fervent Islamists/Radical Left, were quite pleased by the attacks and their results. Demonstrations in various locations—Pakistan, Egypt, Iraq, the West Bank in Palestine, and even Detroit, with its relatively high concentration of Muslims—provided evidence of this joy. Osama bin

Laden, the head of Al Qaeda, the terror network alleged to be responsible for the September 11 attacks, also displayed his pleasure at their outcome as recorded on a tape of him at a social evening in Kandahar, Afghanistan, about a month after the attacks. The joy of the Israelis is of a different order. For more than a year they had been targets of terror stemming from the most recent Intifada, the Palestinian uprising. Their aggressive response to acts of terror did not win them much praise. But the attacks on the United States have given Israelis the feeling that now they are going to be more appreciated, both for striking back at terrorists, as the US is doing, and for what they see as their measured response in doing so.

Shame results from acting in a manner that warrants that one does not deserve the status one has been receiving or is claiming. Moderate Islamists and US Muslims, generally, experienced shame because the terrorists claim to be acting according to the tenets of Islam. Those who feel shame dispute this but feel themselves cast in a poor light by the terrorists' acts. Airport Security Agents may have experienced shame for their poor performance at security check points, although it is not clear that even the closest scrutiny, given the methods of examination in place at the time, would have detected the terrorists' weapons and foiled their plot. But, given that the security agents were placed precisely at the point where the terrorists might have been detected, the attacks cast a shadow over all who are involved in airport security. The hypothesis that security agents did feel shame is less firm that the previous emotion hypotheses and is, thus, marked with a question mark.

Guilt results when one senses one has used excess power toward another. Only Airport Security Agents are tentatively supposed to have felt this emotion. The rationale is that agents may have felt they abused their responsibility, which is to defend the flying public. A lack of defense in this area is tantamount to a loss of status by flyers, who depend on the security agents to protect them from attack. Again, the hypothesis is considered tentative, thus is marked with a question mark.

I contend that the power/status theory adequately predicts, in the sense of prediction used here, the emotions of the different publics. But the effort to do so, with groups about which there is considerable knowledge, leads to some possible elaborations, not so much of the basic theory, but of the conditions for its application. Principally, this entails the different grounds that different groups may have for experiencing the same emotion. As indicated above when considering the emotion fear, the same nominal event, namely the September 11 attacks, precipitated fear in eight of the ten groups, but for at least seven different reasons. It is even possible that for some groups the reasons may have overlapped, but this is only noted here; the analysis will not be carried to this degree of refinement.

In order to retain the validity of the theory in a close analysis, it would be necessary to examine each group and specify the particular other with respect to whom there has been a relative loss of power, the interactional outcome that is theorized to produce fear.

In the case of New Yorkers/Most Americans, the interactional other is the Al Qaeda terrorist group. The interaction outcome, reflecting the fundamental proposition of the theory set forth at the outset, was real. The terrorists actually dealt New Yorkers/Most Americans a blow. In the case of both the Authentic and Opportunistic allies of the US, the interaction is not real but imagined as a possible future event in which terrorists would strike them as they did the US Airport Security Agents also project interaction imaginatively into the future. But their interaction partner, producing the fear, is actually at a remove from the proximate partner, namely the company they work for, that might actually harm (fire) them. The more distant other is Americans, collectively, or represented by the US government, whose wrath over the attacks would spill over into blaming them (the security agents) for America's vulnerability. For Pacifists/Academic Left, the other is, not surprisingly, the US which, in taking military action against Al Qaeda in Afghanistan, would harm civilians, with whom the Pacifists/Academic Left identify. Moderate Islamists also fear potential attack by the US were the war against terror to become a clash of civilizations. Since Moderate Islamists also identify with the Palestinians, any increase in the intensity of Israel's response to the Palestinian uprising is fearful. Finally, US Muslims fear fellow Americans, some few of whom did react violently and/or with discrimination against putative Muslims after September 11.

This examination and breakdown of the differential interaction partners of the different publics in respect to fear after the September 11 attacks, testifies, even if only modestly, to the complexity of large-scale historic events. To predict emotions using power/status theory requires at least this degree of sensitivity to the differential construal and significance of the event to different groups.

The utility of predicting emotions

Let us provisionally suppose that all the predictions discussed above are correct, also the theory from which they are derived. Then one may legitimately ask: So what if the theory can predict emotions correctly? Is there any *sociological* value in that? Actually, it may astonish the reader to learn, relatively little. Not nothing, but not very much either. Let us begin with what little benefit there is in predicting emotions. Taking individuals first, for after all, since emotion is felt within the body, it is manifestly an individual phenomenon, and most theories of emotions have begun at this point. (The issue of group emotions is treated in the last section.)

The utility of predicting the emotions of individuals has mainly what can be called *enlightenment* and *control* functions. Many individuals do not grasp fully what they are feeling, which may be due to various causes, for example, they may have a poor emotion vocabulary, hence can't name their feeling; or they may have learned to repress emotions and are now unable easily to capture them cognitively before they go underground, so to speak. A theory that clearly allows individuals to examine systematically their prior social interactional circumstances as clues to what they may be feeling can provide insight into ambiguous affect and make possible the naming of it by working up from the social context. This is a valuable contribution for individuals.

Further, individuals who want to control their emotions would also profit from an accurate theory that predicts their emotions as a consequence of inter-action outcomes. It becomes, thereby, easier to enhance desirable emotions and avoid undesirable ones by arranging one's social interactions to achieve the given goal (Thoits, 1990). This is also a valuable outcome for individuals of a good predictive theory of emotions.

Taken together, the enlightenment and control benefits of predicting emo-tions entail a view of emotions as more or less *endpoint* variables. But beyond this, we have gained very little sociologically when we know the emotions, even with a certainty. For example, to be able to predict that a given interaction will produce anger in a participant is a severely limited result, since it does not indi-cate how the individual will socially cope with his or her anger. That is, what further interactions and social relations will result from the anger? By and large, considering anger, let us suppose that one could cope either by *fighting* or *not fighting*. If the fighting option is taken, will it be overt combat (*mano a mano*, for example), or verbal combat, or will it be covert fighting, such as discredit-ing the one who instigated the anger, either by telling the truth or lying about him or her to third parties.

And, if fighting has alternative paths, so too does not-fighting. For example, one can exit the situation (Hirschmann, 1970). Or one can suppress the anger and act toward the other deceptively, as if one were not angry, while awaiting an opportunity for retaliation. Or one can repress the anger and beguile oneself into thinking it does not exist, only to have it burst out in aggressive action in a relatively unprovoked situation. Or perhaps it will be displaced onto a surro-gate other. Or one can sublimate the anger so that its 'energy' is dissipated relatively harmlessly, perhaps even creatively. All these are possible sequels to anger, which an emotions theory, even successfully predicting anger, is not likely to deal with.

Similar examination of other emotions would reveal similar variety in social coping options. Given this view of how a theory of emotions may be insuffi-cient for sociological purposes, we may think of emotions as merely *intervening variables*, by contrast with the endpoint view discused above.

No theory of emotions has thus far developed the necessary propositions that would enable the prediction of the coping response, given the emotion. Heise (1989; 1999) is a possible exception. Clearly, this extension of theory could require consideration of a great many additional circumstances beyond out-comes of social interaction, including especially the 'personality' of the actor and his or her evaluation, perhaps through a rational choice analysis (Coleman, 1990) of the advantages and disadvantages of one or another response. But some sociological conditions that reflect the power/status structure can also be relevant to determining the social coping response.

For example, we might consider the degree of power disparity between the two actors. When power disparity is extremely large, we would not ordinarily expect an overt fight reaction when the actor with lesser power is made angry by the actor with greater power, since the disparity would most likely make overt aggressive response nugatory and result in severe punishment. In cases of great power disparity, we might more often expect covert aggression, as the terrorist acts of September 11 demonstrate.

Conversely, when the power disparity is very great, an attack by the one with lesser power on the one with greater power is highly likely to evoke a strong, overt-fight response from the one with greater power. Barbalet (1998) has usefully pointed out the high probability of a fear reaction when élites are attacked by lower social groups. When the fear is augmented by anger, as is the case with New Yorkers/Most Americans after September 11, the chance of a strong fight reaction is intensified. Finally, given the great disparity in power, for the one with greater power a strong fight response is usually available at relatively low cost.

A second structural consideration is the potential for amassing power *via* recruiting allies to assist in a fight response. Indeed, the US did this as a coping response in both the Gulf War of 1990 and before launching military action against Afghanistan after September 11. Gaining allies may not increase one's own power arithmetically, but multiplicatively. This is more likely when new allies are recruited from among former supporters of the enemy. A crucial instance of this was the US recruitment of Pakistan, a former supporter of the Afghan Taliban, against its former clients.

A third structural factor in assessing a power response is how many enemies of the enemy there may be. Again reflecting on the September 11 attacks, Russia and China might normally have been expected to resist the projection of US power into a region that is high on their list of vital interests. Except that these countries are themselves contending with Islamic insurrections, the Russians in Chechnya and the Chinese in Xianjang province, bordering Afghanistan.

While these several structural conditions that helped the US amass power or the ancillary resources of power (eg, airbases near Afghanistan) certainly helped to determine the US coping response to its anger after the September 11 attacks, this is not to say that the US would not have acted entirely alone, both in venting its anger and in the effort to kill or capture terrorist leader Osma bin Laden. The US is, after all, at this point in time, the dominant military power in the world, hence it can, without assistance, pretty much, even if not wholly, do what it wants militarily.

This consideration adds a fourth structural condition to those mentioned, namely the absolute amount of power available as a coping response. In this case, nuclear retaliation against Afghanistan must also have been considered as an option in the period shortly after September 11. Nor can it be guaranteed that, had the US been unable to recruit a world-wide coalition against terrorism—both authentic and opportunistic—including nations on the very border of Afghanistan, the nuclear option would not have been taken.

But the complexity of the issue is not exhausted by naming structural features that reflect the extant power/status situation. These must be augmented by yet another feature of power relations, namely whether the power inspires sufficient fear to gain the desired compliance. For example, as demonstrated by the September 11 attacks, ideology, such as consummate faith in God, can turn even the weakest actors into highly dedicated, highly destructive combatants, willing to suffer self-immolation as long as they exert disproportionate injury to an enemy. Introducing religious faith or other ideology into the prediction equation makes for an extremely complex basis for assessing coping response. Those who do not fear to die in confronting their enemy, to a large extent, although not completely, nullify the power of the other. Generally speaking, all resistance movements that adopt guerilla tactics, suicide bombings and the like have more or less neutralized the power of their more powerful opponent. With one exception: if the more powerful actor destroys the weaker actor(s) entirely, as might be the case in a nuclear response.

To date, no theory of emotions has shed much light on the sociological consequences of emotions. The task is made even harder when we consider the emotions of groups, by contrast with those of individuals.

Emotions in groups

Although the power/status theory of emotions presented above was constructed mainly with individuals in mind, it can be applied to groups. The power and status dimensions are arguably fundamental not only in interindividual interactions, but also in interactions between larger entities, including nations (Kemper and Collins, 1990; Kemper, 1992). Thus, it was entirely legitimate to apply these dimensions and the predictions previously tested on individuals to various large publics in the aftermath of September 11. But this is not to say that individual emotions and group emotions are identical or, that, given the same circumstances, they lead to equivalent coping responses. It is not automatically precluded that individuals and groups experiencing the same emotion may react similarly. What is precluded is that they must do so.

In respect to the similarity between individual emotions and group emotions, it is useful also to dismiss any antiquated notion of 'group mind.' Emotion is fundamentally and incontrovertibly an individual level phenomenon. Only individuals experience emotions. Thus, when we speak of a group emotion, we can mean only that some aggregate of individuals is feeling something that is sufficiently alike to be identified as the common emotion of that aggregate. This common emotion may be the most prominent affective face of the group. Yet, as Lofland (1985: 39) has put it, when we are looking at a 'dominant emotion,' which he defines as 'the publicly expressed feeling perceived by participants and observers as most prominent in an episode . . . it is not to say that an especially large portion of the collectivity feels that emotion.' Thus, only a relatively small number of group members may actually be feeling the emotion as such, that is, with all the cognitive and physiological attributes that distinguish that emotion. In tandem with them, however, may be a very large number of group members (a 'silent majority') who do not fully feel the emotion themselves, but do not reject the propriety of feeling it in the given situation. Thus, while not personally experiencing the emotion, these bystanders, so to speak, add substance to any observation that it is the emotion the group is feeling.

Yet another way in which a group may be said to feel an emotion is through its expression by representative members, those who are especially charged with carrying the symbolic and practical aspects of the group and its purposes into interaction with the representative members of other groups. Heads of state at summit meetings with other heads of state, ambassadors executing their mission, trade negotiators bargaining for market advantage, these are all carriers of the group's interests and it would be reasonable to assume that their representations to their counterparts are backed by their group's feelings about the matter under consideration. Here arise issues of leadership and legitimacy. Representatives cannot indifferently conclude agreements that defy their group's prevailing sentiments without courting a legitimacy crisis. An outstanding example of this was the doomed effort of President Woodrow Wilson in 1919–20 to bring the US into the League of Nations, when the national mood was opposed to such 'foreign entanglements.' In totalitarian states, the dominant emotion is something to be manipulated and mobilized via various strategies of emotional arousal (see Berezin, 1997).

One of the major differences between individual and group emotions is that an individual, even if conflicted, feels a given emotion fully despite its competition with another emotion, while in the group only some may feel the given emotion. When an individual is in a state of conflicted arousal, as when one is angry with a loved one, but also feeling joyful toward him or her, coping actions based on either emotion may be deferred or moderated by comparison with the response in a nonconflicted state. When a group is in a similar state of conflicted arousal two (or perhaps more) loci of emotions are contending for dominance. The emotions of American citizens during the Viet Nam war portray such a case. What ensued was a power struggle between the groups most committed to the competing emotions. The winner of the struggle was then able to implement the coping strategy it wanted in the name of the entire group. In the case of the Viet Nam war, the domestic struggle was mainly won by the US government until some time in 1970, when the Kent State University shootings by National Guardsmen of unarmed students turned the sentiments of the anti-war movement into the dominant emotion of the country. Extrication from the war, even by those who favoured it, became the desired coping response.

What this illustrates is that the resolution of emotional conflict in groups takes place as a social process, usually political and sometimes bitter, with violent and destructive consequences. By contrast, although emotional conflict in individuals can be intense, the resolution rarely leads to the 'death' of some part of the individual, as may be the case of similar emotional conflict in groups, where members may die when the conflict can no longer be contained.

We can speak here, further, of a division of labour of emotions within groups. Only in exceptional circumstances does the dominant emotion become virtually universal. Events such as Pearl Harbour and the September 11 attacks are of such an order. So consequential were the power and status effects unleashed that it would have been difficult for anyone to avoid a common visceral reaction to them. Regardless of situation or condition, virtually all Americans could feel themselves both imperiled and reduced in standing, since the enemy, in both instances, acted successfully to achieve these effects.

Notwithstanding any tendency toward a universal effect, in a large group, some will, by delusion or by ideology or by conscious refusal to accommodate the prevailing emotional current, *not* respond to the power and status outcomes as these are recognized by most others. These types of nonreactors or dissenters introduce the first division in the othewise universal distribution of emotions.

A second division manifests itself in the intensity with which constituent elements of the group experience an emotion, for example, after September 11, power and status loss and their consequent emotions, fear and anger. In large geographical spaces, such as the United States, distance from the first impact of the event is an important moderator of the intensity of response. In the case of Pearl Harbour, the West Coast of the US sensed itself to be more vulnerable than the Middle West or eastern part of the country. Hence the emotions were heightened in the states on the Pacific shore. Conversely, the September 11 attacks on New York and Washington, D.C., inspired far greater fear in the East than elsewhere and a correspondingly greater sense of vulnerability.

In addition to spatial differentiation of felt power and status effects and emotional reactions, there is the full gamut of social and demographic variables—principally, age, sex, and class—that summarize the location of different groups in the division of labour and in the power and status structures of society. Together, these locations mark the degree of investment, both material and symbolic, that different groups in society possess. Doubtless, those on the margins of society will have less of a stake, hence less of a sense of loss when the overall national power and status standing is reduced. For example, blacks could feel that an attack on the US was less damaging to them than to whites, who have a greater investment in a racist society. This was an issue too in the period of the Viet Nam war, although in that national crisis, age was the dominant social denominator of emotion. The young, especially men, who felt themselves subject to the draft, were particularly antagonistic to US policy. Older cohorts, with less to lose in the short run (they wouldn't have to fight) and more to lose in the long run (should Communism succeed in Southeast Asia) were more supportive of the war. Yet even within broad demographic categories, individual variation in emotion was common.

In sum, the relative unity that prevails in the individual experiencing a given emotion is, except in rare cases, offset in groups by the multiplicity of interests and degrees of involvement of group members. These make coping responses in groups more likely to be caught up in processes of negotiation, manipulation, or outright violence. In the latter case, the emotion-based policies of one day

64

can succumb overnight to opposite emotion-based policies, as when a revolution topples an existing regime.

Conclusion

Although it would seem to be a desirable achievement in any science to be able to predict the phenomena the science attempts to explain, in the case of emotions, the efficacy of prediction is somewhat limited. This is somewhat less true in the case of individuals, where simple knowledge of what one is feeling is itself of value. Knowing what one is feeling resolves cognitive uncertainty and allows for rational control of the emotions, where this is indicated. Individuals in interaction with other individuals may also benefit from a successful predictive theory, since it provides understanding of what interaction moves will likely evoke what emotions. Despite these benefits, this knowledge alone does not afford much insight into what the individual will actually do, how the person will cope. And it is the latter that is of sociological interest.

In the case of groups, the problem is compounded by the fact that the enlightenment and control aspects of emotional knowledge are of little value. There is no central cognitive processor that would find advantage in clarifying its understanding of what the group is feeling. Indeed, it would be unnecessary, since in most instances of group emotion, there are individuals who are fully aware of the group's emotion and are able to name it. But even more than in the case of individuals, the group's coping response is sociologically problematic. It requires an extensive understanding of the power-status structure of the group in relation to the group's interaction partner, and, where there are competing emotions for dominance, an understanding of the group's internal power-status structure, and how the groups feeling the competing emotions are related to each other. There is a degree of complexity here that no theory of emotions has begun to address.

Not to end on an entirely negative note, a good predictive theory of emotions serves in one positive capacity in respect to emotions in groups: as in the case of interacting individuals, it enables understanding of what interaction moves are likely to produce given emotions. That could be of benefit to interaction partners who are either trying to provoke a given emotion or who are trying to avoid provoking it. Not because the given emotion is itself of great import, but, rather that it would set the stage for either a desirable or undesirable coping response, respectively. Interaction partners, even at the level of groups, are interested in such knowledge, even if knowledge of the coping response is not assured.

Notes

* I want to thank Edgar M. Mills, Jr., for comments and suggestions on this paper.
1 Space does not permit examing Heise's approach to emotion prediction here.

References

Barbalet, J. (1998) *Emotion, Social Theory and Social Structure: A Macrosociological Approach.* Cambridge: Cambridge University Press.

Berezin, M. (1997) *Making the Fascist Self: The Political Culture of Inter-war Italy,* New York: Cornell University Press.

Coleman, J. (1990) *The Foundations of Social Theory.* Cambridge, MA: Harvard University Press.

Heise, D.R. (1989) 'Effects of Emotion Displays on Social Identification,' *Social Psychology Quarterly,* 52: 10–21.

Heise, D.R. (1999) 'Controlling Affective Experience Interpersonally,' *Social Psychology Quarterly,* 62: 4–16.

Hirschmann, A. (1970) *Exit, Voice and Loyalty: Responses to Decline in Firms.* Cambridge, MA: Harvard University Press.

Kemper, T.D. (1978) *A Social Interactional Theory of Emotions.* New York: John Wiley.

Kemper, T.D. (1987) 'How Many Emotions Are There? Wedding the Social and the Autonomic Components,' *American Journal of Sociology,* 93: 263–289.

Kemper, T.D. (1991) 'Predicting Emotions from Social Relations,' *Social Psychology Quarterly,* 54: 330–342.

Kemper, T.D. and Collins, R. (1990) 'Dimensions of Micro-Interaction,' *American Journal of Sociology,* 96: 32–68.

Lofland, J. (1985) *Protest: Studies of Collective Behavior and Social Movements,* New Brunswick, NJ: Transaction Books.

Simmel, G. (1964 [1923]) 'The Isolated Individual and the Dyad,' *The Sociology of Georg Simmel,* trans. Wolff, K. New York: Free Press.

Thoits, P. (1990) 'Emotional Deviance: Research Agendas.' *Research Agendas in the Sociology of Emotions,* Kemper, T.D. (ed.). Albany, NY: State University of New York Press.

Weber, M. (1946) *From Max Weber: Essays in Sociology,* trans. Gerth, H. and Mills, C.W. New York: Oxford University Press.

Appendix 1

Hypotheses about the emotional aftermath of September 11

I offer here some hypotheses concerning the emotions that the September 11 tragedy has activated in ten different publics. I derived the hypotheses from my work, *A Social Interactional Theory of Emotions* (Wiley, 1978). Doubtless many will dispute my proposals here. At a minimum, I hope to stir some discussion on the theoretical grounds for predicting emotions. I have not studied the different publics, but have relied on impressions derived from the media. Doubtless I may have erred in one or another case. The hypotheses are the emotions I attribute to the various publics and these are shown in Table 1.

The publics as well as the emotions are 'ideal types.' Individuals may belong to more than a single public, which may entail some emotional conflict, if the publics have contrary emotions.

I do not consider intensity of emotion here, but only try to locate the presence of the emotional category in the given public.

Some emotions are numbered and the numbers are discussed in footnotes.

Table 1

PUBLICS	EMOTIONS					
	Anger	Sadness	Fear	Joy	Shame	Guilt
New Yorkers/Most Americans	X	X	X1			
Airport Security Agents		X	X2		X(?)	X(?)
Pacifists/Academic Left		X	X3			
Fervent Islamists/Radical Left				X		
Moderate Islamists		X	X4		X	
Israelis		X		X5		
US Allies: Authentic		X	X			
US Allies: Opportunistic			X6			
Terrorists				X		
US Muslims		X	X7		X	

X1—New Yorkers and most Americans fear another attack
X2—Airport Security Agents are fearful over the possible loss of their jobs
X3—Pacifists and academic left fear the US may strike civilian targets
X4—Moderate Islamists fear US retaliation and believe Israel may be more aggressive in responding to terror
X5—Israelis are joyful that at last the US can better understand Israel's daily torment
X6—Opportunistic US allies fear US displeasure if they do not cooperate with the US, but also fear attacks by terrorists if they cooperate too much
X7—US Muslims fear they will be attacked for the deeds of their co-religionists

Definitions

Anger stems from witting or unwitting punitive actions by other(s) that deprive the self of the usual, normative, or legitimately expected benefits and advantages that accrue to one's status, or that inflict such deprivations and punishments on others with whom one is identified.

Sadness stems from witting or unwitting punitive actions by self or by other(s) that deprive one irremediably of the usual, normative, or legitimately expected benefits and advantages that accrue to one's status or that inflict such deprivations and punishments on others with whom one is identified. Irremediability, such as in the case of death, is crucial here.

Fear stems from possible actions by other(s) that make one vulnerable to punishment and deprivation, or that make others with whom one is identified so vulnerable.

Joy stems from receiving benefits and advantages from other(s), especially when these go beyond what is usual, normative, or legitimately expected.

Shame stems from the sense that one has acted in a manner to reduce the level of one's standing and status, ie, that one does not deserve as much status as one has claimed from others, or that others with whom one identifies have so acted.

Guilt stems from the sense that one has acted in a manner to cause pain and/or deprivation to another who does not deserve it.

(For more detail, see *A Social Interactional Theory of Emotions*)

Emotions and economics

Jocelyn Pixley

Abstract

This chapter examines approaches to emotions in orthodox and various Keynesian-influenced economics, with regard to 'interest' and expectations, and compares it to sociological emotions research. First it shows how economics ignores 'passions' like greed or avarice by transmuting them to the allegedly more predictable, less emotional and completely 'rational' motives of interests. Interest, in contemporary orthodox accounts, is said basically to account for expectations but the accounts are derived from the Renaissance view that 'interest will not lie'. In contrast, the less orthodox economic view argues that expectations are merely imagination and hope, however much data, expertise and information are used, and are thus far from predictable. The chapter then compares Keynesian concepts of emotions such as 'animal spirits' with sociological understandings of them. The contribution that emotions research can make to emotions in economic decision-making is then considered. Financial organizations, in particular, are obsessed with the future, hence the future-oriented emotions of confidence, optimism, pessimism, fear and trust are unavoidable, but this is an endlessly unlearned and regenerative process. Finally, the chapter touches on the policy implications of an alternative understanding of the typical emotions deployed in decision-making by financial organizations.

Introduction

Economic sociology—despite its significant revival in the past twenty years—has not had much impact on economics. One reason is the legacy of the 'gentlemen's agreement' between Parsons and Robbins to a strict division of labour between the means of economic action and its underlying values (Ingham, 1996b). For many economists, sociology still deals with the 'residue of "irrationality"... and "tosh"' (as Ingham recounts 1996b: 244–5). Dialogue is rare—with the exception of an honourable small group of individuals and institutionalized offerings like the *American Journal of Economics and Sociology*.[1] Alongside mutual ignorance of each other, while sociology is marginal in contemporary public debate, economics is as much a perceived source of social problems that Barbalet (in this volume) mentions of science.[2] After twenty years of neoclassical hegemony at policy level and within the academy, its irresponsibility and lack of credibility even within economics are public knowledge.[3]

Yet neoclassical prescriptions, now long implemented, have made governments particularly mindful of financial markets and paralyse policy-makers from seeking economic alternatives. The Third Way sociology of Giddens, Beck, Etzioni and even Castells, which some allege has influenced Tony Blair, Bill Clinton and various labour parties (Frankel, 2001), is not economic sociology and fails in social democratic terms. What these sociologists by and large offer governments are communitarian 'solutions'—redefined as workfare—for the failures and fallouts from economic policy. Third Way sociology provides no analytic means to subordinate economic policy to social policy, as was more or less achieved by Keynesian policies of equitable wages and full employment.

Despite this pessimistic backdrop, new developments in economic sociology give reason for optimism. Research on emotions in particular has much to offer economic sociology, especially when combined with select schools of thought in economics.

In the last twenty years, economic sociology has taken two directions. The first accepts the primacy of economics by taking the rational actor model for granted. Jon Elster and other 'analytical Marxists' fall resolutely into this strand, with the latter's sole gesture to social policy their proposal for a guaranteed or basic income (eg Van Parijs, 1992). This kind of analysis leads to similar policy prescriptions as Milton Friedman's, and it is homologous to postmodern celebrations of an aesthetic, consumerist 'self' (Pixley, 1997; 1993). Rather differently, the general sociology of Third Way approaches largely accepts neoclassical tenets of the state (= bad) and market (= good). Poorly defined concepts, 'information', 'trust', 'social capital', to name the most obvious, are held to cushion *socially* excluded groups from purportedly unstoppable processes of 'globalization'.

The second direction, led by Mark Granovetter and Richard Swedberg, challenges orthodox economics and rational choice, largely at the 'micro' level of economic life. Economic sociology tends to focus on the 'embeddedness' of norms, personal networks and role performance as critical to market activities (Zuckerman, 1999; Uzzi, 1999). Yet, as Geoffrey Ingham points out (1996b: 267), this approach rarely moves to more abstract levels, including macroeconomic concepts like 'growth', 'inflation' or forces of 'supply and demand'. While economic activities are 'embedded' in interpersonal relations, macro levels remain beyond the scope of sociological analysis. Exceptions include sociological treatments of inflation (Hirsch & Goldthorpe, 1978; Swedberg, 1987), also explored in a sociological manner by an economist like Hirschman in his aptly entitled *Essays in Trespassing* (1981).

Trespassing into economic territory by sociologists is equally important. Emotions research finds an entry point with Keynes's concept of 'animal spirits', despite its superficiality and methodological individualism. But more importantly, economics, even the most orthodox, is fundamentally the study of expectations. This point cannot be stressed enough. Unaware of this shift, sociologists tend to set up straw economic persons complete with predictive foresight.[4] While the Keynesian 'revolution' was defeated thirty years ago, few economists can avoid Keynes's concept of uncertainty. All economists agree that expectations are their object of study. Non-orthodox economics, including Post Keynesians, emphasize uncertainty. Orthodox economics, in contrast, holds that while the future cannot be *predicted*, risk can be substituted for uncertainty, and probability distributions of risks can be developed (but see Keynes, 1937; Shackle, 1967; Knight, [1921] 1965).

Expectation, so central to economics, is a key cite for research on emotions. Sociology offers an emerging literature on intrinsic emotional elements of expectations in general. It will be shown below that research on emotions not only demolishes rational actor models of expectations more thoroughly than most critiques (such as Lane, 1991 or Wolff, 1993) but also offers an alternative. It can achieve this at both the 'micro' level of interpersonal relationships and at more 'macro' impersonal inter-organisational levels.

Rational actor models assume that decision making involves optimizing expected benefits. But expected benefits *ex ante* are only hopes (Shackle, 1972)— they involve emotions—as the outcome *ex post* is uncertain. In monetary economies, outcomes are always uncertain as decisions between liquidity and investment options can be deferred; expectations can collapse. Rational models, in denying this fundamental uncertainty, refuse to accept that expectation entails mere hope. Uncertainty concerning the future cannot be dissolved by application of a probability distribution on current 'indicators' of expectations. It is, though, appropriate to focus upon hopeful and confidence-inducing practices and rituals arising out of fundamental uncertainty. Emotional interpersonal relations, creative imagination and emotional attachment to indicators of average opinion are essential in generating expectations.

Application of emotions research to economics here avoids a cognitivist understanding of passions and emotions (see Barbalet, 1998: 22–6; Collins, 1990). Manipulation of emotions can occur in all social action, thus 'trust us' was the overt message of firms like Bankers Trust. But passions are not only a conscious manipulation ('once more, with feeling') because the managed emotion itself can give rise to 'uncontrollable', less consciously-managed passions like smugness (we are more enthusiastic than they are) or to guilt, self-disgust or shame about such manipulations. Importantly, in the face of radical uncertainty at the peak of economic decision-making, there is an obsession with forecasting built into the standard operating procedures of firms, and this focus gives rise to below-the-threshold emotions, or overt fear and panic. My thesis is that the contemporary financial sector is continually in a state of denial about (a) the problem that none of these impersonal organizations know the future; (b) that they must therefore rely on emotions to make decisions; (c) that corporate ends or aims are increasingly for greed than 'innocuous' interest and (d) that this is an endlessly unlearned regenerative process.

As Randall Collins points out, the objects of any decision—the 'utility' of each preference—are emotionally preferred and chosen through a dynamic generated by 'interaction rituals' in specific organized and/or group situations (Collins, 1993). From this basis emotions research can move to 'macro' aspects of economic life. Emotions do not merely 'shape preferences' externally, because aggregated business confidence surveys—all those desperate searches for clues to the future—highlight the dynamic nature of emotions in economic life. Sociological emotions research can show that impersonal, inter-organization relationships are relations of trust and mistrust, over-confidence, distrust, hope and sometimes fear. Outcomes *ex post* generate new chains of interaction rituals, and new levels of emotional energy and responses. As Flam (in this volume) argues, many corporations are emotional, if 'non-feeling'. But if all decision-making draws on emotions, which are not necessarily 'irrational' because they cannot be avoided in formulating expectations and deciding to act, then all corporations must be emotional as well as rational (if 'non-thinking' as only individual persons think and feel). 'Impersonal' emotions (Pixley, 1999a) are part of corporate relations and, through the ritual duties and obligations imposed on office-bearers, are generated and then 'felt' personally by those actors in decision-making positions. Of particular interest is the process whereby emotions in economic decision making can turn into their contraries *ex post*. This process tends to personalize and incorrectly attribute the impersonal, organizational requirements entailed in decision-making to corporate scapegoats and heroes.

This chapter begins by examining approaches to emotions in orthodox economics, with regard to 'interest' and expectations. It then considers Keynesian concepts of emotions and sociological understandings of them. The contribution that emotions research can make to emotions in economic decision-making is then considered. Finally, the chapter looks at the policy implications of an alternative understanding of emotions in finance.

Emotions and 'interest'

It is appropriate to begin by stressing that economics is deeply attached to the conventional distinction between emotions and rationality. Equally, it should be remembered that economic rationality is not the rationality of the conventional 'disinterested pursuit' of the natural scientist, or the rational exegesis or hermeneutical analysis of texts. Economic rationality refers to a means-end procedure of decision-making with the end overwhelmingly assumed in the literature to be interest—in economic terms the single 'maximand' is money (Lane, 1991: 43). The link between interest and greed renders all this problematic (see Hirschman, [1977] 1997).

Hirschman, an economist, argues that the historical transformation of the meaning of passion for money (or 'purely private pursuit of riches') into mere 'innocuous' interest was endogenous to Western thought and Western political establishments (Hirschman, 1997: 129). This was the intention but not the result (passion cannot be 'ruled out' (1997: 135) and, for Hirschman, triumphant capitalism has not exactly been 'innocuous'). He contrasts this with Weber's thesis of an unintended consequence of an excluded, albeit emergent, set of Protestant sects who sought asceticism but found self-interest to be their 'calling'. Hirschman begins with St Augustine's medieval view—well known—about the three major sins, passion for power, passion for gold and sexual passion. His main thesis dwells on emerging Renaissance arguments about how various passions (for Vico 'ferocity, avarice, and ambition': cited Hirschman, 1997: 17) could be 'harnessed' (1997: 16) and act to countervail each other. Bacon sought 'to set affection against affection and to master one by the other' (cited 1997: 22). Greed is eventually seen to be 'tamer', more prudent and 'reasonable' than the 'wild' passions (1997: 31, 35) and, as transformed into 'advantage' and innocuous 'interest' (1997: 19) the intention was that it could 'tame' the other passions. Machiavelli's prudent, calculating *ragioni di stato* is a long way in principle from when, by the end of the 17th century, the interest or reason of the state went to the market place. By then 'interest acquired a specifically economic meaning' (Raab, cited Hirschman, 1997: 37).

Thus Barbalet points to Weber's contradictory insistence on separating rationality from emotions. For example, Puritans rationally, as in purposefully, pursued their calling but in Weber's own word 'hated' superstition (Barbalet, 1998: 37). Hirschman cites another history of Western ideas when the traditional dichotomy between reason and passion seemed capable of transcendence with a third category. It is an inspired passage:

> Once passion was deemed destructive and reason ineffectual [in the late 16th century] . . . a message of hope was therefore conveyed by the wedging of interest in between the two traditional categories of human motivation. Interest was seen to partake in effect of the better nature of each, as the passion of self-love upgraded and contained by reason, and as reason given direction and force by that passion. The resulting hybrid form of human action was considered exempt from both the destructiveness of passion and the ineffectuality of reason (Hirschman, 1997: 45–6).

Interest as a hybrid of passion (avarice) and reason is rarely entertained in economics beyond a distinction between altruism and a passion-less or 'dispassionate' but not impartial self-interest (eg, Gill, 1996; Rowthorn, 1996)[5]. But in popular usage this hybrid is ubiquitous and naturalized—either in cynical or innocuous form. Sociology has opposed the reductionism and abstraction from the social context but, often, at the expense of considering greed behind self-interest or as emotion.[6] In contrast, and nearly as an aside on Machiavelli's pessimistic diagnosis (the Prince can safely assume that humans are invariably 'ungrateful, voluble, false, hypocritical, cowardly, greedy': cited in Hirschman, 1997: 49), Hirschman hints at how useful the up-graded view of an 'interest-governed world' is to economics. The use lies in the 'predictability and constancy' thought to reside in subsequent allegations that 'Interest Will Not Lie' (cited 1997: 49).

Emotions according to 'received wisdom' in economics

'Interest' is the heart of economic theory, neoclassical, Marxist, even Post Keynesian deconstructionists.[7] Orthodox economists' concept of expectations are focused on allegedly 'predictable' self interest, or upgraded self-love. Against this backdrop of a story of the development of ideas, and bearing in mind that popular conceptions of interest still equate it with greed, let us consider economic views of emotions relevant to expectations. Jon Elster, who defends rational choice 'as a way of coming to grips with ourselves . . . [about] what we should be' (Elster, 1993: 179), provides an excellent case.

Recently in the mainstream *Journal of Economic Literature*, Elster accused economics of refusing to consider that emotions could be part of 'the tool kit of economics' (1998: 47). An interesting challenge at first sight, it in fact accentuates and 'legitimates' the point that economics avoids emotions. Elster treats a vast literature in his subsequent *Alchemies of the Mind: Rationality and the Emotions* (1999), but ultimately to diminish the challenge of emotions to rational choice. He draws on psychological, philosophical, literary and neuroscientific approaches to emotions, but excludes most relevant developments in sociology.[8] More seriously, he leaves unexamined the presumption that rational choice is unproblematic. At the end of his lengthy discussion he concludes that emotions get in the way of rational decision-making.

It might be noted that Elster's only mention of *The Passions and the Interests* is the statement that:

> Albert Hirschman has shown that in the eighteenth century *passion and interest* were frequently held up against each other, the latter being thought capable of holding at bay the more destructive aspects of the former. Hence the dominance of interest over passion in a commercial society constituted a 'political argument for capitalism before its triumph' (Elster, 1999: 336–7).

Thus, in a chapter on transmutation and misrepresentation (through shame or guilt) of what he describes as three key motivations—reason, passion and interest—Elster elides Hirschman's entire account of interest as passion. Indeed, 'with regard to the transmutation of interest into passion, I can imagine illustrations but not actually cite real or fictional examples' (Elster, 1999: 334), and none entail greed or avarice (1999: 355–6). But love of gold, from King Midas to Scrooge, are hardly unknown cultural and literary topics: many popular films, thousands of websites and numerous journalists constantly focus on greed: few scholars do so (Robertson, 2001: 2–6). When Elster explores reason (as aiming for understanding), there is a brief discussion of Habermas's approach,[9] before giving his own conception of reason. 'I shall count any impartial, disinterested, and dispassionate motive as a reasonable one'. As Elster sees it, this impartiality can easily be transmuted to, or misrepresented from, passion or interest (Elster, 1999: 339). 'By *interest* I mean any motive, common to the members of some proper subgroup of society, that aims at improving the situation of that subgroup in some respect such as pleasure, wealth, fame, status, or power' (Elster, 1999: 340, his emphasis). Passion, he reiterates, is not the same. Yet, one only need substitute his mild 'aims at improving' in the above passage, with more urgent terms ('relentless pursuit', for example) to arrive at all three 'medieval' passions. Interaction rituals of the boardroom, as suggested by Collins, can turn finance groups into 'money-making junkies' (1993: 220). At least, interest is hardly immune to passion.

A key issue is Elster's view of emotions in rationality as decision-making. While he argues finally that emotions have a dual role in 'shaping choices as well as rewards' and that an 'interest in survival' or material gain may check other emotions (1999: 413), it is essential to outline his full discussion of emotions and rational choice. Elster lists how 'the traditional view' of rationality conceives emotions as an interference. He then looks at two 'revisionist' accounts, first that emotions may 'promote' rational decisions by 'acting as tie-breakers in cases of indeterminacy' or by making us consider 'salient features of the situation'. A second revisionist account is the 'sadder but wiser' hypothesis of the incompatibility of 'rational belief formation' with 'emotional well-being' (Elster, 1999: 284).

Elster's subjectivist notion of rational choice (1999: 284) entails three 'optimizing operations': an optimal chosen action relative to 'desires and beliefs'; optimal beliefs given available information, and optimal resources spent on acquisition of information. From this, 'rationality can fail in two ways: By indeterminacy or by irrationality' (Elster, 1999: 285). Passion primarily subverts rational choice through a 'lack of regard for consequences—including the lack of regard for more information' (1999: 287) or through social norms. The most interesting discussion concerns the idea of learned somatic markers (Damasio, 1994) or 'gut feelings' as an aid to rational choice. Elster believes the 'key idea' (1999: 287) is that emotions can help expedite decisions but he rejects the stronger claim of a causal link between emotions and decision making (1999: 288). He accepts emotions as a tie breaker may help in the 'indeterminacy' of indifference, 'when two options are equally and maximally good' (1999: 288), but he argues that non-emotional tie-breakers also exist. In the case of the 'indeterminacy' of incommensurability where one cannot make up one's mind (say, between two brands of a car), Elster suggests flipping a coin instead of consulting 'gut feelings' (Elster, 1999: 288). The same is proposed—the coin flip or the gut feeling—for an indeterminacy of 'ignorance' but this is only about whether the costs of getting 'more information may exceed the benefits' (1999: 289).

Elster does not admit that rationality is dependent on emotions for lack of any reliable guide to action about the unknowable future. The focus on the costs of gathering information neglects that today's information cannot foretell any outcome *ex post*. A bank may expect that claims on future wealth generated by a firm will be realized, it might not. Keynesian uncertainty does not exist for Elster, only indeterminacy (either indifference or incommensurability: 1999: 288). The flippant image of tossing a coin is, however, exactly what Luhmann proposes (1979: 24) for trust: trust is involved at the precise moment of decision-making as 'trust is a gamble' which depends on lack of contrary knowledge. Elster uses flippant examples (choice between two cars). What about decisions of great moment? Alan Greenspan cannot emerge from a Federal Open Market Committee meeting and declare that the basis of the interest rate decision—by seven Boards of Governors and five district bank governors—was arrived at by tossing a coin. Public confidence would collapse, as when an Australian Treasurer (John Kerin) was forced to resign after acknowledging that he did not know the future. But Elster omits trust and confidence *per se*: for Elster the future is knowable (if it were not for the costs of gaining information: as New Keynesians also argue against the notion of uncertainty).

Elster suggests that Damasio presents a 'strawman of rational choice theory' that always accounts for every outcome of every possible situation (1999: 290). This is not quite so, as Damasio (1994: 58) also emphasizes how emotions foster creativity and enable futures to be imagined. Damasio's inability to acknowledge uncertainty (Barbalet, 1998: 42) is similar to Elster's, but Elster's solution is more facile: 'a rational person would know that under certain conditions it is better to follow a simple mechanical decision rule than to use more elaborate procedures with higher opportunity costs' (Elster, 1999: 290–1). This might entail his coin tossing or 'a little click in my mind' (1999: 296). For him, 'the emotion serves as *a functional equivalent for the rational faculties it suspends* . . . that reason, if left undisturbed, could have come up with by itself' (1999: 291 his emphasis). Elster and Damasio accept that the time taken on counting every contingency might prevent a decision, Elster however takes the view that there is reliable information today about the future, it's just too costly to get it. But the future holds countless and unimaginably more possibilities than will ever be realized. Elster's 'solution' is facile because the outcome of a decision cannot be known *ex ante*. So one would necessarily hope, trust or even pray that the 'cool' mechanical rule or coin flip will work out *ex post*. Any genuine gambler knows this, but not the rational actor. Thus Elster's 'hunch' is that successful stock market investors are those who deploy his similar 'click' in the mind of 'vastly more complex mental calibrations, not because they consult their emotions' (1999: 296). These 'calibrations' are, of course, only over the data of past and present—not the 'future'. In my view, the decision requires an emotional preparedness to launch into it—an imaginative projection that emotionally but not actually reduces uncertainty.

Robert Shiller has popularized behavioural finance with *Irrational Exuberance* (2000). Jon Elster's examples of mechanical rules are the opposite to Shiller's evidence. Shiller tries to explain financial volatility (1989; 2000), using extensive aggregated data from his surveys of investors just after the 1987 stock market crash. His conclusions do not match his evidence. Like Elster, he concludes that emotions get in the way of correct market evaluations because 'millions' of 'diffusion' investors were swayed by emotions, 'suggestion' and rumour from the media. In contrast, 'smart money' investors do gain 'relevant' information about the future, and arrive at correct prices by arbitrage and these prices reflect fundamental values—the Efficient Market Hypothesis (Shiller, 1989: 49; 2000: 228–232). But Shiller's distinction between smart and foolish emotional investors cannot be made from his own data. He finds that nearly double the percentage of 'institutional investors' (to individual investors) reported that on Black Monday October 19, 1987 they experienced 'unusual symptoms of anxiety', including 'difficulty concentrating, sweaty palms, tightness of chest, irritability, or rapid pulse'. The same results obtained to his question about experiencing a 'contagion of fear' (1989: 389). They barely looked at 'technical analysis' or news of some change in 'fundamentals'. Rather, institutional investors reported following what they called the philosophy of 'the trend is our friend' (Shiller, 1987: 392).

It seems, then, that among the orthodox economists who study emotions, most refuse to acknowledge that, however much information is gained to form expectations, humans cannot have knowledge about the future.[10] Even when emotions are freely admitted to play a major role by professional investors, most economists studying these decisions cannot admit that expectations comprise merely 'hope and imagination' (Shackle, 1972: 66). But this is what Post Keynesians who deconstruct received wisdom insist. Thus the cognitive psychologists are correct in suggesting that humans are bad at calculating probability (see Rabin, 1998). These errors are defined mainly as over-confidence (Dequech, 2000). But such errors in calculating probability distributions are irrelevant for economic decision making. Probability works best for gambling.

A post-war interpreter of Keynes, G.L.S. Shackle, argues that there are two opposing meanings of probability. One involves the counting of objective cases—a 'kind of knowledge'. The other 'stands for a language for expressing judgements' about the weight of a variety of rival hypotheses (subjective probability). For 'objective' probabilities to be meaningful, measurements need to be obtained 'by examining a concrete, existing and delimited system' with 'an underlying stability and invariance' (Shackle, 1972: 17–18). A pair of dice is usually invariant and, compared to the unknown economic future, even the weather is 'only moderately uncertain' (Keynes, 1937: 214). Shackle points out that statistical probabilities are knowledge but, if we are uncertain, we can only imagine rival hypotheses (1972: 19)—let alone things 'incapable of being envisaged'. Decision-makers can compile an 'exhaustive' list of 'weighted' hypotheses (they can 'half-believe' one answer may prove right), but it gives a 'dangerously misleading' air of authority by asserting 'degrees of positive belief in a number of rival ideas', or contrary ones (Shackle, 1972: 21, 447). This means that Damasio's depiction of somatic markers learned, say, in the processes of collective board room decisions or in the required duties of fund managers, can help to build a more adequate view than Elster. In contrast to Elster or Damasio, however, Post Keynesians insist on fundamental uncertainty, but mainly argue that emotions (particularly 'animal spirits') are irrational.

Keynesian 'emotions' and sociology

A growing number of sociologists have drawn attention to sociology's ignorance of Keynes (Barbalet, 1998; Ingham, 1996a and b; Wiley, 1983; DiMaggio, 2002; Pixley, 1999b), where the issue of future time is crucial. This neglect of uncertainty means that key features of modernity also vanish from view. Uncertainty is most 'intolerable' at the peak of economic decision-making; whole industries are obsessed with the future. To point to hierarchy and stratification in the management of uncertainty is an invitation for a social structural understanding of uncertainty, given that the microfoundations of orthodox economics cannot accommodate stratification and power. If Keynes's own work deserves careful attention, so does that of Post Keynesians.

As Barbalet says, much of economics and sociology is largely 'timeless' (1998: 92). Economics has ignored the Keynesian concept of animal spirits 'at their peril', according to DiMaggio (2002), while in sociology the lack of attention to time and emotions may also be from ignorance of Keynes's own work. Neil Smelser (1963: 10) mentions that Keynes drew on 'non-economic assumptions' by showing how the Marginal Efficiency of Capital rested on psychological expectations of future yields. Smelser also briefly discusses businessmen's responses to 'uncertain situations', citing the 'magical beliefs' about the 'aggressive' man of action and other self-images of CEOs which 'provide a rationale for making decisions in an inherently ambiguous situation' (Smelser, 1963: 76). But the problem of uncertainty is hardly central to Smelser.

Giddens (1987), who criticizes the notion of 'non-economic assumptions', has also touched on Keynesian uncertainty. In exploring the reflexivity of rational expectations (or 'ratex' as Paul Davidson calls it: 1991), Giddens acknowledges the 'fundamental influence of time and contingency' in Keynes's economics (1987: 194) but, while he denies predictability in the economic world, he fails to challenge ratex. Giddens just accepts the ratex charge that Keynes minimized expectations (Keen, 2001: 211).[11] Ratex theory alleges there exists 'sufficient information about future probability functions' (Davidson, 1990: 69) to leave no 'crucial' economic decisions where 'ratex' would be unable to draw inferences about how 'behaviour would have differed' (Lucas and Sargent, cited Davidson, 1990: 69). Giddens rejects their 'simplified universe of assumptions', yet says that ratex is more original than it acknowledges (1987: 201) because it introduces reflexivity. Agents revise their activities 'in the light of what they get to 'know'—but also what they believe, suspect, fear or feel optimistic about' (1987: 200). So far so good. Then Giddens says 'the predictability of economic phenomena . . . is in substantial part "made to happen" via the knowledgeability of its constituent actors' (1987: 200–1). Therefore, he goes on, the value of ratex is that it demonstrates that 'Keynesianism can only be effective in circumstances in which . . . certain key sets of business actors, do not know what Keynesianism is. If the policies associated with a Keynesian outlook have become ineffective, it might be because their premises have become widely enough known no longer to apply' (Giddens, 1987: 201).

But this is exactly what ratex argued, that government policies, any government policies were ineffectual, through a presumption that the expectations of agents would be the same as the predictions of conventional macroeconomic models. Assuming ratex implies that Keynesian policies 'work' only by fooling or misleading economic agents as these agents already 'know' the future outcome of expenditure decisions (Davidson and Kregel, 1997: xvi). So in the

1970s all economic decision makers 'expected' an increased money supply to cause inflation (despite its interim employment creation), therefore they put up their prices instantly. Thus, according to ratex, government could do nothing about unemployment (Keen, 2001: 212). Giddens avoids a can of worms he opens about the democratic process, merely concluding that economics should not 'insulate' itself from other social sciences (1987: 202). But while Davidson argues that the 'robot decision-maker' entailed in ratex is determinist and denies choice, Giddens extols Merton's idea that expectations are self-fulfilling (1987: 197). Indeed, Robert C. Merton incorporated his father's positive idea (Dunbar, 2000: 19) into his mathematical models at Long-Term Capital Management (LTCM). Yet Keynes had discussed emotions and convention in terms of 'average opinion' with a far less sanguine view, as Merton Jnr found out after LTCM collapsed.

Starting, instead, with Keynes's thesis, organizations make decisions about the uncertain future primarily through convention and emotions about the available information. In sociology the 'anticipatory emotions' are confidence, optimism or pessimism (Kemper, 1978), about the 'knowledge', including surveys of expectations, they have of the past and present. The 'convention' is then to assume that the future will resemble the present (Keynes, 1937). Barbalet makes a strong case for regarding confidence as an emotion even though it is less 'expressive' (1998: 85). The object of confidence is future or prospective behaviour. The experience of confidence is projected into a possible future, and reimported to the present, providing 'a sense of certainty' about what cannot be known. Confidence is a 'projected assured expectation' about the future, brought back and felt in the present (Barbalet, 1998: 87–8).

Barbalet's important treatment of Keynesian confidence moves the debate on emotions to macrosociology. As he says, few even now appreciate the extent that Keynes changed the foundations of economic analysis when he insisted that prospective time is far more important than retrospective time (1998: 92). At the macrosocial level, the feelings of confidence (*ex ante*) about whether investment decisions will indeed prove to be profitable in the outcome (*ex post*) are based on social relationships. The 'source of confidence is in the relationship business enters into with government, from which its sense of acceptance and recognition arises', and this recognition is the independent variable, not any particular policy which will vary in different contexts (Barbalet, 1998: 100). Thus, an increased money supply by government does not fail because business outguesses Keynesianism (Giddens's thesis) and indeed, that inflation actually saved economies from a debt-deflation (Minsky, 1985). Rather, in that historical context, that policy was a sign that governments did not sufficiently recognize business. In contrast, Greenspan's increase in the money supply during the phoney Y2K 'scare' certainly did recognize business (and prolonged the Nasdaq inflation). In recent times, too, we have seen the ubiquitous 'fundamentals' are changing: 'government deficits' are no longer the shocking refusal by government to recognize 'fundamental' prerequisites for finance and business. Well before September 11, business lobbies in 2001 urged government deficits to 'restore confidence'.

Confidence is a major emotion, Barbalet therefore argues, for 'understanding economic activity' at macro and micro levels (Barbalet, 1998: 100). In a welcome exchange by an economist with a sociologist, David Dequech suggests qualifications. From Dequech's Post Keynesian view, Barbalet's use of the Keynesian concept incorrectly treats confidence and 'animal spirits' as much the same. The same occurs in DiMaggio's argument about animal spirits (2002). For Dequech, in contrast, confidence could rest on a deep pessimism and 'certainty' about gloomy trends—hardly a case of 'animal spirits'. If there is a cognitive element to confidence, based on evidence or knowledge (of the present and past), confidence would then take the sense of 'firmly expected to be confirmed *ex post*' (Dequech, 2000: 3). The conclusion from this, it seems to me, is that confidence is then a sense that whether good or bad, the future is pretty much certain: whereas a lack of confidence is an awareness or feeling of uncertainty *per se*, based on contradictory evidence and knowledge that is acknowledged to be 'imprecise'. The gut feeling is the outcome could be good or bad but evidence is patchy, ambiguous, or cross cutting. Dequech implicitly refers to lack of confidence as 'uncertainty perception' and 'uncertainty aversion' which result in a refusal to act (1999: 425–6), but not what may happen if an actor had complete confidence and sense of certainty about a grim future. He only suggests that confidence of a bleak outlook would not give rise to 'animal spirits'. This is slightly contradictory, as he also says that 'animal spirits' do not draw on knowledge or evidence, that is, on information components, whereas confidence does, to be considered below.

Dequech argues correctly, however, that terminological disputes about confidence and animal spirits have serious policy implications. If confidence has a cognitive (information) element, it may also have 'weight' according to Keynes.[12] That is, if confidence can be boosted by increasing information and knowledge about the stability of organizations, then governments have a role not only in spending to improve business prospects, but also in providing institutions that reduce uncertainty and instability (2000: 5). Dequech suggests a reduction of flexible contracts to reduce uncertainty, central banks as lenders of last resort and an international market maker would reduce volatility of exchange rates and financial capital flows. He aims to remove the emotional elements from confidence (by providing 'certainty'), as we will see. Other initiatives, however, can be defended from an emotions perspective, whereas problems derive from Dequech's model. The problems as I see it seem to relate to the largely deconstructionist approach of Post Keynesians where they cannot 'move on'. Thus, first, the issue of cognition and emotion at the point of decision in the organized form is unresolved; second, the dynamism of future-oriented emotions needs consideration, so too their generation from ritual interactions (Collins, 1993) and the 'kaleidic' nature of expectations (Shackle, 1972); and third, the historical context of 'the state of expectations' (Barbalet, 1998; Minsky, 1985) may be neglected.

Emotions research: sociology contra economics

Dequech argues that the Keynesian concept of 'animal spirits' is a condition of 'optimistic disposition' which can lead to 'spontaneous optimism' and is not based on 'any knowledge' (1999: 418, 420). He sets up a complex model to describe the formulation of the state of expectations. Animal spirits, knowledge and creativity are the ultimate determinants of the state of expectations, and knowledge (both of 'likely' trends and of institutional stability such as legal contracts) feeds into uncertainty perception and, along with animal spirits feeds into confidence (1999: 418). Dequech distinguishes between confidence and expectations to emphasize that radical uncertainty does not imply utter ignorance or complete lack of knowledge. Creativity or imagination is important to the formulation of expectations (though as Damasio, 1994 argues, creativity and anticipatory emotions are linked).

Dequech suggests that because confidence is 'partly based on knowledge' (2000: 5), confidence is not really or it is less an emotion whereas animal spirits are emotional. Yet, when Dequech considers the extent of a decision-maker's perception of uncertainty, he defines the postponement of action as the liquidity preference, which 'corresponds to a refusal to bet' (1999: 426). This is precisely why his sequence is flawed. How meaningful is it to say that 'animal spirits' are based on no knowledge at all but merely on an 'optimistic disposition' which feeds into 'spontaneous optimism'? Why should all that arise from nothing? With the organized nature of business decisions, an innate 'disposition' residing in a person is methodologically irrelevant compared with collective 'willingness' or 'preparedness' to 'take the bet'. Emotions are sparked by knowledge and 'new' information to which incumbents of corporate positions must respond. Their responses arise in a context of the prevailing interpretation of that knowledge through a chain of organized, prescribed interaction rituals. They are also, in part, emotional responses to the outcomes of previous decisions of board meetings, for example. The physical co-presence (Barbalet, 1994: 117) in the formal (or informal) ritual situations required for decision-making fosters particular emotions that cannot be reduced to the Cartesian metaphor of 'animal spirits'.

Kemper's schema of anticipatory emotions (Kemper, 1978: 74–5) is extremely useful in showing the dynamic process. Kemper suggests that in considering the past, the anticipatory emotions are optimism and pessimism, whereas those of the present are confidence or lack of confidence (accepting Dequech's point about a grim confidence resting on gloomy data). Combining the two gives at least five potential emotional states, and systematizes Shackle's insight (1972) that expectations can shift, like the twist of a kaleidoscope. So, the expectation is 'hope' if there is optimism from past successful decisions and lack of confidence about present; or 'arrogance' if both optimistic and confident about past 'success' and 'good' current data. As important, in generating the next set of expectations, the outcome of 'hope' *ex post*, if the result is failure, is mild disappointment, whereas the outcome of arrogance if the result is bad is panic, humiliation.

Let me now turn to the importance of trust. Confidence is an emotion, a projection into the future. It remains, though, a feeling of the present, a preparedness for action or inaction. What about the taking of the decision? Luhmann, as I said, argues that 'trust is a gamble' but not like a game of gambling (with predictable probability distributions). Rather, trust entails taking a conscious decision by 'renouncing' further information and taking a 'wary indifference' (1979: 22, 24). In developing his suggestion that 'trust increases the tolerance of uncertainty' (1979: 15), Luhmann says that trust is not really possible without some previous information (incomplete, unreliable). Yet trust is an extrapolation from, or 'overdraws' that information (like an overdrawn bank cheque) and through 'will' gives an assurance of success that simply cannot be derived from the available information. Trust 'makes good' that 'informational deficiency' and is 'a springboard for the leap into uncertainty' (1979: 33). Thus economist Victoria Chick argues, 'the speculator is not *ignoring* uncertainty or just enjoying taking risk, but is acting on his/her best guess, *as if* certain even though not (1983: 211, her emphasis). But if trust depends on the lack of contrary evidence, once contrary evidence arrives, trust is shattered. This gives a more dynamic view to decision making, which also has policy implications (such as, 'excessive' trust may be placed in the central banker with significant consequences, and a spiral of impersonal trust relations can develop, as will be discussed further).

Where both Barbalet and Dequech suggest confidence is involved in the formation of expectations, Barbalet also introduces Luhmann's ideas about trust in a radical understanding of the role of emotions in decision making, even for narrow, technical forms of rationality. He points to the way that trust as an emotion 'overcomes the uncertainty of the future' and in that sense it is rational (Barbalet, 1998: 49). The trust that is projected for decision making derives its rationality from orienting action 'to meaningful outcomes' (1998: 49). This aligns the argument with Luhmann's persuasive distinction between trust and confidence. It is why in my view the Keynesian concept of 'animal spirits' is not as satisfactory as that of trust, which is ultimately required for the actual decision.

Luhmann's distinction between trust and confidence is between attributions that are made *ex post* (1988: 97–8) and it applies best, in my view, to economic decisions (cf. Heimer, 2001) as the end is gain, with prescribed reward structures for agents that aim to enhance corporate profitability. Trust in Luhmann's sense entails making a decision which, if it proves wrong *ex post*, is the 'fault' of those decision-makers. The decision could have been avoided with often neither loss nor gain. If the decision to trust is successful *ex post*, we have corporate heroes and financial stars—until they fail. Successes are in this sense from lucky combinations of later events, not personal wisdom, 'foresight' or the lack thereof. Mistakes by corporations are equally personalized in scapegoating. The impersonal nature of corporate decisions gets lost from view, as Fisse and Braithwaite argue (1993: 35) about corporate intent and the vexed issue of responsibility and accountability in corporate crime.

In contrast, confidence enables action but this action is less about 'gain,' though it usually cannot be avoided without loss. If confidence proves to be utterly misplaced, blame is directed to an external danger. It may be an improbable calamity. Blame can be attributed to the investment bank that took the decision to trust the creditworthiness of a corporation but, *ex post*, financially ruined those with no other option but to feel confident that their funds were safe. For Luhmann, trust entails the prospect of gain or loss, it is modern in its position towards uncertainty and vulnerability, in comparison with a more pre-modern fatalism or *fortuna* (1988: 96). In the modern world, trust is needed to take a punt *for gain* in an uncertain future, whereas distrust can reduce vulnerability by insuring or hedging against losses (by 'passing' the danger elsewhere). Though Luhmann does not quite say it, trust can be in this context an eminently capitalist emotion! Confidence is the feeling about the present—in the face of possible future dangers, whether they are perceived or not. Individual persons may feel grimly confident about the likelihood of global warming but this danger is not from your or my choices or decisions.

Corporations suffer when an insurance company collapses due to the latter's decisions. The outcomes of confidence and trust, *ex ante*, can interweave into a spiral of different attributions of blame *ex post*. There is also a hierarchy of trust which can be neglected in Luhmann's appreciation of trust as a means of reducing 'system complexity'. If system theory is too reified, it is partly from under-estimating the importance of specific organizations (Pixley, 2002), and from neglecting to identify the hierarchical relations of trust and confidence, betrayals and dangers.

Conclusion

Post Keynesians are among the few economists who readily acknowledge emotions in economic life. They also rightly recognize the socially damaging effects of financial crises and sudden 'bandwagon tides' (Davidson, 1998: 657). Yet their analysis leads to quite different policy proposals from the analysis offered here. While these policy implications can only be touched on briefly, they show the key differences between emotions research and virtually all economic approaches to emotions. Thus Post Keynesians who correctly emphasize uncertainty, still regard emotions as 'biased', irrational 'tides'. Their proposals are concerned with reducing emotions in financial decision making by providing greater stability and 'certainty'. My view is that emotions need serious reconsideration as they are unavoidable, they cannot be 'reduced' and indeed they are not necessarily 'irrational'. That is, the state of expectations cannot be arrived at without emotions, and trust, confidence, fear and so forth can play a rational role in actual decisions. Thus the aim to avoid or resolve the gulf between *ex ante* and *ex post* (from Post Keynesians' very insistence on fundamental uncertainty) is futile. In my view this gulf is inescapable.

Post Keynesians neglect that Keynesian policies are best seen as a defence of 'the convention'—the future must be made to resemble the present, expectations must be rendered 'certain' (Negri, 1988: 24). That is, the state will not 'guarantee the certainty of events, but it will guarantee the certainty of the convention' (Negri, 1988: 25). Yet if post-war state intervention focused on employment and equitable wages, there is no doubt that governments still defend the convention and provide certainty to expectations. The problem is that today's focus is on an undemocratic defence of a now de-regulated financial sector, with its 'expectations' that its host of complex financial 'instruments' are relatively safe or certain.

Dequech and also Paul Davidson (1998) propose a market maker with an active role to provide an 'institutional anchor' to reduce the 'irrationality' or 'bandwagon tide' of too many bulls or too many bears in financial markets (1998: 657). Dequech derives his proposal for a market maker from his argument that 'uncertainty aversion' and 'uncertainty perception' can lead to refusal to act (aka bearishness). Again, this formulation, in relation to 'animal spirits', is less satisfactory than drawing attention to trust at the point of decision-making. The question arises, how did 'uncertainty aversion' arise? Unless aversion to uncertainty is being posited as a fixed attribute of an individual 'personality' (and Dequech claims his arguments are as applicable to organizations as individuals), it could only arise as a consequence of other emotions being shattered. This seems eminently 'reasonable'. It is only 'irrational' if one departs from an atomized, untheorized conception of 'animal spirits'. For example, trust turns to mistrust in the face of 'new' contrary evidence. An 'aversion' to uncertainty is a process arising from antecedent emotional states. It was, for example, a widespread response among investment firms to the collapse of Enron and Arthur Andersen in early 2002.

What the Post Keynesians rightly suggest is that we must recognise uncertainty. But in this deconstructive move, the aim is to reduce the emotional component in economic life by trying to provide the certainty of stability (to whom?):

> Because the future is uncertain [in the Keynesian view] . . . there is no solid foundation for believing in stabilizing economic fundamentals. Consequently, there is no rationale for believing in the stability of financial market prices over time, except if there is some *credible institution that guarantees* price stability or some *widespread convention* which presumes price inertia in normal times (Davidson, 1998: 648, my emphasis).

A 'credible' institution here means that we would trust it to 'guarantee' the convention that present expectations about prices will be validated *ex ante*. Having started with the aim to reduce emotions (aka 'irrationality') from the sphere of finance, Davidson's proposal ironically increases the extent that impersonal emotions are required. It sets up a peak market maker that all must believe is credible, that all must trust. It puts a further spiral of impersonal trust organizations over the large number of existing ones.

In contrast, other proposals—from an emotions perspective that accepts the existence of emotions—may be more appropriate for reducing financial crises. The Tobin Initiative could be one possibility, since a very small tax on currency transactions might induce, through the market, slower financial movements. An alternative way to slow the pace of trading is simply a regular day's shut down.[13] Where Dequech and Davidson aim to reduce emotions, the emotions approach offers quite different policy implications. It accepts emotions like trust and confidence and allows emotions to be reconfigured. A slow-down or shut-down gives something like 'cooling off periods' to re-consult 'gut feelings' away from the frenetic pace of speculative transfers.[14] It changes several ritual aspects of finance decision-making, and is thus a procedural change. It also moves towards democratic control over the finance sector (this would be a first), not a 'market maker' which, like many Central Banks, would be independent of democratic control to maintain 'credibility'. These ideas are no panacea for all speculative problems, since re-regulation of the finance sector also seems necessary (Kaufman, 1986).

The aim of prevention can also be justified from the emotions perspective. Instead of aiming to reduce uncertainty, which is not possible, it may be preferable to consider precautionary principles that attempted to reduce the generalization of non-probabilistic risks in finance, where whole populations are positioned in indirect trust-risk relationships for high gains—and losses. These are passed off as risks, 'freely chosen' and including an element of greed for new 'rentiers'. Yet they are dangers for many populations and whole regions, and even for those with small amounts of discretionary income, given that there are compulsory pension and employee share ownership schemes. And a huge financial sector wanting more of them.

The condition of uncertainty is a stratified experience, it is managed differently by various economic groups and organizations. Impersonal emotions between corporations and bureaucracies are not irrational and not removable. Yet, there is a hierarchy of those with the greatest power to manage uncertainty and to manage trust problems. The further heights may be engaged in the greater levels of 'foolishness' (Minsky, 1985: 52), the less they acknowledge that trust, rather than 'certainty', drives their decisions.

Emotions research has an alternative theory to offer about economic life, which is strengthened by drawing on the rich literature from Keynesians and Post Keynesians. The study of expectations is, however, more adequate with these sociological approaches to the generation, transformation and dynamism of expectations or anticipatory emotions.

Notes

1 Space prohibits citing further exceptions.
2 This is not to say that sociology does not have 'blood on its hands' either, in Stephen Turner's words (1996: 16).

3 We can point to cases such as US economists' role in the catastrophic 'shock therapy' imposed on post-Soviet Russia (Gray, 1998: 133–65).

4 My economic colleagues (Paul Ormerod, Steve Keen and Flora Gill) told me this with some impatience, only in 2000. Among sociologists, Uzzi, 1999 and particularly Zuckerman, 1999 are both concerned with the issue of expectations; and DiMaggio (2002) also explores uncertainty and animal spirits.

5 Rowthorn discusses the 'jaundiced' view in economics of interest, which implicitly assumes opportunism, cheating and dishonesty, and interest is unconstrained by moral considerations (1996: 20, 30). Gill's important point is that the assumptions of economics are abstracted from the social context, AND these are taken to be adequate (1996: 145).

6 A.F. Robertson's *Greed: Gut Feelings, Growth, and History* disputes the 'scholarly cover-up' of greed for the past thousand years, highlighting the gulf between public and scholarly interest in greed (2001: 6–9).

7 Hirschman's point here about interest recalls Marxist debates on false consciousness—the precise 'vanguard' method of rational choice theorists. Post Keynesians seek more rational decisions—by minimizing the alleged irrationality of 'animal spirits'—and do not see interest as passion.

8 For example, William James and Simmel are cited, but not Durkheim. There is no reference to Luhmann, Kemper, Collins, Barbalet; trust and confidence are not included, and the closest to confidence is self-esteem and 'self-serving bias'. There is no entry for greed or avarice, the nearest is envy (Elster, 1999). Aristotle, who includes confidence among many emotions, is dealt with at length (pp. 52–75), but Elster avoids confidence. Habermas, not Luhmann, is the major sociologist cited, possibly because Habermas defends 'reason' via a normative view of democratic procedures, whereas Luhmann is a system theorist, a position incompatible with rational actor models. But Luhmann also deals extensively (and far more persuasively than his systems theory in my view) with emotions of trust and confidence.

9 Elster recognizes from Habermas, 'that by its objectivity truth can serve as a strategic resource: By restating a threat as a warning, a speaker may present an interest-based claim in the language of reason' (Elster, 1999: 338). This acknowledges the purpose for Habermas's emphasis on consensus is 'as a *contrast* to the potentially coercive orientation to *success* that characterizes strategic action and instrumental rationality' (Markell, 1997: 389 his emphasis). But why are the reasons for and motives of 'orientation to success' and coercive power not conceived as emotional? It seems to me that purposeful plans and calculations about the future are cast in Weberian means-ends 'rational' terms but are pointlessly divorced from the emotions that may drive such plans and inspire decisions. Revenge (aka 'competition') is often wrought via a 'dispassionate' plan in a boardroom or Faculty office.

10 It is remarkable that Shiller quotes such 'philosophies' as 'the trend is our friend' but makes absolutely no reference in either text cited to Keynes or Post Keynesians, who have tirelessly drawn attention to speculators' sole focus on guessing average opinion about average opinion.

11 Giddens suggests that 'stochastic' processes are recognized in ratex as 'unknowable' (Giddens, 1987: 194). As Davidson points out, ratex assumes that 'the future structure of the economic system is already determined in the current period at least in a stochastic sense' (1990: 66). Therefore, for ratex, these processes are knowable. Davidson argues: 'If economists do not possess . . . and conceptually never will possess an ensemble of macroeconomic worlds, then it can be logically argued that objective probability structures do not even fleetingly exist, and a distribution function of probabilities cannot be defined. The application of the mathematical theory of stochastic processes to macroeconomic phenomena would be therefore highly questionable, if not invalid in principle' (Davidson, 1991: 132).

12 Though Dequech rightly says 'confidence can fall with new evidence' (1999: 424) it is not clear whether he stresses the reduction of uncertainty in a contradictory way. Yet he correctly suggests that the socially conditioned nature of knowledge can itself reduce uncertainty perception, which includes those economic theories that neglect fundamental uncertainty (2000: 4).

13 Economist James Tobin, in 1978, proposed a Currency Transaction Tax (CTT) to throw 'sand in the wheels' of international finance, and to provide a 'modest national autonomy in monetary and macroeconomic policy' (Eichengreen, Tobin, and Wyplosz, 1995: 163), although it

might not reduce risks of a massive crisis or 'excessive volatility'. A second tier, a prohibitively high tax, is proposed to prevent exchange rate runs (Wahl and Wardlow, 2001).

14 This resembles house buying on the spur of the moment, where a week's cooling period is mandatory before exchange of contract in some countries. Also personal discussion with Meghnad Desai on the Tobin tax, 21.3.02.

References

Barbalet, J.M. (1998) *Emotion, Social Theory and Social Structure* Cambridge: Cambridge University Press.

Barbalet, J.M. (1994) 'Ritual Emotion and Body Work: A note on the uses of Durkheim' *Social Perspectives on Emotion*, Vol 2, pp. 111–123, JAI Press.

Chick, Victoria (1983) *Macroeconomics after Keynes: A Reconsideration of the General Theory* Oxford: Philip Allan.

Collins, R. (1990) 'Stratification, Emotional Energy, and the Transient Emotions' in T.D. Kemper (ed.) *Research Agendas in the Sociology of Emotions* Albany NY.: SUNY Press.

Collins, R. (1993) 'Emotional Energy as the Common Denominator of Rational Action' *Rationality and Society* 5 (2) pp. 203–230.

Damasio, A.R. (1994) *Descartes' Error: Emotions, Reason, and the Human Brain* New York: G. P. Putnam's Sons

Davidson, P. (1991) 'Is Probability Theory Relevant for Uncertainty?' *The Journal of Economic Perspectives* 5 (1): 129–143.

Davidson, P. (1990) 'Shackle and Keynes vs. Rational Expectations Theory and the Role of Time' in Frowen, S.F. (ed.) *Unknowledge and Choice in Economics* London: Macmillan.

Davidson, P. (1998) 'Efficiency and Fragile Speculative Financial Markets: Against the Tobin Tax and For a Creditable Market Maker' *American Journal of Economics and Sociology* 57 (4): 639–662.

Davidson, P. and Kregel, J. (1997) 'Introduction' in *Improving the Global Economy* (eds) Davidson, P. and Kregel, J. Cheltenham: Edward Elgar.

Dequech, D. (2000) 'Confidence and action: a comment on Barbalet' *Journal of Socio-Economics* 29 (6): 503–515 Downloaded from www. sciencedirect.com/science? ob=ArticleURL&_udi.

Dequech, D. (1999) 'Expectations and Confidence under Uncertainty' *Journal of Post Keynesian Economics* 21 (3): 415–430.

DiMaggio, P. (2002) 'On animal spirits' in *New Directions in Economic Sociology* (eds) M.F. Guillén, R. Collins, et al. New York: Russell Sage Foundation.

Dunbar, N. (2000) *Inventing Money: The story of Long-Term Capital Management and the legends behind it* Chichester: John Wiley.

Eichengreen, B., Tobin, J., and Wyplosz C. (1995) 'Two Cases for Sand in the Wheels of International Finance' *The Economic Journal*, 105 (January): 162–172.

Elster, J. (1998) 'Emotions and Economic Theory' *The Journal of Economic Literature* XXXVI (1): 47–74

Elster, J. (1999) *Alchemies of the Mind: Rationality and the Emotions* New York: Cambridge University Press.

Elster, J. (1993) 'Some Unresolved Problems in the Theory of Rational Behaviour' *Acta Sociologica* 36: 179–190.

Fisse, B. and Braithwaite J. (1993) *Corporations, Crime and Accountability* Cambridge: Cambridge University Press.

Frankel, B. (2001) 'The Rise of the Sociologist King' *Arena Magazine* 52: 20–26.

Giddens, A. (1987) *Social Theory and Modern Sociology* Cambridge: Polity Press.

Gill, F. (1996) 'On Ethics and Economic Science' in *Economics and Ethics?* (ed.) P. Groenewegen, London: Routledge.

Gray, John (1998) *False Dawn: The Delusions of Global Capitalism* London: Granta Books.

Heimer, C. (2001) 'Solving the Problem of Trust' in Karen S. Cook (ed.) *Trust in Society* New York: Russell Sage Foundation.

Hirsch, F. and Goldthorpe, J. eds (1978) *The Political Economy of Inflation* London: Martin Robertson.

Hirschman, A.O. (1981) *Essay in Trespassing* New York: Cambridge University Press.

Hirschman, A.O. (1997) *The Passions and the Interests* Princeton NJ: Princeton University Press.

Ingham, G. (1996a) 'Money is a Social Relation' *Review of Social Economy* LIV (4): 507–529.

Ingham, G. (1996b) 'Some recent changes in the relationship between economics and sociology' *Cambridge Journal of Economics* 20: 243–275.

Kaufman, H. (1986) *Interest Rates, the Market and the New Financial World* New York: Times Books.

Keen, S. (2001) *Debunking Economics* Sydney: Pluto.

Kemper, T.D. (1978) *A Social Interactional Theory of Emotions* New York: John Wiley & Sons.

Keynes, J.M. (1937) 'The General Theory of Employment' *Quarterly Journal of Economics*, 51 (February): 209–233.

Knight, Frank H. (1965 [1921]) *Risk, Uncertainty and Profit* New York: Harper Torchbooks.

Lane, R. (1991) *The Market Experience* New York: Cambridge University Press.

Luhmann, N. (1979) *Trust and Power* Chichester: John Wiley & Sons.

Luhmann, N. (1988) 'Familiarity, Confidence, Trust' in *Trust* ed. D. Gambetta, Oxford: Basil Blackwell.

Markell, P. (1997) 'Contesting Consensus: Re-reading Habermas on the Public Sphere' *Constellations*, Vol 3, No 3, pp. 377–400.

Minsky, H.P. (1985) 'The Financial Instability Hypothesis' in P. Arestis and T. Skouras, eds *Post Keynesian Economic Theory* Sussex: Wheatsheaf Books.

Negri, T. (1988) *Revolution Retrieved: Writings on Marx, Keynes, Capitalist Crisis and New Social Subjects* London: Red Notes.

Pixley, J.F. (1993) *Citizenship and Employment: Investigating Post-Industrial Options* Cambridge: Cambridge University Press.

Pixley, J.F. (1997) 'Employment and Social Identity: Theoretical Issues' in *European Citizenship and Social Exclusion*, M. Roche and R. van Berkel (eds), Aldershot: Ashgate.

Pixley, J.F. (1999a) 'Impersonal Trust in Global Mediating Organisations' *Sociological Perspectives* 42 (4): 647–671.

Pixley, J.F. (1999b) 'Beyond Twin Deficits: Emotions of the Future in the Organizations of Money' *American Journal of Economics and Sociology* 58 (4): 1091–1118.

Pixley, J.F. (2002) 'Finance organizations, decisions and emotions' *British Journal of Sociology* 53 (1): 41–65.

Rabin, M. (1998) 'Psychology and Economics' *The Journal of Economic Literature* XXXVI (1): 11–46.

Robertson, A.F. (2001) *Greed: Gut Feelings, Growth, and History* Cambridge: Polity.

Rowthorn, R. (1996) 'Ethics and Economics' in *Economics and Ethics?* ed. P. Groenewegen, London: Routledge.

Shackle, G.L.S. (1967) *The Years of High Theory: Invention and Tradition in Economic Thought 1926–1939* Cambridge: Cambridge University Press.

Shackle, G.L.S. (1972) *Epistemics and Economics* Cambridge: Cambridge University Press.

Shiller, R.J. (1989) *Market Volatility* Cambridge, MA: MIT Press.

Shiller, R.J. (2000) *Irrational Exuberance* Princeton, NJ: Princeton University Press.

Smelser, N. (1963) *The Sociology of Economic Life* Englewood Cliffs, NJ: Prentice-Hall.

Swedberg, R. (1987) 'The impact of an exogenous event' *International Social Science Journal* 113 (3): 323–336.

Turner, S.P. (1996) 'Introduction' in S.P. Turner (ed.) *Social Theory and Sociology* Cambridge, MA: Blackwell.

Uzzi, B. (1999) 'Embeddedness in the Making of Financial Capital: How Social Relations and Networks Benefit Firms Seeking Financing' *American Sociological Review* 64: 481–505.

Van Parijs, P. (1993) *Arguing for Basic Income* Cambridge: Cambridge University Press.

Wahl, P. and Wardlow P. (2001) 'Currency Transaction Tax—a Concept with a Future' *WEED Working Paper* World Economy Ecology and Development Association: Bonn.

Wiley, N.F. (1983) 'The Congruence of Weber and Keynes' *Sociological Theory 1983* (ed.) R. Collins, San Francisco: Jossey-Bass Inc. pp. 30–57.

Wolff, R.P. (1990) 'Methodological Individualism and Marx: Some Remarks on Jon Elster, Game Theory and Other Things' *Canadian Journal of Philosophy* 20 (4): 469–486.

Zuckerman, E.W. (1999) 'The Categorical Imperative: Securities Analysts and the Illegitimacy Discount' *American Journal of Sociology* 104 (5): 1398–1438.

Corporate emotions and emotions in corporations

Helena Flam

Abstract

Although sociology of organizations never banned emotions from its field of inquiry, first the sociology of emotions elevated them to central research objects. Disparate research on various types of enterprises shows that both managers and employees are much more emotional than most scientists would care to admit. Under constant pressure not to display their fears, anxieties or worries, they have to balance a mixture of emotions attending solidarity and competition with their peers. Whereas managerial roles actually call for occasional displays of anger at subordinates, anger is beyond the pale for subordinates who are supposed to swallow anger, humiliation or fear. Capitalist labour, no matter whether this of managers or that of workers, exacts a heavy emotional toll. While in handling their work managers rely heavily on the emotional support of their peers and secretaries, employees spin nostalgic stories or take to subversive workplace humour. Against this broader perspective, Arlie Hochschild's research and its critique have focused exclusively on the workers' emotional toll. In centre of interest is emotional labour exacted by employers and the many ways of managing undesired feelings which this labour requires. Hochschild's critics stress that subordinates often find ways of evading supervision and playing with rules for emotional display, so that they are much less subject to emotion management than her research agenda implies. Although Hochschild's research and its echo produced the only coherent body of theory-guided research to emerge so far within the sociology of organizations under the influence of the sociology of emotions, the chapter ends with an argument that her valuable yet work-focused approach has become constraining in times of disjointed, turbulent capitalism. Social change demands that we enlarge our scope of inquiry to include the experience of lay-off and unemployment as well as work-unrelated emotions and the broader society into our purview.

Perhaps more than other fields of sociological inquiry, sociology of organizations has never quite lost its sensitivity to emotions. Although after World War II scholars did not posit emotion as an independent analytical unit, they did not ban it either. In the body of this chapter I will repeatedly refer to 'regular' sociologists of organization to substantiate this claim. For now let me ask the reader to guess the author of the following citation:

> Kindness and friendliness become aspects of personalized service . . . rationalized
> to further the sale . . . [R]ules and regulations . . . stereotype . . . relations with the

customer . . . and loyalty to . . . organization requires that [they] be friendly, helpful, tactful, and courteous at all times . . . Many . . . are quite aware of the difference between what they really think of the customer and how they must act . . . The[ir] smile . . . is a commercialized lure . . . 'Self-control' pays off. 'Sincerity' is detrimental to one's job, until the rules of salesman-ship and business become a 'genuine' aspect of oneself. Tact is a series of little lies about one's feelings, until one is emptied of such feelings.

Those familiar with Arlie Hochschild's 'modern' classic in the sociology of emotions, *The Managed Heart*, probably thought that this excerpt comes from her book. Well, they were wrong. The author is C.W. Mills and the book is an 'old' classic: *White Collar*. In this particular section Mills addresses a new phenomenon of his time—work in large department stores, a new form of formal organization, situated within 'the large anonymous market of the metropolitcan area' (Mills, 1956:182–3). Mills and Hochschild also arrive at a similar basic conclusions about the instrumentalization of employee emotions by large corporations 'In the normal course of her work, because her personality becomes the instrument of an alien purpose, the salesgirl becomes self-alienated' (Mills, 1957:184).

Before I turn to Hochschild's 'classic', and the debates and research that it inspired, I will deal with the question of whether we can consider organizations emotional. I will then turn to corporations and the main intra-corporate actors of our time—managers and workers—to have a look at emotions attributed to them in the literature. This literature consists mostly of disparate conceptual pieces and journal articles reporting various research projects. Although I do my best to link them, one should not expect a presentation of a coherent body of thought in this section, since it simply does not exist. When I finally turn to discuss *The Managed Heart* and its research echo, the focus will remain on corporate organizations, their managers and employees, but in the end I, along with some of Hochschild's critics, will argue for enlarging our scope of inquiry to include work-unrelated emotions and the broader society into our purview.

Emotional corporations?[1]

The usual perspective on corporations is either rationalistic or normative. They are treated as cognitive, goal-oriented, problem-solving, decision-making and intervening actors with their own interests and strategies or with their own value-systems and norms. Upon closer inspection not all, but sufficiently many, of these formal organizations can be analysed as a set of legal-rational rules for emotion management *and* a substitue for authentic feelings. What these organizations produce, apart from everything else, are *tempered* (restrained, disciplined) but solidified and permanent emotions in place of unpredictable and wavering, often boundless feelings. For example, a corporation—one of the supposedly most rationalistic corporate actors—can be seen as a complex system of legal-rational checks, restraints and balancing procedures imposed on the otherwise boundless and irrational impulse of acquisitiveness, on the one hand, and on the equally boundless and self-indulgent impulse to consume, on the other (Weber, 1978:9). Corporate rules specify the desired intensity, direction and duration of acquisitiveness and consumption when they specify the levels at which profits and investments are to be made, require that profits be made in a peaceful manner, and set up the time frames within which the profits are to be achieved.

From the same perspective, such corporate goals as 'profit-realization' or 'help to the needy' or 'solidarity' can be seen as intentions to construct and sustain specific emotions, while corporate rules can be seen as emotion-managing rules which prescribe in what ways these emotions should be constructed and displayed. Many trusts, philanthropic foundations, welfare organizations and state departments are systems created, among other reasons, in order to solidify and regulate otherwise intermittent, arbitrary and unplanned feelings of compassion for the needy (Barber, 1983; McGill, 1941–2:280). Professional and trade organizations, finally, have as a goal to stabilize and regulate intra-group solidarity, but also to inspire and stabilize public trust (Barber, 1983).

Following Weber's cultural-historical analysis, it can be proposed that certain passions, feelings and sensibilities have existed in an unorganized, cultural-historical form in the West and that some of them have motivated the establishment of a rational organization—a corporation—which would stabilize and rationalize their pursuit. But, and here is the structural part of the argument, once these corporations are established, they may be said to construct new emotions by modifying formal rules and procedures. These emotions differ but remain related to the original feelings which initiated the entire process. Moreover, corporations also generate emotions in another sense. They impose the constructed emotions on the individuals working for and living off them.

If this reasoning is accepted, then it follows that many corporations are non-feeling, but emotional. Corporate emotions should be understood as intended constructions, formed according to obligatory-coercive rules, in this case according to the organizational rules.

Corporations require emotional display and deep acting from their members to sustain their self-definitions which are related to their goals. Corporate charters and mandates often translate into formal and informal norms requiring the individuals working for an organization to manage their emotions in specified ways—to display particular emotions and to suppress particular feelings. Just like many jobs so many corporations 'call for an appreciation of display rules, feeling rules, and a capacity for deep acting' on the part of their members (Hochschild, 1979:570).

Of importance in this context is also that individuals acting on behalf of corporations are supposed to construct 'representative' emotions to help sustain their self-image. It is true that as a rule, for example, bankers have to display reserve, discretion, delicacy, sensitivity as well as inspire trust and confidence, 'ideal' state bureaucrats and scientists have to display 'affective neutrality', while business executives 'may be required . . . to sustain a definition of self, office, and organizations as "up and coming" or "on the go", "caring", or "reliable"' (Hochschild, 1979:570).

As much of the material presented below suggests, corporate employees have to overcome many intense feelings to play and sustain their organizational roles. In particular, managers, to whom I will turn next, do not quite succeed in following managerial prescriptions. A few, instead of neutrality, display intense passion and work enthusiasm. Others act their parts in spite of their fears, anxieties and disillusionment, but their play-acting does not quite follow the script. They fail to feel enthusiastic when they should. Anxiety- and fear-ridden, they do not take risky decisions. Instead they follow routine or introduce new bureaucratic rules. Sometimes they shock others by their inability to carry on. Worse, some turn into corporate critics. The emotions which cause the failure to act perfectly one's role are one important reason why corporations do not single-mindedly pursue their goals and why they increase their distance to their initial goals over time.

The myth of managerial rationality

It is a fairly accurate statement of fact that organization research, no matter whether it was hosted by the organizational studies, sociology departments, departments of economics, or business schools, increasingly came to focus on managers and their 'rational' decision-making after World War II. In his Nobel-Prize speech, Simon (1978) dethroned corporate manager understood as an embodiment of perfect rationality. The new manager displayed a mere bounded rationality. He had to work hard to gather and process information, to identify problems and their solutions, to cope with uncertainty about the future. He no longer maximized but settled for satisfactory solutions:

> The classical model calls for knowledge of all the alternatives that are open to choice. It calls for complete knowledge of, or ability to compute, the consequences that will follow on each of the alternatives. It calls for certainty in the decision maker's present and future evaluation of these consequences. It calls for the ability to compare consequences, no matter how diverse and heterogeneous, in terms of some consistent measure of utility. The task, then was to replace the classical model with one that would describe how decisions could (and probably actually were) made when the alternatives of search had to be sought out, the consequences of choosing particular alternatives were only imperfectly known both because of limited computational power and because of uncertainty in the external world, and the decision maker did not possess a general and consistent utility function for comparing heterogeneous alternatives (Simon, 1978:285).

Other critical economists and sociologists, even when they did not abandon the basic assumption of rationality and even when they saw emotion as detrimental, did much to weaken the myth of rationality, even if this was not their intention. They infused decision-making with emotion. Some argued that emotions affect only the parameters of choice in that they colour costs and benefits associated with different options (Elster, 1999:284,287,301). Their opponents proposed that in cases of indeterminacy emotions hasten decision-making since they help to choose. Or they recognized that emotions improve the quality of decision making by making us focus on salient features of the situation. Together they showed that the notion of 'pure', 'perfect' managerial rationality cannot be sustained. One way or another emotions play a role in the managerial decision-making.

Managers as emotional 'men'

The precursors of the sociology of emotions on the anxiety-ridden managers

Analysing managers from the perspective of the sociology of emotions helps us move away from the narrow focus on managerial decision-making and posits the conflicts between the managerial role requirements and the actual feelings experienced by managers in a more forceful way. It casts managers in a much broader light, although we only have a few studies done explicitly from this perspective. By presenting them alongside those conducted by 'regular' sociologists of organizations, I demonstrate how seriously they modify our view of the manager as the rational and in-control decision-maker. The 'regular' studies because they span over forty years suggest that fears and anxiety, and to a lesser extent enthusiasm, are endemic to corporations and managers, not just a result of structural change and downsizing[2] so prevalent in the last two decades of the last century.

In his 1950s-study of the succession problem, Gouldner (1981) paid as much attention to the fears and anxieties of the successor plant manager as to those of the unreplaced managers and workers. The new plant manager feared failure, his counterparts lay-offs. Gouldner actually managed to demonstrate that these very fears and anxieties, paralleled by mutual lack of trust, led to the formalization of the hierarchical relationships and thus to the increased bureaucratization of the plant as such. His case study shows that emotions have serious structural consequences. In her 1970s-study of women and corporate giants, Kanter (1981) took managers and organization sociologists alike to task for equating corporate reality with masculinity and rationality. No matter whether they adhere to Taylorism or the Human Relations approach, she argued, they propagate the view that managers are rational and highly competent, while repressing emotions, women and workers (Kanter, 1981:404–12). The repression is so intense that it has led to the exclusion of women and emotions from the scientific purview as well as from the management. In his 1970s analysis of corporate managers at work, Weick (1981) proposed that they, just as regular people, construct their reality following already established definitions of situation and representations—in this case, the organizational. Fear of failure explains why these managers exclude many action courses from consideration.

94

Rather than taking risk or innovating, as organizational studies and the rational choice approach suggest, they rely on the organizational experience and replicate choices made in the past. A final example: Jackall (1988) devoted much space to the fears of the American corporate mangers he interviewed. In the first two-thirds of his book, fears of authority, loss of career chances and instant career termination surface on nearly every second page. Jackall argues that corporate managers live with the foreboding sense of organizational contingency and capriciousness. They cope with the uncertainty created by the absence of fixed loyalties, and insufficient and unreliable information about their peers and bosses, the very people on whom their life chances depend. Facing constant social and economic uncertainty, corporate managers feel endemic anxiety, but display work enthusiasm (Jackall, 1988:35,69,79).

Although Gouldner, Weick or Jackall did not focus on emotions, they deserve to be treated as the precursors of the sociology of emotions because they show just how pervasive emotions are in corporations. They demonstrate that fear and anxiety hide behind daily corporate routines. These two emotions are the key to understanding why managers fail to play their prescribed roles. They also show that they have structural and action consequences.

As Jackall helps us see, when managers are allowed to speak freely, they admit that they fear corporate and career failure. As Gouldner, Weick and Jackall show they are afraid of decisions which could have fatal implications for them and the corporations they manage. They therefore avoid risk-taking. Anxiety drives them to follow decision-making routines. Anxiety and fear also persuade managers to impose more bureaucratic rules[3] instead of communicating with subordinates. From a newer, psychoanalytic perspective on organizations 'rationality itself—the use of quasi-scientific procedures such as forecasting, planning, monitoring, evaluating, testing and so on—[amounts to] no more than . . . rituals whose function is entirely the allaying of managers' anxieties in a highly unpredictable and even chaotic environment.' (Gabriel, 1998:305) Corporate managers often experience the two unsettling feelings fear and anxiety, but they repress them just as they repress all other emotions in the name of masculine rationality.[4] As Kanter shows, they seem willing to pay this price to retain their corporate dominions.

Managers as neurotics and actors

'Whether the management of the professions, the state or business, management is centrally concerned with the management and control of emotions . . .' (Hearn, 1993:160–161). Male managers control the (emotion) work of others— women and less powerful men, who, in turn, manage the emotions of the clients, patients, passengers or the public. At times they have to employ anger to assert their control. With other managers, they experience 'a complex mixture of solidarity and competition, with the associated emotions of joy, when these are realized and sadness, anger and fear when they are challenged or threatened.' (Hearn, 1993:154) As bosses they draw emotional strength from their secretaries who provide them with empathy and supportiveness (Pringle in Putnam and Mumby, 1993:45). These dub as office wives, slaves or nannies and take care of their bosses' informal emotional needs. They are expected to anticipate these needs, to encourage, to care.

A fascinating American study of laid-off managers supports the image of a corporate make-up to which a sense of control and rationality is central, routine soothing. Based on tens of autobiographical, narrative interviews, Newman (1988; see also Koeber, 2000) reports schock, anger, frustration and deep shame which overwhelm laid-off managers. Since they believe in self-reliant individualism, meritocracy, mastery of one's own destiny and the American myth of success, they cannot but blame themselves for what happened. Suddenly deprived of their wealth, high occupational position, and related privileges that until then constituted the very measures of their moral worth, they experience shock, anger and frustration. Their entire world collapses. Many of them cave in under the burden of unemployment and job search. The protective routine is gone. The unemployment time places them on an emotional seesaw. Laid-off managers experience deep anxiety, high hopes and, when they are not offered an interview or a job, unmanageable frustration and disappointment (Newman, 1988:48). In Newman's view: 'They are victims of their belief in meritocratic individualism as much as they are victims of economic adversity.' (Newman, 1988:94)

Managers in the public sector

Our knowledge about the public sector in times of organizational change suggests that even in this sector managers are no strangers to intense, yet undisclosed emotions. Vince and Broussine (1996) asked managers of six British public service organizations to draw their emotions about the ongoing change. These drawings revealed very intense, sometimes contradictory emotions at top- and middle-management level. They showed anger, anxiety, doubt as well as excitement, humour and enthusiasm. The feeling of impotence prevailed:

> Some drawings revealed fear or dread, either in terms of the consequence to which [managers] felt emotionally attached. Some managers conveyed powerful images concerning the fear of personal catastrophe resulting from change. For example, one person drew himself receiving his . . . unemployment card; another drew gravestones; there were miserable faces; and there were menacing clouds on the horizon . . . In most cases, the managers felt themselves to be powerless, debilitated, somewhat weakened by change . . . (Vince and Broussine, 1996:14).

Also in this case, a research project was necessary to reveal (and to articulate) the emotional consequences of the ongoing organizational change. Vince and Broussine (1996:3–4) argue that managers steeped in the 'rational' cultures of their organizations usually find it difficult to articulate their own feelings. Nor do they consider 'irrational' emotions relevant to the problem-solving task at hand. On the contrary, these are to be suppressed in organization and in oneself as they are the prime causes of inefficiency (see also Kanter, 1981:404,408–9).

In Jackall's study of the anxiety-ridden, but enthusiasm-displaying corporate world the very nature of their work organizations makes managers, the great actors of our time 'who, in order to remain upwardly mobile, have to follow the rules of the game and display iron self-control' to mask all emotions and intentions (Jackall, 1988:47,51,56–62).

Also Albrow posits a glaring disparity between the public and the personal. Only in his argument the central figure is a passionate leader in the public service who hides in public his intense and positive job-related feelings. Leading reformers of the British civil service between 1939 and 1945 and in the 1980s were men characterized by passion, zeal and enthusiasm felt for their work (Albrow, 1992:320–323). They induced admiration, enthusiasm and exhilaration in civil servants working for them. They were charismatic leaders in Weber's sense. In contrast to the leaders and managers depicted so far, not only did they feel and display positive emotions in confrontation with change, but were also capable of transmitting these emotions to others. Albrow uses this evidence against post-World War II theorizing that sees (state) bureaucracy and public officials as soulless and passionless.

Albrow also reminds us that much of the managerial theorizing that was concerned with corporate failure in the West since the 1980s proposes that passionate, charismatic leadership capable of producing a state of emotional contagion in the corporation promises a way out of crisis. The managerial literature associates passion with leadership in politics or economy, while it denies it to civil servants and corporate bureaucrats (Albrow, 1992:322),[5] Consequently, it has political leaders or entrepreneurs waging battles against supposedly lifeless (state and corporate) bureaucracies. From this perspective, charismatic corporate leaders actually embody emotion—the very enthusiasm necessary to bring corporations out of their current crisis. I am not aware of systematic research to prove that they are 'for real' and not a mere embodiment of corporate hopes in difficult times.

The literature that I have cited so far, however, indicates that not enthusiasm but rather fear and anxiety are endemic to managers and corporations—a fact which managerial theorizing completely ignores. Only where it addresses subordinates does it recognize that they are tense or fearful, and, therefore, advises managers to rely on humour to diffuse these feelings (Rodrigues and Collinson, 1995:741 3). It remains blind to the feelings of the managers it wants to advise.

Managers in 'strong culture' corporations

'Strong culture' corporations constitute a distinct type of profit-oriented enterprises. They require intense identification with the corporation from the employees. Höpfl's and Linstead's (1993:83–85) study illustrates a sub-type which unashamedly preys on human weakness and naïveté. Its sales personnel is hired for door-to-door or friend-to-friend product marketing. The study suggests that these corporations recruit people burdened by personal problems, be they of financial or personal nature. They bind newcomers to themselves by offering

them a dream of success, by promising respect and recognition. The corporations incorporate individuals by appealing to their emotions. For this purpose
they stage personal conversion testimonies, regular company meetings, and
luxurious-expressive regional or national events. Group directors, taught how
to recruit and how to deliver oft required scripted motivational talks, play a key
role in the incorporation process. They carry the emotional burdens of their
teams—a 24-hour job. Once group directors, despite their high salaries and all
the perks, become disillusioned and can no longer sustain their belief in the
'dream,' this dream '. . . become[s] the source of dread, disgust, aversion.' (Höpfl
and Linstead, 1993:82) From this point on until they quit, if they quit at all,
they have to convince themselves daily that their corporate life offers any
meaning or emotional rewards. Although repulsed and weary, they have to 'bear'
the effort of 'carrying on' (Höpfl and Linstead, 1993:76,86).

Worn out and suddenly sceptical managers constitute no exception. It can
happen to any manager that he or she cannot sustain corporate illusions and is
unable to continue to play the expected role (Höpfl and Linstead, 1993:89–90).
The triggering event may be the new corporate values, 'unfair' lay-offs, environmental damage caused by one's company or the rat-race and high mort-
gage—anything that increases pressure to bring two views of oneself—one
corporate and one personal—together.

When a manager reveals his ambivalence about his company, his colleagues
are likely to feel profound discomfort. They become disconcerted, avert their
gaze or shift their bodies: 'They [become] anxious for the speaker to finish or to
comport himself to the task and to remain within the consensual frame of
action' (Höpfl and Linstead: 90–91). The show must go on. On occasion it
happens, however, that middle managers as a group take to cynical humour,
parody and irony to mark their distance from the current corporate policy
and thus the senior managers (Rodrigues and Collinson, 1995:742). A study of
managerial humour in a large, multinational computer company located in the
U.S. showed that also senior managers engage humour to express amusement
about, mild aggression towards, dissatisfaction, discomfort and tension about,
even outright resistance against their organization or organizational rules they
are to implement (Hatch and Ehrlich, 1993:518).

The whistleblowers

Once they become members in an organization, many individuals develop deep
loyalty to it, even turn into strong identifiers (Hirschman, 1970; Pizzorno, 1986).
Despite organizational deterioration or a developing split between the corporate and individual morality, these individuals do not abandon their organizations. As Flam shows (1993, 1998) this applies as much to managers as to
workers, as much to the members of Western corporations as to the communist
party members in the Soviet bloc before its collapse in 1989. Apart from loyalty
and identification with their organization, powerful fears and anxieties prevent

critical members from acting on their new insights. Individuals fear jeopardizing their careers, living standards and families. They also feel anxious about their uncertain future. They fear the void. They have to overcome their fear of authority and also to condemn their own past contribution to the wrong-doings of which they have become critical. Not only the self-deception that if they stay they will be able to prevent the worst (Hirschman, 1970), but also these fears and anxieties hinder leaving.

This explains why it takes some organization critics several years before they decide to quit. This also explains why others never decide to take this step. As much research indicates, peer or community dissent is of crucial importance (Milgram, 1974; Cole, 1969; Cole, 1980; Fireman *et al.*, 1979; McAdam, 1988; Moore, 1978; Rüdig, 1990; Scott, 1990). In its presence organization critics feel shame about their own cowardice and feel encouraged to speak out.

An accumulating literature on the 'whistleblowers', employees who warn the public about corporate dangers, shows that they aim to alleviate corporate wrongdoings. Whistleblowers are rare birds. Corporations cultivate individuals who experience constant mobility anxiety and fear both their peers and bosses. They put their employees under constant pressure to ignore or keep secret corporate failures and transgressions. Most corporate employees are only capable of situational and organizational morality (Jackall, 1988). Corporations fear whistleblowers (Jackall, 1988:109,111,146,206). Their initial critical remarks or reports are ignored and discouraged. When this does not work and the whistleblowers go public, corporations retaliate by firing, black lists, character assassination, legal charges as well as by organizing physical threats, police harassment and imprisonment (Glazer and Glazer, 1999:277–8, 291–2). Whisleblowers are the exceptions to the rule—they are the managers or employees who overcome their fears and risk their jobs, family tranquility and life chances to expose corporate transgressions (Jackall, 1988; Flam, 1993:72–3; Flam, 1998:87–93; Glazer and Glazer, 1999:280–1, 289).

Interviews conducted in the US, Israel and the former Czechoslovakia show that whistleblowers overcome their fear of retaliation, and their anxiety about rejection and isolation in that they define corporate dangers as more threatening. They feed on their anger. This anger motivates them and then turns into their primary emotional resource (Glazer and Glazer, 1999:289–291). When applicable, they depend on the trust and comradeship of their peers.

Employees and their feelings

Fear, loyalty, astonishment, disappointment

In Terkel's *Working* (1972) the narrators often mention spiritually demanding play-acting in which they feel compelled to engage in their work life. They explain it with the fear of losing their jobs or incurring the disfavour of their bosses. Fearless individuals who refuse to play-act or play unconvincingly, display 'insubordination through manner' (Terkel, 1972:82–3). They acquire a 'reputation' and are labelled 'trouble-makers', which makes it difficult for them to get and hold on to a job (see also Nowak, 1988). Terkel's book with its massive evidence suggests that the Western, supposedly rational work organizations require a core emotional ingredient—fear.

Job scarcity and the fear of hierarchy on the job are the two most important preconditions for obedient play-acting (Hochschild, 1983:102,116–7). Job scarcity implies that one's chances of finding an alternative job are small, and so magnifies the fear of unemployment and of the boss (Barbalet, 1998:158,160). Factors which enhance job security, be they national laws, tenure, or strong unions, help to minimize both fears.

In the 1950s and the 1960s the capitalist economy was in a phase of expansion. It made full employment and long-term career orientation possible. A booming economy generated and also could sustain institutional and individual expectations concerning a 'standard' life course which included the educational, occupational and retirement phase (Kohli, 1985; Sennett, 1998:15–27).

As long as capitalism provided stable employment and as long as firms attempted to mould individuals working for them so that they would strive to realize the long-term goals of the firms they worked for, it was possible to assume that enterprises resembled a Weberian bureaucracy. They offered job security, a career path and remuneration in exchange for loyalty and subordination. Thus, not only fear, but also loyalty were crucial. Since the onset of the economic crisis in the early 1970s, labour markets have no longer been able to sustain 'standard biographies.' As Newman (1988), Kanter (1991), Sennett (1998), Beck (1986) and Brose *et al.* (1993) note, capitalist enterprises seek profits in new ways: they merge, streamline, re-structure, outsource, etc. For their employees this implies repeated lay-offs, work searches and, if successful at all, a string of employers. Loyalty evaporates, only fear and cynicism remain.

A German study from the early 1980s demonstrates that at least some workers thought of their employers in terms implied by the Weberian model (Esser, Fach, and Väth, 1983:206). The way they saw it, all along they had offered loyalty and high work motivation in exchange for steady wage increases, status and paternalistic type of protection. When their job situation was terminated or modified, they were astonished by what they believed to be their employer's breach of trust. They were shocked that discipline, dependability, accountability and high achievement—work norms which company leadership demanded and which they internalized—did not secure their work places. Once laid off, they felt intense disappointment: they had done their best but were robbed of their due reward by the incompetent or evil enterpreneurs.

Esser, Fach, and Väth (1983:208) propose that these workers lived in a state of 'organized dependency'. As long as they worked, they felt anchored in their firm. When they were laid off, their organizational anchorage shifted from the employer to their union, political party and the state. Let down by their employers, they turned to 'security-bureaucrats' in the hope that these would compensate them for their unfullfilled hopes. They felt that their past, long-term good conduct as union members, voters and citizens justified their cries for help. They expected help in exchange for continued loyalty and good conduct. Alone they were not capable of acting, but as soon as they defined these organizations as their saviours, they found their own actions superfluous (Esser, Fach, and Väth, 1983:208–209).[6] They felt powerless and pinned their hopes on the union leaders. In times of employment just as in time of unemployment, they did not take responsibility. They wanted to be taken care of but left in peace.

Study after study has dealt with widespread employee discontents in both industrial and service sector (Sennett, 1980:106–7; cf Barrington Moore in Scott, 1990:91–2). Missing intrinsic work satisfaction, 'unfair' 'indecisive' or 'incompetent' bosses and material deprivations are the chief reason for these discontents. Sociologists sensitive to emotions help to refine and extend this list. First let me turn briefly to boredom, then a range of emotions conveyed by organizational stories, such as pride, fear, love or nostalgia and, finally, close with joy in subversive humour.

Boredom, pride, anger and love

Following Barbalet, 'boredom is a type or form of anxiety about the lack of meaningfulness of an activitiy, a condition, and (possibly) a life' (Barbalet, 1999:637). It is accompanied by the distortion of time-sense—time appears to come to a standstill. Empirical studies suggest that employees feel bored when they do uninteresting work de-coupled from wage increases in social isolation and at a steady pace without breaks (Barbalet, 1999:637–40). Barbalet argues that boredom is 'restless', 'irritable' and presses one to construct meaning. He proposes that boredom 'is a ready conduit to participation in intergroup conflict' (Barbalet, 1999:643; see also Barbalet, 1998:181), since such conflict averts boredom, bestows meaning on one's activities (and possibly life), strengthens group cohesiveness and helps define one's place within a group. As studies depicted below imply, organizational stories and humour are equally important in averting boredom and constructing meaning. So is gossip or interpersonal conflict.

For his research project on workplace stories and construction of meaning, Gabriel collected 400 stories from 126 employees in five different British organizations (Gabriel, 1995:480). Most of these taped workplace stories expressed pride and amusement or resignation, bitterness and anger—only 10 per cent spoke of gratitude, appreciation or love (Gabriel, 1995:489–490). In the stories marked by the first set of emotions the narrators portrayed themselves as victims, agents of retribution or heroes. They saw themselves as innocent targets or as heroes and heroic survivors victorious over technology or bureaucracy (Gabriel, 1995:482–5). In the stories coloured by the second set of emotions, narrators told of brief encounters between them and a peer/client/patient which entailed a gift as a way of expressing gratitude for compassion or help displayed by the narrator earlier on (Gabriel, 1995:489–491). In contrast to organizational stories which portray the narrators as heroes or victims, these stories paint the narrator as an object of affection. Love fantasies and office romances also surface among typical office-stories. Office romances feature two types of narratives. The first feeds malicious gossip and defines central characters as the 'fools'. The second speaks of romance, whereby the subject emerges as an object of love and affection.

Nostalgia

Similarly to the victim and hero stories, nostalgia is a direct means of attributing meaning to oneself and one's activities in a depersonalizing corporation. It is a way to express the discontents of today:

> ... organizational nostalgia tells us more about the discontents of today than about the contents of yesteryear. Like humour, but in a radically different way, it seeks to provide a symbolic way out of the rigours of bureaucracy, seeking to re-enchant a long disenchanted world. (Gabriel, 1993:137)

As Gabriel (1993:121–31) shows nostalgia signifies a warm yearning for the lost past. It juxtaposes an idealized picture of the past with the present which by comparison is lacking. Within organizations, the leaders, social relationships, technology, products, even buildings may be found wanting. In a nostalgic story a symbolic watershed, such as a move, a corporate merger, or new computerized technology, divides the enchanted past from the present. Organizational nostalgia expresses longing for the past standards of elegance, values, occasional amiable talks with the boss, mutuality in contacts with peers and bosses, etc. The image of organization as a family dominates it. Let me provide some of Gabriel's interview excerpts taken from different organizations:

> The nice thing about Sir Roy ... [was that] he was always around, he was quite visible in the dining room having egg and chips for lunch, or in the bar having a pint and people would go and talk to him if they wanted ... No matter what he did while he was in power, he always seemed a very human person ... The current chairman ... I don't feel I know him at all. [unspecified company] (Gabriel, 1993:128)

> I mean we had, years ago, we had more time to, *for* people ... The old building was a 1920s building, very elegant, *it was a shame to lose* ... [chemical company] (Gabriel, 1993:124–5)

> It used to be like a small community ... everyone knew each other, everyone helped each other ... just like a family ... When we came to this big place here, all those same people were spread across the site and when you pass each other, you don't have the same contact. [a hospital] (Gabriel, 1993:124)

Nostalgic stories attribute quality, caring and altruism to the organizational past and find them missing in the present. They are infused with sadness. When they turn around the departed colleagues, sadness, melancholia, even mourning surface. Gabriel suggests that large, modern organizations with technocratic management are less likely than smaller (and older) organizations to be turned into the objects of nostalgic longing for the past.

Fears, discontent and subversive humour

A more militant image of workers is offered by a Brazilian-British study of workplace humour. Humour does not dwell on the golden past long gone, but instead focuses on the present. In the last two decades managerial theorizing has turned against strict, bureaucratic authority and rigid organizational models because it is believed that they kill innovation and so undermine business success (Peters and Waterman, 1982). As Rodrigues and Collinson (1995:741–3) argue a considerable body of literature advocates that managers relax their control, reduce the hierachy, and 'have fun' in the workplace. From this perspective humour is necessary to reduce nervousness in subordinates, reinforce shared values, facilitate social bonding. The same authors contend that this literature treats humour predominantly as a managerial technique, as a new tool to reinforce managerial power (but see Dweyer, 1991). A 'safety-valve' theory of humour recommends workplace humour as a way of defusing tense situations, even if it is not the management but the employees who crack jokes and laugh.

As Rodrigues and Collinson show, workplace humour has very many functions. For us relevant is that it can be 'a means of handling anxiety and threat: a defensive, distancing strategy for dealing with adversity' and be employed by workers as a means of displaying open, yet relatively safe workplace resistance (Rodrigues and Collinson, 1995:744,749–56). Even though employee humour takes many forms, from joking over pamphlets to satirical cartoons published in a union newspaper, it is intended to de-legitimate and demystify management and glorify the workers, thus inversing corporate values and its hierarchy. In this sense we can speak of the oppositional humour of the subordinates. In a state-owned Brazilian company, Telecom, between 1988 to 1991, this humour focused on current issues, such as decreasing job security, unfair individual lay-offs, over-zealous managerial control and surveillance, non-meritocratic recruitment practices, managerial incompetence or greed, health and safety, etc. In short: subversive, cutting workplace humour expressed employee fears and discontents, it challenged status quo, while it supplied some protection from managerial reprisals (Rodrigues and Collinson, 1995:757–8).

Like nostalgia, subversive workplace humour expresses the discontents of the present and 'seeks to offer partial consolation for the injuries sustained . . . in organizations' (Gabriel, 1993:137). Like nostalgia, workplace humour ennobles the employees, and questions and reverses current corporate values. But subversive workplace humour has a sharp cutting edge and it turns on to the present. Nostalgic myths diffuse discontent, since they dwell on the past.

In his acclaimed book, Scott (1990) argues that we should not see any basic contradiction between mild and strong, hidden and open forms of subordinate protest. His framework abolishes a contradiction of long standing between apparent apathy and protest, 'false' and 'true' consciousness. Whether in a mild form of nostalgia or a powerful form of a subversive employee humour, employees express their discontent with boredom, humiliation, frustration, anger, lovelessness, fear and anxiety that they experience on the job. These emotions are responses to the 'social experience of indignities, control, submission, humiliation, forced deference and punishment' associated with any form of domination (Scott, 1990:111–3).

Scott himself repeatedly warns that specific elements of his framework may be applicable only to the cases of absolute domination, such as serfdom, and slave or caste systems. Collinson's British study of masculinity, joking and conflict in shop-floor relations gives much credence to this warning. It demonstrates that autonomous social spaces are not a sufficient condition to generate ultimately open, yet at the present less risky 'hidden' subversive scripts (Scott, 1990:20,85–6,111,114,118–35). Collinson's study actually questions the connection which Scott posits between an autonomous subordinate culture, solidarity and resistance.

Collinson (1988:182) first refers to his predecessors who showed that humour counteracts boredom, anxiety, even fear of death among miners or hostility between co-workers who belong to various ethnic groups. Citing numerous interviews he then demonstrates that shop-floor humour—highly insulting nicknames, uninhibited swearing, mutual ridicule, pranks—counteracted boredom, strengthened shop-floor cohesion around masculinity and manual work, and helped to express antagonism to white collar staff and managers at a lorry-making factory in the North West of England that he investigated between 1979 and 1983. These forms of humour helped 'to alleviate any feelings of inferiority', to maintain 'a very conscious sense of a difference and ideological support for their own world', and to turn upside down the official hierarchies of shop-floor/office, manual/non-manual, worker/middle class, uneducated/educated, unpolite/polite (Collinson, 1988:186–7,189,197–8). They were the very forms of workplace resistance. At the same time, however, insults turned out to constitute attempts to control and discipline those co-workers who did not contribute their fair share to the bonus scheme which was calculated on a collective basis. They also testified to the division between 'virile' single men, set on 'having a laff' at work, and married 'breadwinners', keen on maximizing their earnings. Ultimately, Collinson argues, shop-floor humour that emphasized masculine independence resulted in superficial and largely defensive relationships between the men who, when layoffs came in 1983, turned out so fragmented and individualized that they did not offer any form of resistance.

Emotion management

The Managed Heart, Hochschild's singular contribution to the sociology of organization, caused a strong echo. In her modern 'classic' she opened new research vistas. She put emotions in the centre of analysis while studying their interplay with organizational and societal norms. In the book she shows that firms in the service sector require not only services but also emotion work from their employees. She argues that it depends on the corporate goals which feeling rules employees have to follow and which emotions they have to display. Each firm's goals decide which informal, all apart from formal, qualifications and which emotional attributes play a role in hiring. In the same vein, they also dictate whether the personnel is subject to no, little or much training and supervision in order to acquire and keep up the required emotional habits.

Hochschild investigated two contrasting occupational groups in the service sector: the stewardesses and the credit collectors. Her research shows that stewardesses face pressure to display positive emotions such as sympathy, warmth and caring towards passengers. They are to make them feel comfortable and to upgrade their status. In contrast, credit collectors are supposed to display aggression and contempt. They are to hurl insults at debtors to make them feel loss of status.

Both occupations demand 'deep acting'. The employees have to follow emotion rules which their jobs demand, produce specific desired emotions so that they can act convincingly. This calls for 'emotion management'—suppressing or deeply hiding real feelings in order to display the desired ones. Only when employees engage in emotion management can they deliver emotion work for which they are paid. Stress felt during leisure time, inability to relax and find back to what one really feels came to constitute new occupational hazards.

Hochschild's admirers and critics, blinded only as far as her own contributions to points 1 2 are concerned, found the following aspects of her work wanting:

Even though increasing competition forces management to intensify their attempts to achieve total control over the process of emotion work, the fact is that managerial control of emotion work is often partial, incoherent and contradictory. It makes it easier to resist and depart from managerial rules. Not the discursive but the material and structural power generates pragmatic acceptance of corporate norms. (Taylor, 1998:100; Taylor and Tyler, 2000:88–9) Whereas Hochschild argued that employers and, sometimes, trade unions decide whether and what kind of emotion work becomes part and parcel of one's job, also work teams and professional ethics play a similar role (Dunkel, 1988).

Hochschild's work does not grant employees enough sovereignty. It fails to recognize that these are aware of the employer manipulation to which they are subject, and activate different strategies to circumvent this manipulation and supervision. They resist and negotiate managerial prescription. Very few experience anything akin to alienation. (Taylor, 1998:94–8; Taylor and Tyler, 2000:88–90; Bogner and Wouters, 1990:278). Shifts in the general power balance to the benefit of subordinates have led to increased informalization of power relations in the last decades of our century (Bogner and Wouters, 1990:272–277). Societal norms have lost much of their binding force. This means that the conduct standards are re-interpreted in concrete situations. For stewardesses this means that they have a much greater room for maneuvre than Hochschild believes. It is expected of them to exercise spontaneity and discretion which actually demands more cognitive and emotion work than when conduct rules were set. But they use their discretion and spotaneity to discipline clients and so wrest more freedom for themselves. Finally, Hochschild does not quite appreciate the fact that 'emotional workers' are able to develop and think about their emotions (see point 4 below). They can play with them in their interactions with clients. This can be enriching in ways manual labour is not (Barbalet, 1998:182).

Hochschild does not recognize that specific occupations become construed as gendered when they are carried out predominantly by either men or women. The gendering of occupations not only implies that the positions in these occupations are expected to be filled by either men or women but also that these jobs demand specific emotional performance (Pierce, 1995:1; Taylor, 1998: Taylor and Tyler, 2000). Occupations performed mostly by women are not only less paid or lower in prestige, power and career possibilities. They also demand more emotional labour. Pierce's study (1995) which compares the work demands placed on female in contrast to male paralegals in three different American law firms makes clear that gender plays an enormous role on the job. Male paralegals can take exception to the 'standard' occupational expectations concerning emotional labour by the virtue of being men. Women cannot do this for risk of being fired or stigmatized as unmotivated or uncooperative. Like their male colleagues they are expected to analyse documents and do legal research but, in addition, they have to soothe the feelings of their bosses. On the job interactions between female paralegals, acting their parts as supportive and non-assertive 'office moms', and their bosses, the trial lawyers, acting their parts as 'Rambo litigators', in following gendered work expectations reproduce the gendered division of labour with all its structural consequences. According to her critics, Hochschild missed the association between occupation, gender and demands placed on emotional labour. She also neglected the gendered differences in power which are their consequence.

Emotion plays a role in the service sector as part of self-presentation to manipulate the buyer, as a deeply-felt feeling needed to get on with one's task, and in the form of work on own emotions (Dunkel, 1988:66). Hochschild does not recognize that '[e]motional labour is an experience which remains within the emotional possession of the employee. The emotions generated by that labour have emotional consequences. These lead the emoting person to apprehend their situation emotionally and to form emotional responses to it.' (Barbalet, 1998:181) The contrast between 'surface acting' and 'deep acting' is overdrawn and oversimplified (Taylor, 1998:99). In order to meet targets and earn their income, employees engage in 'sophisticated surface acting' or 'deep acting for pragmatic purposes'. Very few let their jobs influence or modify their private emotions.

Hochschild introduces an unwarranted distinction between authentic and superficial feelings which parallels her distinction between private and public, a distinction which in light of Elias' research on the civilization processes should not be made at all (Bogner and Wouters, 1990:266–8). We are long past any authentic emotions, know only those imposed by our civilization and national cultures. Elias' work on the history of manners also shows that it is not capitalism as such which leads to emotion management but, rather, any relations of power and dependence which create intense pressures to follow the dominant display rules.

Hochschild assumes that emotions on the job are more often subject to management than emotions in the private sphere. This is another unsustainable assumption as not only keeping up a job but also maintaining private relationships calls for much emotion work and emotion management (Bogner and Wouters, 1990:259–62).

We should look at not only work-related but also leisure time emotions. We should shift our focus to a macro-context which, *via* the expanding welfare state, has neutralized work competition after World War II (Wouters, 1992). This competition exists but, in an increasingly egalitarian context, has become a conversational taboo. Individuals suffer its effects in silence. Because of a basic sense of security and, I think, also to relieve competitive work time tensions, they are more than ever willing to risk and experiment during their leisure time—hence more free sex and risky sport.

Conclusion

It is still too early to herald the time of studies on emotion in organizations. As this text (see also Fineman, 1996) shows there is no coherent body of research or thought devoted to this particular topic. I can only repeat once more (Flam, 1999) that the scattered wealth of unrelated research projects on emotions can only hamper, not hasten, persuading others about the viability and theoretical insights offered by the sociology of emotions.

Nevertheless, these disparate studies show that both managers and employees turn out to be much more emotional than most scientists would care to admit. Both are under pressure not to display their fears, anxieties or worries. Both have to balance a mixture of emotions attending solidarity and competition with their peers. But whereas managerial roles actually call for occasional display of anger at subordinates, anger is beyond the pale for subordinates. Subordinates are expected to communicate only positive emotions to clients (unless these happen to be debtors) as well as to those higher up in the hierarchy. They are supposed to swallow anger, humiliation, fear (Scott, 1990:37–41). No wonder that managers take to the emotional support of their peers and secretaries, whereas employees spin nostalgic stories or take to subversive workplace humour. Capitalist labour, no matter whether this of managers or that of workers, exacts a heavy emotional toll.

As the last section shows by citing some examples, Hochschild's modern 'classic' generated an entire flurry of writing. Even at the recent annual meeting of the American Sociological Association yet another criticism of her work was presented (Kriz, 2000). I would like to close by repeating what I also said on this occasion and later published (Flam, 2000:178–92):

When Arlie Hochschild (1983) in the US or Jürgen Gerhards and Wolfgang Dunkel (Gerhards, 1988; Dunkel, 1988; Badura, 1990) in Germany tried to legitimate sociology of emotions, they pointed to the enormous expansion of the service sector. They argued that this particular sector, much more than the traditional industries, called for emotion work. Not surprisingly, although sociology of emotions expanded to cover many areas (for overview, see Flam, 2000 and Fineman, 1996), following this kind of reasoning, many sociologists of emotions concentrate on the service sector. Or they study work-related emotions.

This focus on emotion at work, I believe, has become confining. It prevents us from asking new questions about the nature of Western societies in which we live. Yet, as I argue elsewhere (Flam, 1999), sociology of emotions has arrived at a point where it can and should make a step towards macro-level theorizing. It needs to link its theorizing about emotions in organizations to a theory of society.

Revolving-door labour markets and de-institutionalized biographies set in a pluralistic context supply a new justification for the sociology of emotions and for its additional focus on self- and other-related emotions. Katherine Newman (1988), Richard Sennett (1998), Barbara Ehrenreich (1994), and Koeber (2000) in the US as well as Martin Kohli (1985; 1988) and Ulrich Beck (1986) in Germany sketch a grand narrative which helps us link a macro-concern with the vicissitudes of the capitalist economy with a micro-concern with the emotions of people who have to cope with these ups-and-downs.

As the institutional framework of capitalism becomes disjointed and capitalism itself undergoes yet another in a long series of turbulences, people are no longer securely anchored in work organizations nor rescued by the welfare state. After World War II they could take it for granted that they would have a relatively stable and predictable life. Since the 1970s, though, they face an unknown and unstable future. It is extremely probable that they will face unemployment, even if they are well educated. Nobody can count on a safe organizational harbour.

A good point of departure for linking these macro-level phenomena with the micro-level emotional experience is the following question: What are the emotional costs of coping with revolving-door labour markets set in a context of pluralistic societies with their great supply of life models? At least three distinct research niches can be idenitified: career pursuit, lay-offs and occupational discontinuity. Emotions typical of each can be studied in their own right. Important is that not only work- but also self- and other-centered emotions should come into focus.

Macro-level sociological theorizing about the main generators of meaning, such as religion or mass media, turns out less useful than expected in answering the question about managing the emotional costs of capitalism for two reasons. First, scientists such as Luckmann, Giddens or Bauman cannot agree whether religion, family, mass media, therapies, social movements, etc. do or do not help to make sense of reality and whether they reinforce or only further weaken social bonds. Secondly, as biographic research shows, religion, family or the mass media are seldom harnessed to cope with the deeply upsetting experience of lay-off or competition.

The same biographic research suggests that the emotional effects of lay-offs and occupational discontinuities vary considerably depending on how they are interpreted. Individuals draw on a number of interpretative schemes to frame their painful experiences, ranging from specific definitions of gender and success to national myths and state-ideologies. Individuals and groups switch between self-blame and other-blame frames. A worrisome fact is that they turn xenophobic with amazing regularity. We need to understand this social fact.

The classical sociologist, Emile Durkheim, already noted more than 100 years ago the demoralizing and disorienting effects of competition and social mobility. As other classical sociologists, he tried to distance sociology from psychology and economics. However, in accounting for different types of suicide, he paid close attention to the unsettling emotions which exposure to social mobility and weak social bonds cause. The sociology of emotions delivers tools with which Durkheim's classical research agenda may be rejuvenated.

Notes

1 This section draws on one section of my 'Emotional "Man"' (1990b).
2 Many companies which were once thought invulnerable operate since 'at the edge of abyss' or collapse 'which creates feelings of realistic anxiety' (Stacey in Gabriel, 1998:305).
3 Bureaucratic impersonality generates anxieties in its own right (Baum, and Fineman and Gabriel in Gabriel, 1998:306). It creates space for fantasies, for strong emotions associated with attributions of blame, credit and scapegoating. Gabriel distinguishes between two views on anxiety in organizations. The first sees the manager set in a highly unpredictable environment as an anxious individual, a creator of managerial rationality. The second sees bureaucratic organization and its procedures as a cause of anxiety. The authors presented in the following do not focus narrowly on bureaucracy *per se*. Instead most of them show that various aspects of corporate life evoke fear and anxiety in managers who then respond to these feelings in various ways.
4 Even female managers 'endorse the dominant discourse of 'rational' organizations and 'scientific' management . . . it is difficult for the managers to represent themselves as good managers in any other way vis-à-vis emotion.' (Swan, 1994:103)
5 Weber offered an image of a passionate, charismatic leader as a head of bureaucracy as well as posited the problem of disciplining affectivity in mass organizations, but he denied 'the passionate commitment of the dutiful bureaucrat' (Albrow, 1992:317–9,324). Albrow stresses that Weber, in contrast to his many followers, counterposed rationality and affectivity—everywhere but in the bureaucrat or the bureaucratic organization. Albrow explains that this was a consequence of Weber's drawing on the German theory of the rational legal administration of the modern state rather than on a theory of human co-operation so prevalent at his time.
6 They justified their own passivity in various ways. They explained their lacking sense of efficacy by pointing out to competition about jobs and lacking solidarity among workers. They argued that workers' common actions always petered out. They declared that in contrast to a single worker (the powerless little man) organizations have the necessary expertise and negotiating skills or explained their passivity by the German need for leadership and authority figures. Or they expressed the hope that things would not come to worst.

References

Albrow, M. (1992) 'Sine Ira et Studio—or Do Organizations Have Feelings' *Organization Studies* 13, 3: 313–329.
Badura, B. (1990) 'Interaktionsstress' *Zeitschrift für Soziologie* 19, 5: 317–328.

Barbalet, J.M. (1998) *Emotion, Social Theory, and Social Structure*. Cambridge: Cambridge University Press.

Barbalet, J.M. (1999) 'Boredom and social meaning' *The British Journal of Sociology* 50, 4: 631–646.

Barber, B. (1983) *The Logic and Limits of Trust*. New Brunswick, N.J: Rutgers University Press.

Beck, Ulrich. (1986) *Risikogesellschaft. Auf dem Weg in eine andere Moderne*. Frankfurt a.M: Suhrkamp.

Bogner, A. and Wouters, C. (1990) 'Kolonialisierung der Herzen? Zu Arlie Hochschilds Grundlegung der Emotionssoziologie' *Leviathan* 18, 2: 255–279.

Brose, H.-G., Wohlrab-Sahr, M., and Corsten, M. (1993) *Soziale Zeit und Biographie*. Opladen: Westdeutscher Verlag.

Clegg, S.R., Hardy, C., and Nord, W.R. eds, (1996) *Handbook of Organization Studies*. London: Sage.

Cole, S. (1969) *The Unionization of Teachers: A Case Study of the UFT*. New York: Praeger.

Cole, S. (1980) *The Sociological Method*. Chicago: Rand McNally.

Collinson, D.L. (1988) 'Engineering Humour: Masculinity, Joking and Conflict in Shop-floor Relations' *Organization Studies* 9, 2: 181–199.

Dunkel, W. (1988) 'Wenn Gefühle zum Arbeitsgegenstand werden' *Soziale Welt* 39, 1: 66–85.

Dweyer, T. (1991) 'Humor, Power and Change in Organizations' *Human Relations* 44, 1: 1–19.

Elster, J. (1999) *Alchemies of the Mind. Rationality and the Emotions*. Cambridge: Cambridge University Press.

Ehrenreich, B. (1994) *Angst vor dem Absturz: Das Dilemma der Mittelklasse*. Reinbek bei Hamburg: Rowohlt Taschenbuch (first printed in 1989 as *Fear of Falling*. New York: Harper Collins).

Esser, J., Fach, W., and Väth, W. (1983) *Krisenregulierung*. Frankfurt a.M: Suhrkamp.

Fineman, S., ed. (1993) *Emotion in Organizations*. London: Sage.

Fineman, S. (1996) 'Emotion and Organizing' in *Handbook of Organization Studies*. Edited by S.R. Clegg, C. Hardy, and W.R. Nord. London. Sage, pp. 543–564.

Fireman, B., Gamson, W.W., Rytina, S., and Taylor, B. (1979) 'Encounters with unjust authority' in *Research in Social Movements, Conflicts and Change*. Vol. 2. Edited by L. Kriesberg. Greenwich, CT: JAI Press, pp. 1–33.

Flam, H. (1990a) 'Emotional "Man": I. The Emotional "Man" and the Problem of Collective Action' *International Sociology* 5, 1: 39–56.

Flam, H. (1990b) 'Emotional "Man": II. Corporate Actors as Emotion-motivated Emotion Managers' *International Sociology* 5, 2: 225–234.

Flam, H. (1993) 'Fear, Loyalty and Greedy Organizations' in *Emotion in Organizations*. Edited by S. Fineman London: Sage, pp. 58–75.

Flam, H. (1998) *Mosaic of Fear: Poland and East Germany before 1989*. Boulder. East European Monographs distributed by Columbia University Press.

Flam, H. (1999) 'Gillian Bendelow and Simon J. Williams (eds) Emotions in Social Life: Critical Themes and Contemporary Issues. London: Routledge, 1998' *European Journal of Social Theory* 2, 1: 115–119.

Flam, H. (2000) *The Emotional 'Man' and the Problem of Collective Action*. Frankfurt a.M: Peter Lang.

Gabriel, Y. (1993) 'Organizational Nostalgia—Reflections on the "The Golden Age"' in *Emotion in Organizations*. Edited by S. Fineman. London: Sage, pp. 118–141.

Gabriel, Y. (1995) 'The Unmanaged Organization: Stories, Fantasies and Subjectivity' *Organization Studies* 16, 3: 477–501.

Gabriel, Y. (1998) 'Psychoanalytic Contributions to the Study of the Emotional Life of Organizations' *Administration & Society* 30, 3: 291–314.

Gerhards, J. (1988) 'Emotionsarbeit. Zur Kommerzialisierung von Gefühlen' *Soziale Welt* 39, 1: 47–65.

Ghiloni, B.W. (1994) 'Women, Power, and the Corporation: Evidence from the Velvet Ghetto' *Power* (Critical Concepts. Vol. 3). London: Routledge, pp. 232–244 (first printed in 1984).

Glazer, M.P. and Glazer, P.M. (1999) 'On the Trail of Courageous Behavior' *Sociological Inquiry* 69, 2: 276–295.

Gouldner, A.W. (1981) 'Succession and the Problem of Bureaucracy' in *The Sociology of Organizations: Basic Studies*. Edited by O. Grusky and G.A. Miller. New York: The Free Press, pp. 280–302 (first printed in 1954).

Grusky, O. and Miller, G.A. eds, (1981) *The Sociology of Organizations: Basic Studies*. New York: The Free Press (first printed in 1970).

Hatch, M.J. and Ehrlich, S.B. (1983) 'Spontaneous Humour as an Indicator of Paradox and Ambiguity in Organizations' *Organization Studies* 14, 4: 505–526.

Hearn, J. (1993) 'Emotive Subjects: Organizational Men, Organizational Masculinities and the (De)construction of "Emotions"' in *Emotion in Organizations*. Edited by S. Fineman. London: Sage, pp. 142–166.

Hirschman, A.O. (1970) *Exit, Voice and Loyalty*. Cambridge, MA: Harvard University Press.

Hochschild, A. (1979) 'Emotion Work, Feeling Rules, and Social Structure' *American Journal of Sociology* 85: 551–575.

Hochschild, A. (1983) *The Managed Heart: Commercialization of Human Feeling*. Berkeley: University of California Press (deutsche Übersetzung: 1989a. *Das gekaufte Herz*. Frankfurt a.M.Campus).

Hochschild, A. (1989) *The Second Shift*. New York: Viking-Penguin.

Hochschild, A. (1990) 'Ideology and Emotion Management: A Perspective and Path for Future Research' in *Research Agendas in the Sociology of Emotions*. Edited by T.D. Kemper. Albany: State University of New York Press, pp. 117–142.

Höpfl, H. and Linstead, S. (1993) 'Passion and Performance: Suffering and the Carrying of Organizational Roles' in *Emotion in Organizations*. Edited by S. Fineman. London: Sage, pp. 76–93.

Jackall, R. (1988) *Moral Mazes: The World of Corporate Managers*. New York: Oxford University Press.

Kanter, R. Moss. (1981) 'Women and the Structure of Organizations: Explorations in Theory and Behavior' in *The Sociology of Organizations: Basic Studies*. Edited by O. Grusky and G.A. Miller. New York: The Free Press, pp. 395–424 (first printed in 1975).

Koeber, C. (2000) 'Downsizing, Displacement and High-Tech Workers' paper presented in the session on Work and the Workplace at the 95th Annual Meeting of the American Sociological Association in Washington, D.C., August 12–16.

Kohli, M. (1985) 'Die Institutionalisierung des Lebenslaufs' *Kölner Zeitschrift für Soziologie und Sozialpsychologie* 37, 1: 1–29.

Kohli, M. (1988) 'Normalbiographie und Individualität: Zur institutionellen Dynamik des gegenwärtigen Lebenslaufregimen' in *Vom Ende des Individuums zur Individualität ohne Ende*. Edited by H.-G. Brose and B. Hildenbrand. Opladen: Leske + Budrich, pp. 33–54.

Kriz, Katrin (2000) 'Emotional Labor Revisited: Theorizing the Psychological Aspects of Interactive Service Work' paper presented in the 92nd Regular Session in the Sociology of Emotions convened at the 95th Annual Meeting of the American Sociological Association in Washington, D.C. on August 12–16.

McAdam, D. (1988) 'Micromobilization contexts and recruitment to activism' in *International Social Movement Research*. Vol. 1. Edited by B. Klandermans, H. Kriesi, and S. Tarrow. Greenwich, CT: JAI Press, 125–154.

McGill, V.J. (1941–2) 'Scheler's Theory of Sympathy and Love' *Philosophy and Phenomenological Research* II: 273–291.

Milgram, S. (1974) *Obedience to Authority: An Experimental View*. London: Tavistock.

Mills, C.W. (1956) *White Collar*. New York: A Galaxy Book. Oxford University Press (first printed in 1951).

Moore, B. Jr. (1978) *Injustice: The Social Bases of Obedience and Revolt*. White Plains, NY: M.E. Sharpe.

Newman, K. (1988) *Falling from Grace: The Experience of Downward Mobility in the American Middle Class*. New York: Free Press.

Nowak, K. (1988) 'Covert Repressiveness and the Stability of the Political System: Poland in the End of the Seventies' *Social Research* 55, 1/2: 179–208.

Pizzorno, A. (1986) 'Some other kind of otherness: a critique 'rational choice' theories' in *Development, Democracy and the Art of Trespassing: Essays in Honor of Albert O. Hirschman*. Edited by A. Foxley *et al*. Notre Dame: University of Notre Dame Press, pp. 355–373.

Peters, T.J. and Waterman Jr., R.H. (1982) *In Search of Excellence: Lessons from America's Best-Run Companies*. New York: Harper & Row, Publishers.

Pierce, J.L. (1995) *Gender Trials. Emotional Lives in Contemporary Law Firms*. Berkeley: University of California Press.

Putnam, L.L. and Mumby, D.K. (1993) 'Organizations, Emotion and the Myth of Rationality' in *Emotion in Organizations* Edited by S. Fineman London: Sage, pp. 36–57.

Rodrigues, S.B. and Collinson, D.L. (1995) '"Having Fun": Humour as Resistance in Brazil' *Organization Studies* 16, 5: 739–768.

Rüdig, W. (1990) *Anti-Nuclear Movements: A World Survey of Opposition to Nuclear Energy*. Harlow, Essex: Longman.

Scott, James C. (1990) *Domination and the Arts of Resistance: Hidden Transcripts*. New Haven: Yale University Press.

Sennett, R. (1998) *Der flexible Mensch*. Berlin: Berlin Verlag (first printed in 1998 as *The Corrosion of Character*. New York: W.W. Norton).

Sennett, R. (1980) *Authority*. New York: W.W. Norton.

Sennet, R. and Cobb, J. (1972) *The Hidden Injuries of Class*. New York: W.W. Norton & Company Inc.

Simon, H.A. (1978) 'Rational Decision-Making in Business Organizations' Nobel Memorial Lecture, 8 December (1977) *Les prix nobel* 1978: 275–302.

Swan, E. (1994) 'Managing Emotion' in *Women in Management: A Developing Presence*. Edited by M. Tanton. London: Routlege, pp. 89–109.

Taylor, S. and Tyler, M. (2000) 'Emotional Labour and Sexual Difference in the Airline Industry' *Work, Employment and Society* 14, 1: 77–95.

Taylor, S. (1998) 'Emotional Labour and the New Workplace' in *Workplaces of the Future*. Edited by P. Thompson and C. Warhurst. London: McMillan, pp. 84–103.

Terkel, S. (1972) *Working: People Talk About What They Do All Day and How They Feel About What They Do*. New York: Pantheon Books.

Vince, R. and Broussine, M. (1996) 'Paradox, Defense and Attachment: Accessing and Working with Emotions and Relations Underlying Organizational Change' *Organizational Studies* 17, 1: 1–21.

Weick, K.E. (1981) 'Enactment and Organizing' *The Sociology of Organizations*. Edited by O. Grusky and G.A. Miller. New York: The Free Press, pp. 265–280 (first printed in 1979).

Wouters, C. (1992) 'On Status Competition and Emotion Management: The Study of Emotions as a New Field' in *Cultural Theory and Cultural Change*. Edited by M. Featherstone London: Sage, pp. 229–252.

Managing the emotions of competition and recognition in Academia

Charlotte Bloch

Abstract

In the sociology of science, social relations have been discussed in terms of competition and recognition. The purpose of this chapter is to enlarge our understanding of the social relations of Academia by incorporating the emotional dimensions of these relations into our discussion. To this purpose the results of an empirical study of emotions and emotional culture in Academia is presented. These results are based on analytical distinctions between the structural conditions of emotions, the emotional culture of Academia, lived or felt emotions and the management of emotions. Within this analytical framework different ways of managing the emotions of uncertainty, shame, anger and pride are identified and presented. It is shown how these feelings emerged from the structural conditions of the social relations and it is shown how persons try to manage the mentioned emotions according to the tacit rules of feelings of Academia. The study shows how these emotions are managed according to the representative feelings of Academia. It is also shown, however, how these emotions and their management relate to damaged social bonds. These unintended consequences of the emotions and the emotional culture of Academia are interpreted as emotional fuel to the prevalent basic moods of academic departments and their research environment.

When I tell my colleagues that I am researching emotions in Academia, they smile and some even laugh. According to the literature, laughter springs *inter alia* from an awareness of incompatible frames of reference.[1] My colleagues laugh because they experience emotions and Academia as incompatible entities. Indeed, laughter is an emotional response to an apparently cultural incompatibility between Academia and emotions. This cultural incompatibility is not merely expressed in laughter but also in the philosophy and sociology of science where, as a rule, emotions are classified and evaluated as disturbing, subjective elements that impede scientific cognition.[2]

We are, however, always emotional (Heidegger, 1927; Bollnow, 1974; Scheff, 1997). Human emotionality is an ongoing stream pervading every aspect of our social lives. Thus the question is not whether emotions and Academia are compatible, but rather what characterizes emotions and their management in Academia.

In this chapter I present some preliminary results from a qualitative study of emotions in Academia. The objective of the article is to illustrate how the perspective of emotions may contribute to and qualify our conventional sociological understanding and theories of social relations in Academia. Thus a brief outline of conventional approaches to social relations in research and scholarship is first presented. The empirical investigation and preliminary results of my analysis is then presented.[3] Finally I discuss the implications of my results for our understanding of the social relations within Academia.

Sociological theories of social relations in Academia

In the sociology of science, social relations are discussed in terms of both competition and recognition. The theories of Pierre Bourdieu (1975; 1991), Tony Becher & Paul R. Trowler (2001) and Warren O. Hagstrom (1972) are presented in the following. These theories have been selected because they present established approaches to social relations in science.[4]

Bourdieu (1975; 1991) is primarily concerned with the structural conditions for social relations in science. In accordance with this theory, science is analysed as a system of relations between positions that are mutually distinguished by different volumes of capital, ie, competence and characteristics that allow access to the profits of the field and thus to valorizing of one's capital. Within science as a field, the fundamental struggle has to do with achieving a monopoly on 'correct' science. As Bourdieu says, science is 'the locus of a competitive struggle, in which the specific issue at stake is the monopoly of scientific authority, defined inseparably as technical capacity and social power, or to put it another way, the monopoly of *scientific competence*, in the sense of a particular agent's socially recognized capacity to speak and act legitimately (ie, in an authorized and authoritative way) in scientific matters' (Bourdieu, 1975:19).

The structure of the scientific field is thus defined at every moment by the state of the relations of power among the protagonists in the struggle just as the scientific field, which, as the locus of a political struggle for scientific domination, assigns each researcher, as a function of his position within it, his indissociably political and scientific problems and his methods. Thus, according to Bourdieu, every scientific 'choice' is a political investment strategy, directed, objectively at least, toward maximization of strictly scientific profit, ie, a potential recognition by the agent's competitor-peers (Bourdieu, 1975:22). Compared with other social fields, however, the scientific field has one special feature, namely that 'the producers ie, the scientists tend to have no possible client other than their competitors' (Bourdieu, 1975:23).[5] That is to say that recognition, the profit in the field, is conditioned by other researchers who, being his competitors too, are the least inclined to grant recognition without discussion and scrutiny.

To summarize, Bourdieu views science as a dynamic field of positions with different volumes of capital. The specificity of this field is that scientists are one another's judge and competitor at one and the same time. These structural relations are not to be reduced to the aggregate of the interactions in the interactionist sense, but are to be seen as structural conditions that in fact determine the concrete relations and interactions in Academia (Bourdieu, 1975:19).

More concretely than Bourdieu, Becher & Trowler (2001), and also Hagstrom (1972), elucidate different aspects of competition and recognition in terms of peer-review or 'peer-group judgement' as an academic institution. Peer review, as a social form, is present in many different academic contexts, from the review of articles for scholarly journals to judgement of oral presentations of research results at seminars, and congresses, for instance. Becher and Trowler focus on the formalized peer review of submissions for publication, research grant applications and application for tenure. They acknowledge solidarity with the peer review, the rationale of which is that only other professional experts are capable of evaluating the quality of research. They also emphasize the problems involved in peer review that stem from the fact that the academic peer group is not well defined. The academic peer group is a floating sociality, consisting of anything from a specialist network or an invisible college to a wider professional community.

There are further limitations on peer review. In highly specialized fields of research there may be no relevant experts to review research. Also, in many cases the relevant experts do not agree. These problems, and others, are confirmed by studies that question the validity of the peer review.[6] Additionally, competitiveness between peers may be the source of unethical evaluations based on personal preferences and antipathies, and even plagiarism. An advantage of peer review is that the responsibility for control of research quality is in principle collective. Whatever their position, every member of a professional field has the right to criticize the work of another and every member has the possibility of having his or her research evaluated. However, this strength also has its limitations. In the real world, according to Becher and Towler, peer validation will most frequently contribute to consolidating the existing power and prestige relations by means of the 'Matthew principle' (to those who have [publications] shall be given more), and through the gate-keeping and selective favouring by academically powerful people of persons on the basis of their academic background and profile.

While Becher and Trowler point to shortcomings in scientific evaluation and recognition through formalized peer review, they do not comment on its symbolic and emotional aspects and effects. This latter is treated by Hagstrom. Inspired by anthropology, he interprets the peer review as an exchange of gifts, in which the researcher presents his or her results to the scientific community and where, on the basis of the logic of gift-giving, acceptance of the gift implies a recognition of the status of the giver, ie, in the world of science, a recognition of the giver as a valued researcher.

The logic of giving gifts, according to Hagstrom, captures the paradox between science as a value in itself and the desire for recognition. By this logic, a gift is given without any expectation or calculation of return. Research is con-

Charlotte Bloch

ducted for its own sake, and many researchers would deny that their research is motivated by a wish to achieve recognition. However, recognition is of significance for the researcher, a fact that is *inter alia* apparent in the reactions and sometimes war-like states that the lack of expected recognition can give rise to. According to Hagstrom this paradox implies that the researcher must constantly find a balance between, on the one hand, selection of topic, methods, style etc. that ensure him or her recognition from colleagues, and on the other hand, falling back on outer conformity with these standards for the sake of achieving recognition. As Hagstrom indicates, this paradox is to be found in all professions based on values. A balance must be found where the values are not compromised.

Hagstrom analyses the symbolic ambiguity in the formalized peer review, but in addition he also applies the gift-giving metaphor to the exchange of information, references and ideas between peers. These gifts should not be given in the expectation of reciprocity—it is not a trade. Instead Hagstrom speaks of an expectation of gratitude, which he elaborates by applying Simmel's clarification of the way in which gratitude 'establishes the bond of interaction of the reciprocity of service and return service, even when they are not guaranteed by external coercion' (Hagstrom, 1972:118).

Thus Hagstrom unravels a special ambiguity in the relation between recognition and the submission of research as a gift. He indicates some emotional aspects in this ambiguity but does not elucidate them further.

I shall conclude this section with Becher and Trowler's theory of the different nature of competition within various research environments. According to Becher and Towler, the nature of competition depends on what they call population density within the discipline in question. It is thus neither the specific discipline nor the harshness or softness of the subject that determine the competition and, for that matter, the nature of the cooperation, but how densely 'populated' the discipline in question is. On the basis of population density, they then distinguish between urban and rural environments. It is a characteristic of the urban environments that the researchers aim at a limited area with clearly delimited problems and some few salient topics. On the other hand, the rural environments are characterized by researchers covering a broader stretch of intellectual territory and spreading themselves over many themes. These different environments give rise to different types of competition. Intense competition most frequently characterizes the urban environments where the costs can be fear and suspicion of colleagues. As Becher and Towler say, one keeps the cards close to one's chest, publishes one's results too quickly and speculates about scientific theft. This type of competition does not exist in the rural environments where people are involved in quite different subjects with no mutual relation. But this does not mean that competition is non-existent in the rural environments. It is merely not expressed in swift publication of results but in a subtler manner by 'an emphasis on publications, aggressiveness at meetings and a high degree of single-mindedness' (Becher & Trowler, 2001:118). People here try to exceed each other with respect to the quality and significance of their

116

work, but they seldom fight within the same area. I incorporate the above-mentioned theory because it qualifies different ways in which the interaction between competition and the struggle for recognition can be played out. Becher and Trowler only sporadically comment on what these different environments mean for life in Academia.

Summary

I have now presented different approaches in the sociology of science to the social relations in Academia. Bourdieu illustrates some structural conditions for these relations, while Becher & Trowler and Hagstrom illustrate different aspects of these relations on a concrete level. These theories have in common that they point to different potential contradictions that may influence the social relations in Academia, the contradiction inherent in being each other's competitor and judge at one and the same time, the contradiction between the peer review as a collective institution for research quality and the peers as an unclear, undefined group, and the contradiction between the norm of the intrinsic value of science and the desire for recognition. These contradictions may be of importance for the way in which social relations are *felt* in Academia. None of the above-mentioned theories try, however, to unravel the emotional dimensions of social relations. In the following the focus is on the emotional aspects of these social relations.

An empirical study

The following is a brief account of the design, materials and method of my study, which involved 54 people selected on the basis of gender, academic position, and faculty (health science, social science and the humanities, specifically). Each faculty was represented by an equal number of women and men distributed over PhDs, junior lecturers and senior lecturers/professors. To ensure anonymity, the interviewees were spread across different sections, departments and institutions of higher education. Data collection consisted of individual interviews with the junior lecturer/senior lecturer/professor group, and focus group interviews with the PhDs in gender and area specific focus groups. The drop out was minimal.

The study targeted social emotions, ie, emotions that by means of role taking have the self and/or others as the target, and at emotion management in Academia. Concretely, questions were asked concerning four groups of emotions: a) pride/joy, b) anger, c) shame/embarrassment/confusion, and d) laughter. The interviewees were asked to describe concrete episodes where they had felt these emotions and the descriptions were subsequently followed up with more elaborate questions to investigate the culture around the emotions in question (eg, management of the emotion, the person's assessment of the way in which others experienced the person feeling the emotions etc.) I also asked for descriptions of emotional work and strategic use of emotions. Finally, I asked about the social relations, eg, about giving and receiving recognition and a lack of appreciation, questions to do with cooperation (reading and commenting on texts), questions about assessment of the nature of the relations, specifically whether the interviewee regarded his/her relations as corrosive or nourishing.

The interviews were phenomenologically oriented in the sense that the interviewees were encouraged to describe the phenomena that the interview was targeted at in as much detail as possible. The transcribed interviews were then processed on the basis of a grounded analysis and an interpretative analysis in which a number of different theories were incorporated.[7] These theories are now presented.

Theoretical frame of reference

The theories of social relations in the sociology of science touch upon the emotional aspects of these relations, but they do not explore them. Thus in my analysis of emotions in Academia I have drawn upon theories of emotions in organisations and theories from the sociology of emotions.[8] In my analysis I distinguish analytically between structural conditions of emotions, emotional culture and felt or lived emotions. The distinctions and concepts that have structured my analysis are now presented.

Gibson's (1997) approach to the structural conditions of emotions focuses on the felt emotions that stem from the power and status relations in the organization. Gibson follows the theories of Theodor Kemper (1978) and Randall Collins (1990), according to which power and status relations release certain emotions. According to Kemper and Collins, emotions are a direct effect of these relations. Gibson, however, modifies this theoretical statement to structural factors framing or limiting emotions (Gibson, 1997:222). However, whereas Gibson focus on emotions that stem from power and status, with respect to the structural prerequisites for emotions in organisations, I have found Bourdieu's analysis of the specificity of the scientific field of particular relevance for my empirical material.

With respect to the emotional culture of Academia, I draw on Flam's (1990a,b) theory of emotions in organizations and on Hochschild's (1983) classical work on feeling rules, expression rules and emotion management.[9] Flam creates a third perspective of organizations, an emotional perspective that supplements rationalist and normative perspectives. To do this she developed the concept of representative emotions. Flam views organizations historically as ways of stabilizing certain passions, feelings and sensibilities which historically have existed in a non-organized cultural form. When these organizations have been established, they construe emotions by means of formal rules and procedures. These construed emotions vary in form but are related to the original emotions that set the whole process in motion. The construed emotions hereafter exist as prescribed representative emotional norms (feeling rules) and proscribed emotions. One example of this is the requirement that scientists must display affective neutrality when presenting their research results. Representative emotions are central to the emotional culture of the organisation. They are similar to Hochshild's 'feeling rules', but their specific function is to represent the organization. I take Hochschild's concepts of feeling rules to refer to the norms for the emotions that are suitable in certain situations, expression rules to refer to the norms for the way in which and the extent to which emotions should be expressed in certain situations, and the concepts of emotion work, emotional labour and emotion management to refer to our handling of our emotions in order to comply with the normative demands.[10]

The relationship between felt emotions and culture of feelings are practically always connected through emotion management. I maintain, however, as do Barbalet (1998), Gibson and Flam, *inter alia*, an analytical distinction between felt emotions and feeling culture. This distinction is for my part grounded on an existential phenomenological understanding of emotions as a non-mediated inner relation between our world and us. This does not mean that emotions are independent of cultural-cognitive categories. They have a cognitive element in the form of an assessment of our emotional condition. This cognitive element stems from our emotional culture, thus emotional culture interacts with the emotions that are lived. It interprets them but does not describe their experiential qualities (Bloch, 2001). Analytically Gibson clarifies the relation between emotions, emotional norms and management of emotions by saying that felt emotions may be expressed as they are felt, or moderated by culture to produce expressed emotions depending on a) the strength of the display rule, b) the strength and type of felt emotions, c) individual differences in capacity and motivation to feel and express emotion, and d) the structure of the situations (Gibson, 1997:234).

The above distinctions are presented in the model in Figure 1 below. These distinctions are, as already mentioned, analytical and ontological, and in real life felt emotions, emotional culture and management of feelings are most frequently interwoven in a complex manner. I have, however, not had the opportunity to study these emotional processes as lived processes but have had to rely on the interviewees' descriptions. That is to say I have interpreted the verbally mediated expressions of these processes. This is a limitation of the interview as method, but those are the conditions. We can never reach lived emotions in a non-mediated form. Thus in my analysis of the interviewees' descriptions of emotional episodes, the structural relations in the scientific field have been interpreted as generative prerequisites for the social emotions, and the management of emotions has been interpreted as institutional ways of handling the emotional culture in Academia.

In the discussion of the implications of my analysis of emotions and their management in Academia, I include Thomas Scheff's theory of emotions and social bonds and Bollnow's theory concerning moods. Scheff (1990, 1994, 1997) explores the emotional side of communication and recognition. According to

Scheff, every interaction is not merely the communication of content but also a communication of respect and esteem or disrespect for the other. This means that every communication is simultaneously a building up of, damage to, or maintenance of social bonds. The emotional sides of social bonds are shame and pride, and in extension of this Scheff has developed a theory of the way in which subtle cues of disrespect release non-acknowledged shame. Shame covers a group of emotional states such as embarrassment, humiliation and uncertainty, signalling a feeling of or a threat of being rejected, an attack on our social selves. These feelings are so uncomfortable that they are repressed before they reach our consciousness (unacknowledged shame). This does not, however, mean that the shame disappears but rather that it continues to live as recursive spirals of emotions as, for instance, shame/rage spirals, which in turn have consequences for the social relations. Bollnow's (1974) theory of moods and emotions is incorporated to assess the significance of Academia's emotions for the academic research environment in general. In Figure 1 I have indicated some cues to the results of the analysis that will now be presented.

Results of the analysis

In the following I present extracts from my analysis of how the emotions of shame, pride and anger are managed in Academia. No differentiation will be made in the presentation according to gender or the different faculties. However, it should be noted that the departments included in the study came closest to what Becher and Trowler term rural environments. While urban environments could have been expected within the area of health science, in my assessment the departments in this study were more rural than urban in nature.

The emotions presented and the forms in which they are managed were found at all levels in Academia, although they were articulated with different degrees of strength. The PhDs and junior lecturers, who were relatively recent arrivals in Academia, were thus more conscious and articulate about certain feeling norms than the professors for whom these feeling norms had become a matter of course.

The deceiving game

'The deceiving game' is my metaphor for a certain way of managing the existential doubt that is inextricably linked with good research. It is a feature of the deceiving game that everyone pretends to have confidence and control in relation to their research. As everybody knows that this is not the case, they play a deceiving game. This game manages the emotions connected with problem solving, and dealing with resistance. Belief, hope and confidence alternate with resignation, despondency, uncertainty and doubt (Jacobsen, 2001:67), and most often this emotional mobility is not limited to the project but includes the

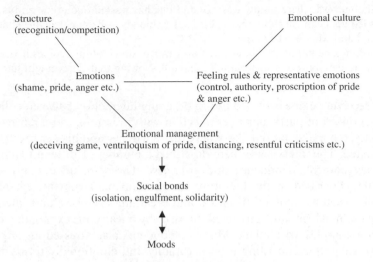

Figure 1: *Analytical model*

self-esteem of the person as a researcher. One interviewee has this to say about the fear of inadequacy:

> The fear, I mean, it is precisely this that is very clear, and not just in the case of PhDs. It is in the culture of research. People are dead scared of being inadequate, aren't they, because they really don't have much more than their brain to present. This is all we have in this culture, and if someone cuts you to pieces in front of a lot of other people, people get scared—yes they are afraid of it. That's my experience.

The fear of the judgement of one's colleagues is indicated in this quotation. The deceiving game is here a way of protecting one's vulnerability in relation to the scrutiny of one's colleagues. As an interviewee says:

> Really tough exclusion on the basis of qualifications takes place the whole way up through the system, so one can't start by saying—'I don't know whether I'm any good at this', can one? But one can start by saying—'I don't really have a handle on this paper yet, I've got into a new area and I haven't really thought the whole thing through yet'.

Thus the deceiving game consists in expressing control as a researcher. This aspect is elaborated in the following quotation where a junior lecturer clarifies the difference between sharing limited fiascos with others and expressing existential doubt.

> I[11]: How about professional fiascos—do you tell your colleagues anything about these and how do they react?
> Ip: Limited fiascos, yes.
> I: What does that mean?
> Ip: That means that if one has spent a month running around some archives and what

one thought was there simply was not and one has wasted one's time and is getting really fed up. I can tell about that—'Listen, I've bloody well done it again. That wasn't so good and what am I to do?'

But fundamental doubt about one's own worth, which always comes if one is in a fruitful research process—I wouldn't dream of showing that. They might just believe it.

The deceiving game is played out in on-going interaction between colleagues but it is utilized in particular in connection with presenting research results at congresses, seminars and the like, where the researcher and his/her results are to be evaluated. The interviewees here described a number of different techniques to display control, confidence and overview. These included many of the techniques described in the literature on emotion management, eg, physical techniques such as taking pills and doing breathing exercises, and intellectual techniques in which one protected oneself by means of expressing oneself through a complex vocabulary. Many respondents also stressed an important cognitive technique consisting in intellectually and emotionally trying to split one's project from one's person. Especially the junior lecturers and PhDs stressed this technique. Finally, collective emotional work and training, such as trial presentations for others as an exercise, was mentioned by this group.

The deceiving game is a complex, institutional emotional management technique. Research as a process provides constant fuel for uncertainty and doubt and the competition-judgement relations create conditions for the deceiving game as a protective measure. At the same time the deceiving game satisfies the demands of the feeling culture of Academia to demonstrate control and authority. However, for many the precondition for this is continual emotional labour. In some cases the deceiving game can develop into bluffing in the sense that one strategically pretends to knowledge and competencies one does not possess. However, in my analysis the deceiving game is in the first instance a protective measure and a way of adapting to the emotional norms of Academia.

Finally: the different facets of the deceiving game were most clearly expressed in the interviews with junior lecturers and PhDs. They were in the processing of learning this game, and the PhDs could talk to each other about it. This is why it was presented in more detail here.

Ventriloquising one's pride

According to Hagstrom's analysis, a paradox exists between the significance of recognition for the academic and the proscription on demanding recognition in Academia. Pride can here be regarded as the emotion of recognition, and this feeling and its institutional management will now be presented.

The interviewees described pride in the context of academic successes such as having an article accepted, publishing and getting one's books reviewed positively, achieving academic positions etc., but they also experienced that it was forbidden to display this pride in Academia. Showing pride was interpreted as boasting: 'One must keep pride or joy to oneself, it is unacademic to display emotions'. As some of the interviewees ironically formulated it, there was no 'Whoopee!' culture in their department. But why are pride and joy regarded as illegitimate boasting when recognition is the prize in Academia? In this context the interviewees emphasized two inter-linked aspects: competitive relations and a solidarity principle. Competitive relations implied the fear of embarrassing one's competitors by telling them about a success. As one interviewee said:

> One just doesn't do that (say that one has had an article accepted) and that's because there's always some competition going on between different persons in a department which means that one doesn't want to embarrass anyone. One doesn't want to, one doesn't want to (laughs a little), that sounds strange. But one doesn't want to seem boastful and if one comes and says—'I've just had an article accepted for *Nature* or *Science*' or another scholarly journal, one keeps quiet about it where others may find it easier to express, I think. But it's got a lot to do with not boasting about it, one just doesn't do that.

The proscription on displaying pride can be interpreted as a kind of etiquette in relation to one's competitors, but can also be motivated and interpreted as solidarity. An interviewee formulated it thus:

> Well it could just as well be an expression of something cultural that one tries to maintain some form of solidarity culture where nobody . . ., well our culture is very marked by this feeling of solidarity where nobody can be more than anyone else in some way or other. After all we are researchers. One could say that the basic idea in such a research institution or behind such a research institution is, after all that it is difficult to compare research, it is difficult to measure research. That's why I think that it is embedded in our culture, and that there is probably something healthy in this anchorage, that it shouldn't be like this . . .

This senior lecturer views the proscription on pride as a means of protecting oneself against competition and inequality by means of a type of solidarity where nobody is more than anybody else. This type of tact also meant that to the extent that one talked about one's successes and thus one's pride, it was most frequently to persons who were not among one's direct competitors.

According to Hagstrom's theory, the proscription on desiring recognition of an academic performance stems from the academic value of research being an end in itself. That is to say that the proscription on pride is a representative emotional proscription. However, the interviewees in this study saw the proscription as a way of handling the competitive relations in a considerate way. In spite of all the different cultural reasons for proscriptions on displaying pride, the interviewees desired and sought recognition and a central institutional manner of managing pride became by these means what I have termed ventriloquism.[12] It is a feature of ventriloquism that one supplies some valuable information or an entertaining or funny story to persons from whom one wants recognition at the same time as one manages to relate one's success as an underlying story or item of information, eg, that one has presented a paper at an important congress, that one has received an important invitation, has had an article accepted etc. As one interviewee formulated it:

> One tells about a funny episode that happened at an annual meeting from which it emerges that I was present, that I read a paper.

Another interviewee describes the principles of ventriloquism as follows:

> It has to do with choosing one's story, doesn't it? It's a matter of telling a story which is special and funny along the lines of 'a funny thing happened on the way to the baker's'. It's the same type of anecdote and nothing else. It's not a big, pompous presentation of having achieved a breakthrough.

And he clarifies:

> It belongs to the code that one puts oneself into the background in favour of some material that one, so to speak, ventriloquizes through giving one the opportunity to say, 'Isn't it interesting?'. But at the same time it is also possible to present oneself as the person who has seen it and now is presenting things in an order that makes it look like something new and fantastically interesting.

One has to learn this ventriloquism:

> One probably does that through imitation just as one learns the invisible codes of behaviour anywhere. A one-sided, jubilant presentation of one's own success is not favourably viewed—that is if one is at the centre of the story. I think that it is permissible within the local anecdote because it is presented as an amusing little story. But it is not appropriate to place oneself at the centre of the story.

According to the interviewees, telling about one's successes was a breach of academic manners and was regarded as embarrassing and stigmatizing. If these successes were indirectly communicated through a good story, on the other hand, they received recognition. Ventriloquism was a widespread institutional way of managing pride with consideration for Academia's norms of emotion and expression. I have already described the way in which the proscription on pride can be interpreted as cultural management of competitive relations in Academia. However, ventriloquism as a form of management has the structure of gift giving. The good story is a gift (entertainment or information), but acceptance of the gift implies tacit recognition of the performance which is ventriloquized in the good story. Similarly, this technique was in particular employed in relation to persons whose recognition was important for one's academic career.

Shame, anger and broken social bonds

The peer review is the academic institution for professional assessment and awarding of recognition. It can take place in an atmosphere of friendliness and mutual respect in spite of scholarly disagreement, but it can also release strong feelings that have certain social consequences. In the following I shall briefly describe such feelings among the judges after which I focus on the judged.

In the peer review, peers are colleagues who are assigned the right to judge the research of others, but this assignment also implicate a power as judges of others. Several of those interviewed describe here how as judges they could feel great anger vis-à-vis the person or persons being judged.[13] They could be alone with their anger but it could also be shared with others in the appointments committee as collective anger. As one interviewee formulates it:

> When we have expressed our irritation then we know where we have each other. This produces a relationship of confidence which is a precondition for a high degree of openness.

The interviewee here describes a well-known process in group formation where, by means of common feelings, an in-group is created vis-à-vis an out-group. However, the collective confirmation of solidarity through common anger, where the judges are the guardians of science while the judged are the intruders, shows the way in which the peer review can pave the way for hierarchical position processes and feelings of superiority. As the interviewee says in the quotation, these processes which had the character of an introductory ritual to the judgement, can create a sense of trust within the group that paves the way for a more subtle view of the applicant's products, but they can also be developed into a feeling of superiority, a feeling of power, or into continued collective confirmation of the groups as a community at the expense of the person/persons being judged. An interviewee puts it like this:

> Yes, we didn't mince words (when judging colleagues)—the others were not diplomate either (laughs a little).

But first and foremost the peer review aroused strong feeling in those being judged. This does not mean that the interviewees only had negative personal experience of peer review, but the majority of those interviewed described examples of what they experienced as insulting and disrespectful judgement. These judgements could be interpreted as personal persecution or as an expression of institutional disrespect for the person's scholarly area. The borderline between scholarly criticism and disrespectful criticism is, however, unclear. As one interviewee said:

> After all, anything can be torn to shreds. One can always apply the ten criteria for an article and tear the work apart. But I think that some of this criticism in this case was pointless in some way or other. It was more aimed at demonstrating the knowledge and the superiority of the critic than giving a constructive critique of the project in question. It was rather to show that the other (the critic) knows something than to make a contribution. It was not constructive and it was more to bring the man down or else to take revenge. I don't think that it made much of a contribution.

This interviewee describes how personal, destructive motives can get the upper hand in the peer review. These judgements gave rise to shame, rage and disappointment. The following two are examples that according to the person transgress the norms of decent peer reviewing. An interviewee tells about a review of a large-scale work:

On average the reviews were good, but there were certainly some that absolutely expressed what I would call academic malice, hatred, small-mindedness and the like. One becomes very depressed and also ashamed that some people can behave like that, I think.

And another interviewee describes a colleague's reaction to the recommendation of an appointments committee:

He actually was so angry, disappointed and unhappy that he ran up and down the corridors and showed everyone who wanted to look at it that we had pronounced him unqualified. So he was very incensed and really, really upset. It ended with him declaring that he would never talk to me again in his life. Since then every time we have met he has looked right through me and we haven't greeted each other.

These two descriptions illustrate the range of feelings from depression to rage. The interviewees in this study described different ways of managing these emotions. Some described how they transformed their anger to contempt and placed the judge in question and his/her allies at a distance. One interviewee formulates it thus:

It was so dirty, low and bad that I simply will never have anything to do with him again. Others who have experienced the same confront the person in question, but I couldn't be bothered to touch it.

Another frequently employed form of management was not greeting each other—as if the other person did not exist. Several of the interviewees found this type of reaction too childish but all had experienced this form of management in their departments. Finally, the anger could find expression as revenge through criticism of the judge's work in scholarly journals, newspapers etc. As one interviewee said:

If there is somebody who thinks that another person's research was wrong or something like that, they don't talk to each other for a long time. They do not have a quarrel, but they may express their disagreement indirectly through a negative review of the person's work.

The above-mentioned forms of management of anger should be understood in relation to the proscription in the academic feeling culture on displaying anger. Showing anger is a challenge to the representative feeling norms of Academia. As an interviewee says, this is 'a little too primitive for us'. However, the feelings aroused by academic attack were difficult to deal with through emotional work and thus explosions of anger were not an unknown phenomenon. As one interviewee says:

Normally my colleagues here are very well mannered, like at any university, and they know how to rein in their emotions and are very analytical in their approach etc. But once in a while their feelings run away with them and I think that I can safely say in the case of almost all the colleagues I have known in my years here, there have been situations where they have blown their top—and that applies to almost everyone. That is where one has been under pressure in some situation and has expressed it.

The peer review is the dominant form of organization for social relations in Academia. This form, with its built-in contradictions, created the basis for strong feelings of shame, disappointment and anger.[14] These feeling are precisely the emotions of damaged social bonds. These damaged social bonds created the basis for suspicion and mutual isolation. Isolation as a form of management was in particular found among senior lecturers.

Discussion

According to my study, life in Academia gives rise to strong feelings of pride, anger, uncertainty and shame which are prohibited in the academic emotional culture. Thus life in Academia presupposes competent management of these emotions in accordance with the academic feeling rules and our position in the social structure.

In my analysis I have pointed to the structural conditions of competition and recognition as the frame of these emotions and to the emotional culture of Academia as the frame of our managing these emotions. I have stressed the deceiving game as a way of protecting one's doubt, uncertainty and potential shame in relation to the academic relations of competition and judgement, I have pointed to the relation between competition and the proscription on pride as a way to show tact in competitive relations or a solidarity concerning equality, and I have described ventriloquism as a widespread institutional way of managing pride, having consideration for the emotional and expression norms of Academia. I have, moreover, shown the way in which the social structure of the peer review can create feelings between colleagues that affect the social bonds and create the preconditions for mutual isolation.[15]

The deceiving game and ventriloquism may be viewed as forms of management that both satisfy the representative emotional norms of affective neutrality and distance while simultaneously being efficient in the competition for recognition. However, the peer review releases feelings that appear to be difficult to manage within the emotional norms of Academia. Thomas Scheff's theory can be employed to illustrate why. On the basis of Scheff's theory, the peer review is not merely the communication of an assessment of a colleague's research, but also the communication of esteem and respect for the other as an equal. This aspect is often overlooked, intentionally or unintentionally, thereby creating the basis of what Scheff terms unacknowledged shame, which continues to live in emotional chains of shame, anger, guilt, rage etc. These emotions are the psychological side of what Scheff calls damaged social bonds. Damaged social bonds fuel the grounds for what Scheff terms alienation. Scheff distinguishes between two sides of alienation: isolation and engulfment. It is characteristic of isolation that one stops listening to others. One only hears oneself. On the other hand, it is characteristic of engulfment that one merges with others in conformity at the expense of oneself. These two forms were found in Academia. Isolation was primarily characteristic of senior lecturers in my sample.

They could have a few confidants but the main impression was one of professional and human loneliness. However, they could gather a small circle of persons, most frequently younger people, around their research. In the present investigation this was particularly noticeable in the field of health science. This group then became a faction in the department, marked by engulfment internally and isolation externally.[16]

The theories of social relations in Academia indicate an awareness of the potential contradiction inherent in being one another's judge and competitor, but what specifically takes place on the socio-emotional level and the consequences of this remain unclear. Scheff's theory here points to some overlooked emotional dynamics, but what is the significance of these? In order to assess this, Bollnow's theory of moods is to be incorporated.

According to Bollnow (1974), human beings are always tuned, that is, always in a mood state. Our moods are pervasive states colouring our world of action, feeling and thinking. They are the underlying bearing of life, a way of being in the world, and the primary source of our experience of self, other persons and the world. Moreover, moods are not situated on the level of the individual. Our moods spring from the inner relationship between the human being and its life-space. They do not come from the outside, nor from the inside. They arise as a way of being from this way of being itself. Whereas emotions are focussed upon an object, moods by contrast do not have an object as such. However, emotions do build upon specific moods in the sense that moods constitute the frame of emotions that are possible. (Bollnow, 1974:35–37) Thus Bollnow sees moods as determining the possible emotions. According to a previous empirical study (Bloch, 2001), it can be shown that the relationship may operate the other way around. That is, an accumulation of certain emotions may also give rise to the development of specific moods. Thus there is a dynamic mutual relationship between moods and emotions. In terms of this theory, an accumulation of negative feelings can create the basis of a mood of structural paranoia just as confirming emotions may give rise to a mood of trust. Moods or tuning are considered to be flimsy phenomena. However, according to a Danish investigation of 250 scholars (Jacobsen, 2001a,b), the basic mood of their departments is a demonstrable social reality. The scholars were able to characterize their department in terms of its prevalent basic mood. According to the same study, a good basic atmosphere was a precondition for what the interviewees experienced as a good research environment. On this basis a preliminary hypothesis can be formulated about a connection between emotions in social relations, the basic atmosphere in the department and the research environment.[17]

This chapter was introduced by a presentation of conventional theories of social relations in Academia. In the analysis I have focused on the emotional aspects of these relations. In connection with Bourdieu's approach, emotional dynamics of the structural conditions of competition and mutual recognition have been illustrated. Becker and Trowler's analysis of the peer-review ignores its emotional aspects while describing many of its shortcomings. From an emotional perspective these shortcomings may, however, be interpreted as fuelling the emotions leading to damaged bonds. Concerning Hagstrom's theory of gift-giving, the emotional perspective may also enlarge our understanding in terms of how we emotionally manage the contradictions between our desire for recognition and the proscription of this desire in Academia. However, the emotional perspective also shows how the social relations in Academia imply a serious amount of emotional labour. There is nothing wrong with performing emotional labour in so far as we are able to integrate and contain our emotions in a personally and a culturally accepted way. If that is not the case, it may have unintended consequences on the level of the individual and on the level of the organization. Using the theories of Scheff and Bollnow, some of these unintended consequences have been suggested.

Conclusion

In this paper I have shown how an emotions approach can contribute to qualifying our understanding of the social relations in Academia. I have, furthermore, pointed to the manner in which emotional dynamics in Academia can have some unintended consequences for research environments. The perspective of emotion here contributes to illustrating some important aspects of academic life that are excluded by the self-understanding of Academia.

Acknowledgements

I am endebted to Poul Poder Pedersen, Inge Henningsen, Lis Højgård, Hanne Nexø Jensen, and Dorte Marie Søndergård for comments on the first draft of this paper, and I am endebted to The Danish Research Councils for their support of the present study. I also want to thank Jack Barbalet for adding flow to the English language of this paper.

Notes

1 Cf, Douglas 1975, Mulkay, 1988 and Hatch & Ehrlich, 1993.
2 Cf. Barbalet's chapter in this monograph for a more subtle evaluation of the view of emotions within the philosophy of science.
3 The study is a sub-project within a cross-council research initiative entitled 'Gender barriers in higher education and research', which runs from 1996–2002. As indicated in the term 'preliminary results', only some dimensions in my empirical data are included in the present presentation. The gender perspective, for instance, does not comprise part of in this chapter.
4 Merton's normative imperatives for the scientific community, popularly called CUDOS, also belong among the established theories. Merton analyses ideal norms for relations and communication between scientists. These norms are based on values traditionally regarded as the opposite of emotions. The values are the suspension of the personal and attitudes that precisely have an emotional component, detachment and impartiality (Merton, 1942). Today Merton's ideal norms are still effective elements in scientific self-perception.

5 This specificity shares science as a field with the artistic field (Bourdieu, 1991:8).
6 Cole (1983) has investigated the validity of peer reviews on the basis of their ability to identify the researchers who are promising in the long term. Cole found that the researchers who had been rejected were in the longer term more productive than the applicants who received a positive evaluation.
7 My transcription includes a number of non-verbal signs, and the non-verbal aspects play a role in my interpretation in analysing the interviews. I was here inspired by Susanne Retzinger's and Thomas J. Scheff's theories and methods for analysing emotions in discourse (Scheff, 1997; Retzinger, 1991; Bloch, 1996 and 2001).
8 Cf. Fineman (1993) for a more detailed account of emotions in organizations.
9 In English the term feeling connotes a milder physical sensation than the term emotion does. In the present context the two terms are used interchangeably.
10 Emotional labour refers to the management of feeling to produce a certain feeling and/or display of feeling. Emotional labour is sold for a wage and has exchange value. Emotion work refers to the same act performed in a private context where it has use value (Hochschild, 1983:7). Emotion management includes both emotional labour and emotion work.
11 I is an abbreviation for the interviewer and Ip stands for the interviewee or interviewed person.
12 I owe this metaphor to one of the interviewees.
13 For many academics, anger was a way of mobilizing themselves for the academic battle. On the other hand the judges could also experience great enthusiasm and joy in relation to an applicant's work, and the positioning activity could go the other way. The peer review is, thus, not an emotionally neutral institution.
14 Apart from the peer review, the competitive relations found more general expression in forbidden feelings such as envy and malicious enjoyment. The competitive relations implied that the success of the one was potentially the fiasco of the other, and as the goal of most people is success and professional prestige on the basis of 'publish or perish', envy and malicious enjoyment were unavoidable social feelings.
15 It must be mentioned that the emotions analysed and their forms of management in Academia only constitute a selection of these emotions and forms of management. Other forms of management, such as humour, which is an important way of managing emotions in Academia, have not been included in this presentation. It should, furthermore, be stressed, that this is a qualitative study of the nature of some phenomena and not their dissemination.
16 Scheff describes some of these social dynamics in Scheff, 1995.
17 The concept of mood has features similar to what Barbalet in the present monograph calls unnoticed or background emotions.

References

Barbalet, Jack M. (1998) *Emotion, Social Theory and Social Structure.* Cambridge: Cambridge University Press.
Becher, Tony and Trowler, Paul R. (2001) *Academic Tribes and Territories.* Philadelphia: The Society for Research into Higher Education and Open University Press.
Bloch, Charlotte (1996) Emotions and Discourse. *Text,* 16(3): 323–341.
Bloch, Charlotte (2001) *Flow og Stress.* København: Samfundslitteratur.
Bollnow, Otto Freidrich V. (1974) *Das Wesen der Stimmungen.* Frankfurt: Vittorio Klostermann.
Bourdieu, Pierre (1975) The specificity of the scientific field and the social conditions of the programs of reason. *Social Science Information,* 14(6): 19–47.
Bourdieu, Pierre (1991) The Peculiar History of Scientific Reason. *Sociological Forum,* 6(1): 3–26.
Cole, S. (1983) The hierarchy of the sciences, *American Journal of Sociology,* 89(1): 111–39.
Collins, Randall (1990) Stratification, Emotional Energy and the Transient Emotions. In: Kemper, Theodore D. (ed.): *Research Agendas in the Sociology of Emotions.* Albany: State University of New York Press.

Douglas, Mary (1975) *Implicit Meanings*. London: Routledge & Kegan Paul.

Flam, Helena (1990a) Emotional Man: I 'Man' and the Problem of Collective Action. *International Sociology*, 5(1): 39–56.

Flam, Helena (1990b) Emotional Man: II. Corporate Actors as Emotion-motivated Emotion Managers. *International Sociology*, 5(2): 225–324.

Gibson, Donald E. (1997) The Struggle for Reason: The Sociology of Emotions in Organizations. *Social Perspectives on Emotion*, Volume 4: 211–256.

Hagstrom, Warren O. (1972) Gift-Giving as an Organizing Principle in Science. In Barnes, Barry: *Sociology of Science*. Penguin Books, 105–121.

Hatch, Mary Jo and Ehrlich, Sanford B. (1993) Spontanous Humour as an Indicator of Paradox and Ambiguity in Organizations. *Organization Studies*. 14(4): 505–526.

Heidegger, Martin (1927) *Sein und Zeit*. Hall a. D. Saale.

Hochschild, Arlie R. (1983) *The Managed Heart*. Berkeley: University of California Press.

Jacobsen, Bo (2001a) *Hvad er god forskning?* København: Hans Reitzels Forlag.

Jacobsen, Bo, Madsen, Mikkel Bo, and Vincent, Claude (2001b) *Danske forsknings miljøer*. København: Hans Reitzels Forlag.

Kemper, T.D. (1990) Social Relations and Emotions: A Structural Approach. In Kemper, Theodore D. (ed.) *Research Agendas in the Sociology of Emotions*. Albany: State University of New York Press, 207–237.

Merton, Robert K. (1957 [1942]) The Normative Structure of Science. In Merton, Robert: *Social Theory and Social Structure*, New York: Free Press, 550–561.

Mulkay, Michael (1988) *On Humour*. Oxford: Polity Press.

Retzinger, Suzanne M. (1991) *Violent Emotions*. London: Sage.

Scheff, Thomas J. (1995) Academic gangs. *Crime, Law & Social Change*. 23: 157–162.

Scheff, Thomas J. (1997) *Emotions, the Social Bond, and Human Reality*. Cambridge: Cambridge University Press.

Thoits, Peggy A. (1996) Managing the Emotions of Others. *Symbolic Interaction* 19(2): 85–109.

131

Science and emotions

Jack Barbalet

Abstract

Science can proceed only when emotions are excluded. This conventional view is widely held but false; indeed, practically meaningless. On the contrary: the issues must be: Which emotions?, and how do they specifically relate to the activities at hand? The chapter considers the changing fortunes of emotions in the discourse of science. In doing so it demonstrates that emotions can be seriously considered in the sociology of science, even though it is hardly ever acknowledged that they have been. By focussing on the role of emotions in core scientific processes, our understanding of science is broadened and our account of emotions enriched.

Introduction

A discussion of science, in a monograph on the sociology of emotions, is simply out of place. Or so it might seem. It is not only that emotions are typically excluded from considerations of science, but also that sociology has found it difficult to come to grips with science.

The conventional view, that science uncovers the laws of nature, provides sociology with little scope for inquiry: nature is prior to society and its laws are unaffected by social intervention. Such a perspective influenced Karl Mannheim, for instance, when he said that 'natural science . . . is largely detachable from the historical-social perspective of the investigator' (Mannheim, 1936: 261). Thus a sociology of scientific knowledge becomes, if not unattainable, entirely problematic (but see Pels, 1996). With the historically recent sociologization of nature itself, this perspective and its corollary no longer obtain, of course: a sociology of scientific knowledge is not currently held to be contradictory.

It may be a truism that sociology's owl flies out of crises. Robert Merton remarked in the 1950s that 'sociologists would turn seriously to the systematic study of interaction between science and society only when science itself came to be widely regarded as something of a social problem or as a prolific source of social problems' (Merton, 1970: vii). Indeed, the development of a sociological interest in science grew only recently in the history of the discipline. Writing in 1972, Barry Barnes indicated that 'sociologists have scarcely begun to examine

[the] internal structure of science, and systematic investigation of its relationship with the wider society remains a hope for the future' (Barnes, 1972: 9). Such a statement, however, would have been difficult to make by the end of the 1970s and impossible by the end of the 1980s. This periodization coincides exactly with a realization that techno-science has reached the limits of its growth and is undergoing fundamental transformations fraught with potentially debilitating contradictions (see Ziman, 1994). At the same time, the social legitimacy of science can no longer be taken for granted. It is in these circumstances that the social-cultural study of science has grown at an almost exponential rate. Ironically, however, in the resulting studies, the concept of nature is so thoroughly relativized that science itself evaporates into a politics of influence, effectively undifferentiated from every other type of social production (see Cole, 1992; Lynch, 1993). Through such a subversive route the sociology of science fails again, this time for lack of a subject, and its material gravitates instead to various forms of cultural studies (see Jasanoff, Markle, Petersen, and Pinch, 1995). That is one side of the picture. What of emotions and science? To pose the question reveals the abyss.

From its inception, the scientific revolution of the seventeenth century insisted on the impossibility of science under emotional influence. Francis Bacon, the prophet of this new way of thinking, warned in the *Novum Organon* that:

> The human understanding is no dry light, but receives an infusion from the will and affections; whence proceed sciences which may be called 'sciences as one would' . . . Numberless . . . are the ways, and sometimes imperceptible, in which the affections colour and infect the understanding (Bacon, 1620: 267).

This was no idiosyncratic view, but reflected in the Royal Society's recommendation after its foundation in 1662 to abolish eloquence in language as it is contrary to reason and abets passion. Such a radical separation of science and emotion, which will be critically evaluated in the discussion to follow, no doubt arose from the religious background of the day, not only Puritan but also Catholic, in which it was supposed that the sensitive or passionate soul was at war with the reasonable or rational soul (Wright, 1604). This is not the only source of the division between emotion and reason (see Toulmin, 1990; Barbalet, 1998: 54–61), which has been sustained by an enduring misunderstanding of the nature of both reason and emotion, and the relationship between them (Barbalet, 1998; Damasio, 1994; de Sousa, 1987). Yet so pervasive has been this conventional understanding of an oppositional separation of science and emotion, that some historically recent feminist critiques of science, for instance, have posed the emotional basis of science to be not a current reality but an aspiration of a new, alternative, and as yet unrealized utopia (Harding, 1986: 142–4), a position similarly accepted by some Marxist writers (Levins and Lewontin, 1985: 207).

While only two decades ago political radicals envisaged a future prospect in which emotions might be incorporated into science, today it is not unusual for mainstream scientists explicitly to recognize the importance of emotions for the success of their ongoing research. James Watson, for instance, characterizes this move in the title of his recent book, *A Passion for DNA* (Watson, 2000). Similarly, a collection of scientific autobiographical interviews (Wolpert and Richards, 1997), represents the emotional and feeling side of scientific work as both positive and necessary. Edward Wilson insists on the importance of emotions for the production of science, both in general (Wilson, 1998: 112–5) and in terms of his own personal development as a scientist (Wilson, 1996). These instances can be replicated many times.

No doubt this appreciation of the salience of emotion in their work by scientists themselves is part of the larger late-modern inclination to centre the self in terms of its emotionality (Barbalet, 1998: 173–4). Yet there is much evidence that key scientists have acknowledged the supportive role of emotion in science throughout its historical development. A survey of select scientific autobiographies (Darwin, 1876; Einstein, 1949, 1954; Priestley, 1776; Tinbergen, 1968; Wilson, 1996) reveals that when discussing their research and its discoveries the signal role of particular emotions (wonder, joy, sorrow, hope, fear, love) is frequently referred to, even though the same author may state adherence to the principle that science proceeds when emotion is expelled.

As interesting for our purposes as these declarations by scientists of the significance of emotions are, they remain entirely partial. They emphasize individual achievement in science at the expense of any awareness of its social nature, and tend to confine emotions to an idiosyncratic aspect of the scientific process that is ultimately outside of its essential core. They would generally agree with Herbert Feigl when he said that 'flash[es] of insight on the part of a scientific genius are not in themselves scientific activities . . . they do not validate knowledge claims' (quoted in Friedrichs, 1970: 209). It will be shown in the discussion to follow, on the other hand, that emotions are an unavoidable and essential aspect of science in all of its phases, and underlying the social basis of science itself.

Science as activity

It is important to avoid thinking of science as occurring in the mind of the scientist; science includes but is not essentially intellectual or mental processes. At the same time, it is important not to think of science as principally material or physical processes. There is manipulation of physical objects in science, certainly, and instrumentation directed to physical processes, but that is not all of science. Before it is anything else, science is activity, and especially actions of and interactions between scientists. From this perspective, emotions are unavoidable. For in action the whole person participates, and science, then, requires that 'intellect, will, taste, and passion co-operate just as they do in practical affairs' (James, 1897: 92; see also Macmurray, 1961: 12; Polanyi, 1958). The British zoologist John Baker wrote that:

The joy of discovery is a very real incentive to research, despite the rareness of its realization. It is an error to suppose that the scientist is unemotional, or could succeed if he were. The error has arisen through a misconception. The absolute necessity that a scientist's findings shall not be changed from objective truth in response to emotional urges of any kind does not result in his becoming a particularly unemotional person: whether a discoverer or anyone else is pleased with a discovery has no effect on its validity (Baker, 1942: 17–8).

In a word: emotion is understood to be necessary for motivation for scientific discovery even though not validation; and the emotion of joy is held to be central in this, a matter to which we shall return below.

Writing only a few years prior to Baker, Robert Merton made a similar point, namely that 'although it is customary to think of the scientist as a dispassionate, impersonal individual—and this may not be inaccurate as far as his technical activity is concerned—it must be remembered that the scientist . . . has a large emotional investment in his way of life, defined by the institutional norms that govern his activity' (Merton, 1937: 596). It is the threat to the social structure of science, especially by Socialist and Fascist state instrumentalities respectively, that animates Baker and Merton in their separate statements here, and reveals to them the necessity of emotion in science. But there is a difference between them concerning the appropriate conceptualization of motivation.

Merton distinguishes between individual or 'distinctive motives' and the 'distinctive pattern of institutional control of a wide range of motives which characterizes the behaviour of scientists' (Merton, 1942: 613). For Merton, the sociologically more significant emotional attachment is to institutional norms: 'The institution of science itself involves emotional adherence to certain values' (Merton, 1937: 601). The individual or personal motives of scientists are necessarily diverse, and may include, among a host of possibilities, a 'passion for knowledge, idle curiosity, altruistic concern with the benefit to humanity' (Merton, 1942: 613) and so on. Yet the matter is not as cut and dried as Merton leaves it here. In order to consider an important debate concerning the discussion of emotions in science, and explore further the nature of scientific motivation, it is first necessary briefly to state Merton's argument concerning the origins of modern science in religious Puritanism.

Merton's monograph, *Science, Technology and Society in Seventeenth-Century England* (1938), is a landmark text in the sociology of science. It is widely regarded as an application of the Weber thesis to science, namely that Protestant asceticism formed the cultural foundation of the development of modern science, a viewpoint to which Weber himself adhered (Weber, 1905: 249 note 145), but which has a longer history (see, for example, Nietzsche, 1887: 589–92). Indeed Merton's thesis is that Puritanism in 17th century England provided a legitimating ethos for the conduct of science, and tended to direct persons toward scientific research.

Merton's argument is nuanced and measured. While he acknowledges that the class composition of the Puritan congregations may have led them to support science for self-interested reasons (Merton, 1938: 81, 90), this is not the basis of his case. Neither is it Puritan theology, but rather the Puritan ethos, that promotes science, according to Merton (1938: 102). This is because while Puritanism as a social phenomenon serves to legitimate science, Puritan religious leaders and theologians 'vehemently attacked' scientific discoveries as subversive (Merton, 1938: 100–1). The positive relationship between Puritanism and the growth of science is not seen by Merton as historically enduring but obtains for a particular and limited period only (Merton, 1938: 76), for while he insists that the Puritan system of ethics promoted science in the 17th century, he agrees that science later came to undermine that system in ways wholly unanticipated by both Puritans and scientists themselves (Merton, 1938: 79, 99).

The particular attributes of Puritanism that Merton believed contributed to the emergence of science in 17th century England are numerous. He argues that the Puritan advocacy of Good Works as public service (Merton, 1938: 61–2, 73), the Puritan orientation of systematic, methodical and constant labour (Merton, 1938: 63), as well as the high value Puritans placed on learning and education (Merton, 1938: 65), and the Puritan view that the study of natural phenomenon served the Glorification of God (Merton, 1938: 71–2), all contributed to the social legitimacy of science. Additionally, the Puritan assumption of Order in Nature also underpins scientific inquiry (Merton, 1938: 107–8), as did the Puritan support for reason (Merton, 1938: 92) and experimentation (Merton, 1938: 93, 94). Merton is clear, nevertheless, that religion is the historical basis of support for science as an institution, but that it cannot explain particular scientific discoveries: these latter 'belong to the internal history of science and are largely independent of factors other than purely scientific' (Merton, 1938: 75). Merton demonstrates the veracity of his cultural argument by showing that the membership of the Royal Society in the relevant period is predominantly Puritan (Merton, 1938: 113–4).

In all of this Merton insists that underlying the religious ethos are emotional currents or sentiments. 'The Puritan advocacy of experimental science,' says Merton, 'was the inevitable outcome of an emotionally consistent circle of sentiment and beliefs' (Merton, 1938: 115). Those who experience particular sentiments are not necessarily aware of them (Merton, 1938: 82), even though their actions will be encouraged or even directed by such sentiments. Indeed, Merton defines the task of sociology as one of revealing the sentiments themselves: 'When [the sociologist] has uncovered the sentiments crystallized in religious values and cultural orientation which governs their expression, when he has determined the extent to which this led men toward or away from scientific pursuits or perhaps not influenced them at all, then his task is, in its initial outlines, complete' (Merton, 1938: 55–6).

The importance of sentiment, affect or emotion in Merton's argument has gone quite unnoticed in the literature, with two exceptions (Feuer, 1963; Shapin, 1988). This no doubt arises in part from the largely untheorized treatment of the concept in Merton's discussion. Yet there was no need for Merton to dwell on the concept: it would have been known to his readers at the time through contemporary discussion of Pareto's account of sentiments in the work of

Lawrence Henderson (1935: 20–1, 24–5, 63–8). In Merton's account, sentiments lie behind the religious values that promote science. Sentiments are crystallized in values (Merton, 1938: 75). While cultural practices influence the direction of action (Merton, 1938: 56, 91), sentiments remain the source of action (Merton, 1938: 91). This is not simply a causal chain, but an interactive system in which ideas and behaviour reinforce or alter sentiments (Merton, 1938: 56). Thus, for Merton, 'an emotionally consistent system of beliefs, sentiments, and action' that emerge out of ascetic Protestantism 'played no small part in arousing a sustained interest in science' (Merton, 1938 quoted in Feuer, 1963: 3).

In an unfortunately neglected book, *The Scientific Intellectual* (1963), Lewis Feuer engages Merton on the content of the relevant emotions that encouraged the scientific revolution:

> The scientist of the seventeenth century was a philosophical optimist; delight and joy in man's status pervaded his theory of knowledge and of the universe. And it was this revolution in man's emotions which was the basis for the change in his ideas. Behind the history of ideas lies the history of emotions. Every major intellectual movement is preceded by the advent of new kinds of feelings that shape the new mode in which reality is to be intellectually apprehended. Emotions determine the perspective, the framework, for the explanation of the perceived world (Feuer, 1963: 1).

Feuer argues that the emotions congruent with ascetic Protestantism are hostile to science, not its basis. Intellectually, Feuer argues, the 'Calvinist doctrine of original sin was plainly hostile to the pretension of ordinary human beings to understand the world' (Feuer, 1963: 6). Similarly, the general ethos of ascetic Puritanism inhibits the scientific impulses: 'An ascetic ethic', says Feuer, 'is hostile to the direct sense of beauty [required for science], and deprives the thinker of the idle richness of imagery', it is 'sense-mistrusting' and 'image-destroying' (Feuer, 1963: 13). In contrast with the ascetic ethos, that he says inhibits science, Feuer postulates a 'hedonist-libertarian ethos' that 'was the emotional basis of the scientific movement of the seventeenth century' (Feuer, 1963: 7), and which in part emerged in reaction to Puritanism.

Feuer's challenge to the Merton thesis operates principally in the realm of the emotional basis of the scientific revolution at the level of motivation. Implicit in his argument is the idea that in the historical origins of the scientific movement, the social motivation toward scientific practice is prior to the pattern of institutional control of motives which characterizes the behaviour of scientists, to use Merton's terminology. In this regard Feuer's approach is similar to Norbert Elias's account of the requisite changes in the structure of personality in the opening stages of the civilizing process in early modern Europe (Elias, 1939). Through this focus the particular and specific content of sentiment or emotion becomes crucial. Merton's discussion paid less attention to this matter than Feuer's. It could not have been otherwise. The Paretian sentiments at the heart of Merton's account are postulates, not facts, they are deduced from the behaviour of subjects (Henderson, 1935: 20–1), and their content is therefore determined by the hypothesis entertained about the behaviour under consideration, rather than them explaining that behaviour. Merton's culturalist hypothesis not only left sentiments untheorized but was indifferent to the emotional content of the sentiments underlying the Puritan ethos.

The elements of the Puritan ethos Merton points to do not in themselves encourage scientific practices, as he supposes. The things Merton refers to, mentioned above, are: Good works, a sense of vocation, and the prestige of learning and education. These are necessary for all socially valued endeavours, and not particular to science. Similarly, alchemy, magic and astrology as much as science are based on assumption of order in nature, reason, and experimentation (Polanyi, 1958: 161). Neither is it necessarily resolved that the membership of the Royal Society is as clearly Puritan as Merton attempted to demonstrate. Feuer's examination of the evidence comes to a conclusion contrary to the one presented by Merton (Feuer, 1963: 68–76; see also Feuer, 1979). Merton's rejoinder is forceful but not conclusive (Merton, 1970: xxiv-xxviii). And there has never been a consensus among historians accepting of Merton's historical argument, including the religious complexion of the Royal Society (see Cohen, 1990).

Science as organization

The classic presentation of the scientific study of nature assumes that either the scientist's wonder, as with Aristotle, or the utility of the discovery, as with Bacon, drives the research process. But these alternative visions are partial insofar as both disinterested and also applied scientific work are conducted competitively, with the ability to legitimately claim priority for a finding being determinative of standing in a scientific community. Indeed, unlike every other form of producer community, the outputs of the scientific community ideally belong not to the individual producer but to the community as a whole. The individual producer or scientist has only claim to be recognized for their discoveries. Merton describes it thus:

> The substantive findings of science are a product of social collaboration and are assigned to the community. They constitute a common heritage in which the equity of the individual producer is severely limited . . . The scientist's claim to 'his' intellectual 'property' is limited to that of recognition and esteem which, if the institution functions with a modicum of efficiency, is roughly commensurate with the significance of the increments brought to the common fund of knowledge (Merton, 1942: 610).

It is important to note that the institutional emphasis on originality in science and the consequent concern with scientific priority is not a recent development but implicate in the scientific revolution of the seventeenth century, amply demonstrated by Isaac Newton's famous battles over recognition. This characteristic explains, for instance, the predominance of the scientific journal.

The characterization of science, as a collective activity of a community in which the individual members are in competition for recognition of new findings, is widely accepted in the sociological literature. Richard Whitley, for instance, describes modern sciences as 'reputational work organizations' (Whitley, 1984). Warren Hagstrom says that 'the organization of science consists of an exchange of social recognition for information' (Hagstrom, 1965: 13). Hagstrom goes on to make the crucial point that an absence of awareness or acknowledgement of the significance of social recognition is required for it to function properly (Hagstrom, 1965: 13–4). This general model tends to emphasize an aspect of the process of science that is dependent on emotional rather than non-emotional factors. As Hagstrom says, the gift relationship that encompasses the general form of scientific exchange—recognition for information—is without formal rights and obligations, thus 'gifts are felt to represent positive sentiments rather than contractual obligations' (Hagstrom, 1965: 105). Without doubting this latter claim, the general model from which it derives requires qualification.

The reputational or recognition depiction of the basic mechanisms of the scientific community ignores the fact that significant developments in science have occurred outside of such a pattern. A case in point is the theory of continental drift, which revolutionized earth sciences since the 1960s, first seriously proposed by Alfred Wegener in 1912. Wegener continued to present evidence for and develop his theory from that time and throughout the 1920s, even though at the time of his death in 1930 it continued to be almost completely rejected (see Cohen, 1985: 446–66). To refer to 'expected' reputation in cases such as this is simply question begging and not remedial of the original formulation. An alternative approach is to go back one step in the process of science and also to go forward one step. To go back is to consider the question of commitment on which the quest for recognition is based. To go forward is to consider the nature and basis of the scrutiny of the claims to recognition that constitutes scientific validation.

Textbook accounts of science typically warn against emotional commitment as undermining of objectivity. But the assumption of such accounts is that science is an essentially individual and psychological practice: the scientist forms ideas about nature that they then test for the truth of their claims. Thus the individual mind must be pure of logic and free of prior commitment, according to this view. In reality, on the other hand, science is an organizational and institutional practice, essentially social in nature. In this context emotional commitment is not only unavoidable, it is a necessary and positive factor in the processes of science. According to one study:

> ... science advances through a heated adversary process, which is fundamentally social, wherein one [person] tests [their] discoveries against the discoveries of another. [Emotional] energy and commitment infuses the whole process.
>
> ... To remove commitment and even bias from scientific inquiry may be to remove one of the strongest sustaining forces both for discovery of scientific ideas and for their subsequent testing (Mitroff, 1974: 72, 73).

Such commitments are necessary for scientific practice and advances, and, in a context of dependence on experiment and evidence, are elements in the practice of scientific rationality, according to Mitroff (1974: 249), who bases this account on extensive interviews with 42 eminent scientists who studied the Apollo moon rocks (see Mitroff, 1974: 64).

Close examination of the adversary and competitive nature of science, through laboratory studies (Knorr Cetina, 1995) and other essentially cultural accounts of science, tend to suggest that the truth claims of scientists rest on essentially political forms of argument. What this approach ignores, though, is that a non-political arbiter is always at work in science. Whether a finding gains acceptance within a scientific community ultimately depends upon whether it contributes to further and future research (Cole, 1992: 27; Chalmers, 1990; Whitley, 1984). The theory of continental drift, for instance, came to be accepted thirty years after Wegener's death because by that time there was sufficient evidence that ocean floors are real entities, that sea-floor spreading is a real phenomenon, and that the theory of continental drift transformed as the theory of plate tectonics was fertile ground for further research (Cohen, 1985: 458–63). The processes underlying these features of science are best understood as not primarily cultural but emotional.

The emotional basis of scientific discovery and validation can be considered by treating a work generally assumed to prefigure instead the culturalist approach to science, but which in fact operates through a quite different set of assumptions. Ludwik Fleck, *Genesis and Development of a Scientific Fact* (1935), remains effectively unknown to sociologists precisely because it is so frequently cited as a precursor of the Kuhnian approach in the philosophy of science and the strong program in the sociology of scientific knowledge. Its assimilation into the prehistory of these traditions means that it is never read in its own right but through the conventions of a constructionist sociology of science. It has been wholly overlooked that Fleck not only refers to the role of social factors in scientific discovery and validation, but that he also explicitly points to the central role of emotion in these processes, and in doing so points to a new departure of understanding.

Fleck offers a macrosociology of science when he treats the practice and context of science in terms of 'thought collective' and 'thought style' respectively:

> If we define 'thought collective' as a community of persons mutually exchanging ideas or maintaining intellectual interaction, we will find by implication that it also provides the special 'carrier' for the historical development of any field of thought, as well as for the given stock of knowledge and level of culture. This we have designated 'thought style' (Fleck, 1935: 39).

Fleck therefore grounds scientific knowledge, as well as values and practices (culture), in the social structural relations of the persons involved. Thus scientific knowledge is born of the social institution of science. Science, as social organization, and science as knowledge, are thus fundamentally linked, and each is explained sociologically not naturalistically (Brannigan, 1980, 1981). This can be seen in Fleck's rather Durkheimian account of a fact:

140

In the field of cognition, the signal of resistance opposing free, arbitrary thinking is called a fact (Fleck, 1935: 101).

A fact, therefore, is a property of the thought collective, not in the first instance a property of an external reality.

Fleck argues, then, that facts have no inherent primacy but are collectively formed conceptualizations which have both a history and a social basis. He conceives his own work to be sociological epistemology. The particular fact that Fleck (1935) discusses is syphilis, the conceptualization of which, he shows, has a long social, medical, and scientific history. In particular, he examines the Wassermann reaction and the development of serology as socially produced phenomena which historically specified syphilis as a fact in its present form.

Because scientific facts arise through social processes, Fleck holds that an examination of scientific activities will reveal a social structure in which there is 'organized effort of the collective involving a division of labor, cooperation, preparatory work, technical assistance, mutual exchange of ideas, and controversy' (Fleck, 1935: 42). Indeed, Fleck goes on to say that through the social character of scientific activity, persuasive processes involving 'propaganda, imitation, authority, rivalry, solidarity, enmity, and friendship' will occur (Fleck, 1935: 43). All of this is now commonplace, at least since Latour and Woolgar (1979). But to say no more than this would be to entirely miss Fleck's real contribution.

The emotional basis of science is to be found pervasively, according to Fleck. The structure of the thought collective of science, for instance, consists of an esoteric circle and a larger exoteric circle that are distinguished by expertise. The basis of coherence in these is emotion, in particular the emotions of trust and confidence (Fleck, 1935: 105). Each circle is itself stratified by expertise. The distinctive products of these strata are, respectively, journal science, vademecum [handbook] science, textbook science, and popular science (Fleck, 1935: 112ff). Whereas journal science reports on the activities of the esoteric circle, popular science is the product of the outer exoteric circle. These points will be taken up again below.

The basis of scientific knowledge is scientific observation (see Ziman, 1978: 43–53). Fleck's discussion of scientific observation is particularly pointed. First, Fleck indicates that scientific observation is only possible after a period of scientific training (Fleck, 1935: 48). He then goes on to say that the role of training is not in the first instance to produce knowledge but rather to generate appropriate experience. Experience is so important because it is the basis of emotional sensibility, as we shall see. By possessing the appropriate experience the trainee thereby qualifies for membership in the thought collective. This experience and its consequences provide access to observations consonant with the correlative thought collective. Fleck says:

> Direct perception of form requires being experienced in the relevant field of thought
> . . . At the same time, of course, we lose the ability to see something that contradicts
> the form (Fleck, 1935: 92).

The epistemological importance of experience referred to here is precisely in the fact that scientific experience or training produces particular expectations and therefore provides an appropriate focus of attention. Attention is the property of cognition that selects only a portion of the vast range of sensory involvement for conscious awareness. Fleck gives the example of the selection of different bacterial colonies from 102 different cultures. The observations are not 'pure' but 'anticipate' differences (Fleck, 1935: 90). Expectancy is an affective element of a number of particular emotions. It is the fundamental emotional basis of all vision and observation. Because they are not given social representation these emotions are not culturally labelled, and are therefore without names. Thus, scientists are seldom conscious of experiencing them, and they function as back-grounded emotions (Barbalet, 1998: 59–60).

Given the significance of emotions in Fleck's characterization of thought collective it is important to appreciate the consistency of his account of thought style. According to Fleck, truth and facts derive their meaning from particular thought styles. A thought style, Fleck says:

> consists of a certain mood and of the performance by which it is realized. A mood has two closely connected aspects: readiness both for selective feelings and for correspondingly directed action (Fleck, 1935: 99).

As mood changes, so does meaning (Fleck, 1935: 110). The link indicated here between emotions and meaning has been observed in a number of contexts, including empirical observation and theory formation (James, 1890: 312–7; Gouldner, 1970: 37–40; see also James, 1902: 128–9).

While accounts of emotions typically acknowledge their goal-setting function, Fleck's point above reminds us that goal setting is really a consequence of a more fundamental aspect of emotion: that aspect of emotion that instructs the emoting subject on their place in relations with others, that is, the formation of meaning. Emotions are provoked by circumstances and experienced as transformation of dispositions to act within them. For this to occur the subject of the emotion apprehends objects and relations in their environment differently, and is oriented toward them in a new way. Perceptions of things change, through emotional consciousness, and things are valued differently: they are seen in a new light. This is how insights form, and how scientific discoveries are made. Jean-Paul Sartre puts it well when he says: 'through a change of intention, as in a change of behaviour, we apprehend a new object, or an old object in a new way' (Sartre, 1939: 60). More particularly Adam Smith (1795), in a major historical source for the sociology of science, makes a similar point linking scientific discovery with affectual change, when he refers to 'observed [. . .] dissimilitudes' productive of 'anxious curiosity' (Smith, 1795: 40). These lead to the construction of 'connecting principles of nature' (Smith, 1795: 45) which return the mind to a state of composure (Smith, 1795: 46, 61) and thus lead to advancements in understanding, to science.

The formation of new meaning in science thus derives significantly from the emotional direction of observation of anomaly. It is important to emphasize

that experience and experience of anomaly in science is social not naturalistic. It is the relations within the thought collective that produce the tensions productive of emotions that lead to the perception of new facts or new principles. The typical representation of scientific activity holds that the scientist apprehends aspects of nature and reports on the laws of natural processes. But, in fact, the scientist, in apprehending aspects of nature, does so by clearly manipulating social products in social relationships. These social products are not just instruments (Hacking, 1992) but also theories. There is a point to these manipulations, namely to provide a 'correct' and 'useful' account of natural processes. But this is to refer to motive not system. The system science deals with is an essentially social system.

Albert Einstein, for instance, developed the special theory of relativity in 1905 through his relationship with the local time coordinate theory developed by the Dutch physicist Hendrik Lorentz and the radiation law developed by the German physicist Max Planck. Alfred Wegener's stalled revolution in earth sciences through the theory of continental drift, mentioned above, was the result of his confrontation with the theory of intercontinental bridges and with the work of the alpine geologists Rudolf Staub and Franz Kossmat. This is to say that scientific observation and conceptualization take place in an intellectual framework that not only has an essentially social history, but also an exhaustive social context.

Fleck's account of the scientific community and scientific knowledge, through the notions of thought collective and thought style, therefore, takes us directly into the role of emotion in scientific discovery. All that has been reported here concerning Fleck's discussion of the relevance of emotions in science is clear in his text: but not one of the scholarly commentaries on Fleck (Baldamus, 1977; Cohen and Schnelle, 1986; Douglas, 1986; Freudenthal and Löwy, 1988; Löwy, 1990) has noticed the fact. What better demonstration than that of the power of the thought style and its basis in institutions, not external reality!

One issue that arises from the preceding discussion is the relative absence of reference to emotion in the scientific texts, if it is indeed as important to scientific processes as indicated here. Again, Fleck covers this matter quite effectively. First, science works by modelling a 'discovery' into a 'fact'. The epistemological changes from the initial experimental results to the widely accepted new knowledge include conceptual differences which mean that the later truths psychologically preclude access to the earlier findings. Fleck says that 'we can no longer express the previously incomplete thoughts with these now finished concepts' (Fleck, 1935: 86). With rationalization and schematization the affective components of discovery become lost and obscured. The 'collective remodelling of an idea has the effect that, after the change in thought style, the earlier problem is no longer completely comprehensible' (Fleck, 1935: 123).

Behind this epistemological change, consequent upon the collective apprehension of a finding, is the process of personal distancing. Thus, as a provisional finding of an individual researcher becomes public property, the idiosyncratic affective involvement of the discovery moves into the background and obscurity (Fleck, 1935: 144). Fleck explains this in terms of the move through the structure of the thought collective, from journal science to hand-book science:

> [there is movement from] uniqueness and novelty of working material . . . associated inseparably with the author [to the] hidden invocation of the collective . . . [It is the] duty of the individual research worker to remain in the background . . . [P]ersonally colored non-additive journal science . . . is converted next into vademecum [hand-book] science by the migration of ideas throughout the collective (Fleck, 1935: 119).

The transformation from a finding to a fact does not amount to the end of emotion in science, but only an extinguishing of the close association between the emotions of discovery, the discoverer and the discovered. As a fact becomes more broadly accepted in the thought collective and affects the structures of the thought style, more pervasive collective emotions operate.

Fleck makes the point that the 'inclination to objectivize the thought structures' of natural science is itself a characteristic 'mood' (Fleck, 1935: 144). In particular, this is described as a 'mood of solidarity' around particular conventions and fixed meanings (Fleck, 1935: 145; cf also 99). Indeed, Fleck observes that the more scientific knowledge occupies the exoteric periphery 'thinking appears to be even more strongly dominated by an emotive vividness that imparts to knowledge the subjective certainty of something holy or self-evident' (Fleck, 1935: 117).

Thus, all phases of scientific production, Fleck shows, are underlain with distinctive patterns of emotional involvement, unavoidable and instrumental in the realization of science as a social institution.

Discussion

Up to the present time sociologists of emotion have given no attention to science. Yet, as we have seen in the preceding account, a number of writers in the sociology of science tradition, of very different methodological and theoretical persuasions, have referred to the signal importance of emotions in all phases of scientific production. It must be hastily added that there is an absence of a broad awareness within the sociology of science that emotions have loomed large in its concerns. Nevertheless, the record of attention to emotions is clear. This situation is both entirely anomalous and also quite unexceptional.

In a chapter aptly called 'The Neglect of Affects', A.F. Davies indicates the complex set of possible relations between emotions and awareness of emotions: he says that an emotional system 'comprises not merely feelings and impulses, but also the conscious thoughts that help define the situation', that 'unconscious feelings also play a part' and that 'we may or may not know that we are in an emotional system' (Davies, 1980: 301). The emotional system of science includes conscious thoughts that depreciate the constructive role of emotions, significant unconscious feelings predominate, and most practitioners would not know that they were in an emotional system. The emotional system of the sociology of science seems to replicate that of science itself. Nevertheless, as we have seen, a number of key sources in the sociology of science point to the importance of emotions in scientific processes. In the discussion to follow will be indicated the contribution an examination of science might offer the sociology of emotions.

The role of emotions in science, indicated above, covers a range of activities. The emotional nature of motivation for scientific engagement is appreciated by a number of writers. Consideration of sociological characterization of motivation, in terms of institutional control, as with Merton, or socially formed personality structure, as with Feuer (and Elias), raises a number of issues at the core of the sociology of emotions. Indeed, without strenuous modification of frameworks, the difference here is an analog of the debate between constructionists and positivists in the sociology of emotions (Kemper, 1981). These parallel debates in the sociology of science and the sociology of emotions respectively, could be profitably linked.

A connected question concerns the particular emotions that are associated with scientific motivation. At the individual level, such a question is practically devoid of meaning because the personal motives involved will be as numerous as the numbers of persons implicated, indeed more numerous, as most individuals relate to goals with multiple motives. Yet consideration of whether emotions in science are associated with a 'hedonistic-libertarian' or an 'ascetic' ethos is not entirely without purpose. While it is doubtful that a decisive answer could be provided to such a question, and it is probable that these are not the only or most fruitful possibilities, consideration of the emotional background of particular types of activities, including science, is of genuine sociological interest. Such an inquiry would supplement sociology of knowledge appreciations of the ways in which social being affects social consciousness (see Bensman and Lilienfeld, 1991). At the present time, the sociology of emotions would benefit from an application of a structurally grounded middle-range approach to particular emotions, providing balance to the cultural and global inclinations of constructionist approaches. The emotional complexion of science, in the sense suggested here, affords such a case and is of intrinsic interest.

The role of emotional attachment and commitment, associated with the process of competitive claims to priority, is central to an understanding of science and has wider applications. Hagstrom's observation, that positive sentiments rather than contractual obligations characterizes scientific production and exchange, explains not only a key aspect of the social organization of science, but also its economic or pay structure. Scientific workers, and also scholarly and academic workers, tend to tolerate relatively lower wage and poorer employment conditions than comparable workers. This is likely to arise out of the positive sentiments associated with knowledge production in general, in which a significant component of remuneration and standing is in the form of emotional satisfactions and the discharging of emotional commitments. The positive sentiments associated with scientific recognition cannot be directly assimilated into the conceptualization of emotional labour as it is presently constituted. Scientific production is not subject to emotional management or feeling rules, and the affective outcome is enrichment not depletion. But this is just the point: consideration of the unacknowledged but central role of emotion in scientific priority exchange supplements and broadens the emotional labour approach to work organization (see Barbalet, 1998: 179–82).

The emotional patterns of commitment and competition, that characterize the structure of modern science, require a stabilizing framework. In the sociology of science it is widely assumed that this framework is provided by the norms of the scientific community. But norms are inherently ambiguous and notoriously poor regulators (Kuhn, 1977: 330–9; Mitroff, 1974: 11–18). The deceptively simple depiction of the structure of the scientific community, or thought collective, as consisting of esoteric and exoteric circles, structured by trust and confidence (Fleck, 1935: 105), points to an affective means of control, wholly appropriate to a social system framed by competition and commitment. The role of trust as a means of control within science is typically treated in terms of norms (Zuckerman, 1977). But, even then, the essentially affective or emotional nature of the topic is unavoidable and obvious in the exposition. The large and growing sociological literature on trust benefits from consideration of the emotional aspects of trust (Barbalet, 1996). The role of trust within the structure of scientific communities has drawn less attention than the role of trust in relations between scientific and lay communities (Wynne, 1995: 377–8, 381). But this only underlies the point that trust, confidence, and loyalty are modalities of action that regulate institutional behaviour.

To suggest that trust and associated emotional patterns can explain the regulation of scientific activity shows further how consideration of science is not only appropriate for the sociology of emotions but it, in turn, is also beneficial for the sociology of science. For instance, the role of Mertonian scientific ethos in shaping the practices of science is now thoroughly doubted, because the norms and values constitutive of it are too broadly and abstractly conceived (Barnes and Dolby, 1970). But norm or value led explanation of behaviour continues to be advocated, as when Kuhn, for instance, holds that a contextualized and differentiated understandings of values is essential for an account of scientific theory choice (Kuhn, 1977: 330–3). The issue cannot simply be the breadth and focus of values, however. It must be what values can tell us about behaviour at all. The idea that norms and values can lead behaviour ignores the fact that these arise retrospective to events, and that action is led by the emotions that arise in interaction (Collins, 1981: 990–4). Any capacity that values offer agency comes from the fact that values are 'cognitions infused with emotion' (Collins, 1990: 27).

More than any of those already mentioned, the most challenging aspect of emotion in science is its role in thought style, in concept formation. Fleck shows that scientific training provides experience generative of particular expectations or emotional sensibilities. These serve to structure scientific perception. Fleck's account is brief even though the significance of what he reports is large. At the very core of what are widely understood to be cognitive and intellectual processes is the formative influence of emotions. Rather than treat these as founded in psychological processes, Fleck grasps their sociological dimensions. The scientists engaged by these particular emotions experience them below the threshold of awareness. These emotions are not culturally tagged or named. It is the exploration of these emotions that offers the greatest challenge to the sociology of emotions. In taking it up, some of the more limiting aspects of conventional understandings of emotion will be tested and a broader appreciation of the nature of emotions made possible. Thus close attention to the emotions central to scientific insight and discovery will enrich the sociology of emotions.

Unnamed emotions that are not consciously experienced, such as those just mentioned, are likely to be regarded as infrequent if not impossible events. In fact, however, these constitute the largest category of emotional experiences. Consciousness of an emotional feeling is necessarily associated with an ability of the person experiencing it to provide verbal or linguistic reference to the feeling. Much emotional activity, on the other hand, is mediated by areas of the brain unconnected with language functions (Gazzaniga, 1985). Consciousness of emotion is likely to occur, therefore, when those parts of the brain associated with language are also the neurological site of emotional processes (see LeDoux, 1998). Cross-cultural evidence is also relevant to this problem. It has been reported, for instance, that an emotion linguistically tagged in one society may be unnamed in another. The linguistic absence of an emotion word, however, does not mean that members of the affected language group do not experience the emotion they have no name for and of which they are apparently unaware (see James, 1890: 485, also 448, 454; Ortony, Clore and Collins, 1988: 8; de Rivera, 1977: 128).

The social significance of consciousness of emotions resides in its reflexive consequences: consciousness of emotion permits reflection on the concerns represented within it. This 'moral' quality of emotion is simply absent in the back-grounded emotions that typically operate in scientific research. But emotion itself is an apprehension of the experienced world of the emoting person that is registered not primarily in conscious awareness but through bodily processes. At the present time the sociology of emotions is almost wholly occupied with those emotions that persons experience consciously. Such emotions are subject to 'management' and strategically employed in interactions. Emotion in the sense of mere physical engagement of the actors in their relations with others, and the transformation of perception consequent upon such engagement, is almost wholly neglected by the sociology of emotions. Yet this latter is the most prevalent form of emotional experience and, being the more fundamental, is the more important for an understanding of social activity and processes. Sociological study of that aspect of scientific observation consonant with these emotions has the potential, therefore, of revolutionizing the sociology of emotions, as well as the sociological study of science.

Conclusion

What emerges from the foregoing account and discussion is that an emotions approach provides a thoroughly sociological apprehension of science. This is in contrast to the currently prevailing cultural treatment of science that emphasizes values and 'political' relations between scientists. The application of the sociology of emotions to the study of science not only captures the experiences of the scientists in a comprehensive fashion, going beyond both the intellectual and the cultural dimensions of the scientist's activities. In addition, the sociology of emotions engenders an examination of science within an intellectually rich framework that reveals and explores aspects of science that would otherwise not be amenable to sociological investigation.

References

Bacon, Francis (1620 [1905]) 'Novum Organum'. Pp. 256–387 in *The Philosophical Works of Francis Bacon*, edited by J.M. Robertson. London: George Routledge and Sons.

Baker, John R. (1942) *The Scientific Life.* London: George Allen and Unwin.

Baldamus, Wilhelm (1977) 'Ludwig Fleck and the Development of the Sociology of Science'. Pp. 135–56 in *Human Figurations: Essays for Norbert Elias*, edited by Peter R. Gleichmann, Johan Goudsblom, and Herman Korte. Amsterdam: Stichting Amsterdams Sociologisch Tijdschrift.

Barbalet, J.M. (1996) 'Social Emotions: Confidence, Trust and Loyalty'. *International Journal of Sociology and Social Policy.* 16(9/10): 75–96.

Barbalet, J.M. (1998) *Emotion, Social Theory, and Social Structure: A Macrosociological Approach.* Cambridge: Cambridge University Press.

Barnes, S.B. and Dolby, R.G.A. (1970) 'The Scientific Ethos: A Deviant Viewpoint'. *Archives Européenes de Sociologie.* 11: 3–25.

Barnes, Barry (1972) 'Introduction'. Pp. 9–16 in *Sociology of Science*, edited by Barry Barnes. Harmondsworth: Penguin.

Bensman, Joseph and Robert Lilienfeld (1991) *Craft and Consciousness: Occupational Technique and Development of World Images.* 2nd edition. New York: Aldine de Gruyter.

Brannigan, Augustine (1980) 'Naturalistic and Sociological Models of the Problem of Scientific Discovery'. *British Journal of Sociology.* 31(4): 559–573.

Brannigan, Augustine (1981) *The Social Basis of Scientific Discovery.* Cambridge: Cambridge University Press.

Chalmers, Alan (1990) *Science and Its Fabrications.* Minneapolis: University of Minnesota Press.

Cohen, I. Bernard (1985) *Revolution in Science.* Cambridge, MA: Harvard University Press.

Cohen, I. Bernard (ed) (1990) *Puritanism and the Rise of Modern Science: The Merton Thesis.* New Brunswick: Rutgers University Press.

Cohen, Robert S. and Thomas Schnelle (eds) (1986) *Cognition and Fact: Material on Ludwik Fleck. Boston Studies in the Philosophy of Science, volume 87.* Dordrecht, Holland: d. Reidel Publishing Company.

Cole, Stephen (1992) *Making Science: Between Nature and Society.* Cambridge, MA: Harvard University Press.

Collins, Randall (1981) 'On the Microfoundations of Macrosociology'. *American Journal of Sociology.* 86(5): 984–1014.

Collins, Randall (1990) 'Stratification, Emotional Energy, and the Transient Emotions'. Pp. 27–57 in *Research Agendas in the Sociology of Emotions*, edited by Theodore D. Kemper. Albany: State University of New York Press.

Damasio, Antonio R. (1994) *Descartes Error: Emotion, Reason, and the Human Brain.* New York: Putnam.

Darwin, Charles (1876 [1929]) *Autobiography of Charles Darwin.* London: Watts & Co.

Davies, A.F. (1980) *Skills, Outlooks and Passions: A Psychoanalytic Contribution to the Study of Politics.* Cambridge: Cambridge University Press.

Douglas, Mary (1986) *How Institutions Think.* Syracuse, NY: Syracuse University Press.

Einstein, Albert (1949) 'Autobiographical Notes'. Pp. 3–95 in *Albert Einstein: Philosopher-Scientist,* edited by Paul Arthur Schilpp. Evanston, Ill: Living Library of Philosophers.

Einstein, Albert (1954 [1982]) *Ideas and Opinions.* New York: Crown Trade Paperbacks.

Elias, Norbert (1939 [2000]) *The Civilizing Process: Sociogenetic and Psychogenetic Investigations.* Oxford: Blackwell.

Feuer, Lewis S. (1963) *The Scientific Intellectual: The Psychological and Sociological Origins of Modern Science.* New York: Basic Books.

Feuer, Lewis S. (1979) 'Science and the Ethic of Protestant Asceticism: A Reply to Professor Robert Merton'. *Research in Sociology of Knowledge, Sciences and Art.* 2: 1–23.

Fleck, Ludwik (1935 [1979]) *Genesis and Development of a Scientific Fact.* Chicago: University of Chicago Press.

Friedrichs, Robert W. (1970) *A Sociology of Sociology.* New York: Free Press.

Freudenthal, Gad and Ilana Lowy (1988) 'Ludwik Fleck's Roles in Society: A Case Study using Joseph Ben-David's Paradigm for a Sociology of Knowledge'. *Social Studies of Science.* 18: 625–651.

Gazzaniga, Michael (1985) *The Social Brain.* New York: Basic Books.

Gouldner, Alvin W. (1970) *The Coming Crisis of Western Sociology* London: Heinemann.

Hacking, Ian (1992) 'The Self-vindication of the Laboratory Sciences'. Pp. 29–64 in *Science as Practice and Culture,* edited by Andrew Pickering. Chicago: University of Chicago Press.

Hagstrom, Warren O. (1965) *The Scientific Community,* New York: Basic Books.

Harding, Sandra (1986) *The Science Question in Feminism.* Ithaca: Cornell University Press.

Henderson, Lawrence J. (1935) *Pareto's General Sociology: A Physiologist's Interpretation.* Cambridge, MA: Harvard University Press.

James, William (1890) *The Principles of Psychology, volume 2.* New York: Henry Holt and Company.

James, William (1897 [1956]) *The Will to Believe and Other Essays in Popular Philosophy.* New York: Dover.

James, William (1902 [1958]) *The Varieties of Religious Experience: A Study in Human Nature.* New York: Dover.

Jasanoff, Sheila, Gerald E. Markle, James C. Petersen, and Trevor Pinch (eds) (1995) *Handbook of Science and Technology Studies.* Thousand Oaks: Sage.

Kemper, Theodore D. (1981) 'Social Constructionist and Positivist Approaches to the Sociology of Emotions'. *American Journal of Sociology.* 87(2): 336–362.

Knorr Cetina, Karin (1995) 'Laboratory Studies: The Cultural Approach to the Study of Science'. Pp. 140–66 in *Handbook of Science and Technology Studies,* edited by Sheila Jasanoff, Gerald E. Markle, James C. Petersen, and Trevor Pinch. Thousand Oaks: Sage.

Kuhn, Thomas S. (1977) *The Essential Tension: Selected Studies in Scientific Tradition and Change.* Chicago: University of Chicago Press.

Latour, Bruno and Steve Woolgar (1979) *Laboratory Life: The Social Construction of Scientific Facts.* Thousand Oaks: Sage.

LeDoux, Joseph (1998) *The Emotional Brain: The Mysterious Underpinnings of Emotional Life.* London: Weidenfeld and Nicolson.

Levins, Richard and Richard Lewontin (1985) *The Dialectical Biologist.* Cambridge, MA: Harvard University Press.

Löwy, Ilana (1990) *The Polish School of Philosophy of Medicine: From Tytus Chalubinski (1820–1889) to Ludwik Fleck (1896–1961), Philosophy and Medicine, volume 37.* Dordrecht: Kluwer Academic Publishers.

Lynch, Michael (1993) *Scientific Practice and Ordinary Action: Ethnomethodology and Social Studies of Science.* Cambridge: Cambridge University Press.

Macmurray, John (1961 [1995]) *Persons in Relation*. London: Faber and Faber.

Mannheim, Karl (1936 [1968]) *Ideology and Utopia: An Introduction to the Sociology of Knowledge*. London: Routledge and Kegan Paul.

Merton, Robert K. (1937 [1968]) 'Science and the Social Order'. Pp. 591–603 in his *Social Theory and Social Structure. Enlarged edition*. New York: Free Press.

Merton, Robert K. (1938 [1970]) *Science, Technology and Society in Seventeenth-Century England*. New York: Harper.

Merton, Robert K. (1942 [1968]) 'Science and Democratic Social Structure'. Pp. 604–15 in his *Social Theory and Social Structure. Enlarged edition*. New York: Free Press.

Merton, Robert K. (1970) 'Preface: 1970'. Pp. vii–xxix in his *Science, Technology and Society in Seventeenth-Century England*. New York: Harper.

Mitroff, Ian I. (1974) *The Subjective Side of Science: A Philosophical Inquiry into the Psychology of the Apollo Moon Scientists*. Amsterdam: Elsevier Scientific.

Nietzsche, Friedrich (1887 [1992]) 'On the Genealogy of Morals'. Pp. 451–599 in *Basic Writings of Nietzsche*, translated and edited by Walter Kaufman. New York: Random House.

Ortony, Andrew, Gerald L. Clore, and Allan Collins (1988) *The Cognitive Structure of Emotions*. Cambridge: Cambridge University Press.

Pels, Dick (1996) 'Karl Mannheim and the Sociology of Scientific Knowledge: Toward a New Agenda'. *Sociological Theory*. 14(1): 30–48.

Polanyi, Michael (1958 [1974]) *Personal Knowledge: Towards a Post-Critical Philosophy*. Chicago: University of Chicago Press.

Priestley, Joseph (1776 [1965]) Extract from *Experiments and Observations on Different Kinds of Air*. Pp. 139–50 in *Priestley's Writings on Philosophy, Science and Politics*, edited by John A. Passmore. New York: Collier.

de Rivera, Joseph (1977) *A Structural Theory of the Emotions*. New York: International Universities Press.

Sartre, Jean-Paul (1939 [1948]) *The Emotions: Outline of a Theory*. New York: The Wisdom Library.

Shapin, Steven (1988) 'Understanding the Merton Thesis'. *Isis*. 79(299): 594–605.

Smith, Adam (1795 [1980]) 'The History of Astronomy'. Pp. 33–105 in his *Essays on Philosophical Subjects*. Oxford: Oxford University Press.

de Sousa, Ronald (1987) *The Rationality of Emotion*. Cambridge, MA. MIT Press.

Toulmin, Stephen (1990) *Cosmopolis: The Hidden Agenda of Modernity*. New York: Free Press.

Tinbergen, Niko (1968) *Curious Naturalists*. New York: Doubleday.

Watson, James (2000) *A Passion for DNA*. Oxford: Oxford University Press.

Weber, Max (1905 [1991]) *The Protestant Ethic and the Spirit of Capitalism*. London: HarperCollins.

Whitley, Richard (1984) *The Intellectual and Social Organization of the Sciences*. Oxford: Oxford University Press.

Wilson, Edward O. (1996) *Naturalist*. London: Penguin.

Wilson, Edward O. (1998) *Consilience: The Unity of Knowledge*. New York: Alfred Knopf.

Wolpert, Lewis and Alison Richards (eds) (1997) *Passionate Minds: The Inner World of Scientists*. Oxford: Oxford University Press.

Wright, Thomas (1604 [1971]) *The Passions of the Minde in Generall*. Facsimile reprint. Urbana: University of Illinois Press.

Wynne, Brian (1995) 'Public Understanding of Science'. Pp. 361–88 in *Handbook of Science and Technology Studies*, edited by Sheila Jasanoff, Gerald E. Markle, James C. Petersen, and Trevor Pinch. Thousand Oaks: Sage.

Ziman, John (1978) *Reliable Knowledge: An Exploration of the Grounds of Belief in Science*. Cambridge: Cambridge University Press.

Ziman, John (1994) *Prometheus Bound: Science in a Dynamic Steady State*. Cambridge: Cambridge University Press.

Zuckermann, Harriet (1977) 'Deviant Behavior and Social Control in Science'. Pp. 87–138 in *Deviance and Social Change*, edited by Edward Sagarin. Beverly Hills: Sage.

Complex emotions: relations, feelings and images in emotional experience

Ian Burkitt

Abstract

In this chapter I argue that emotions are experienced primarily as structures of feeling which give meaning to relational experience. These feelings can be articulated through speech genres or discourses which give them form as specific emotions that have a place in the emotional vocabulary of a culture. Thus, I seek to distinguish between feeling and thought and attempt to trace the complex process through which feelings become emotions. This involves a reconsideration of the relation between body and thought, and the material and the ideal, as it appears in the work of various thinkers. Central to this is the role of image-schemata (Johnson, 1987) that mediate between the recurring relational patterns of bodily activity in the world, which makes experience meaningful, and the symbolic structures of the social group that can be used to articulate bodily feelings metaphorically. Feelings and emotions, then, while in a complex relationship to one another, are not always identical: they can in fact diverge, giving rise to the ambiguous nature of much emotional experience. Finally, all of this is considered in the light of power relations and the way that emotional dynamics play a central role in power.

Anglo-Saxons who are uncomfortable with the idea that feelings and emotions are the outward signs of precise and complex algorithms usually have to be told that these matters, the relationship between the self and others, and the relationship between self and environment, are, in fact, the subject matter of what are called 'feelings'—love, hate, fear, confidence, anxiety, hostility, etc. It is unfortunate that these abstractions referring to *patterns* of relationship have received names, which are usually handled in ways that assume that the 'feelings' are mainly characterized by quantity rather than by precise pattern. This is one of the nonsensical contributions of psychology to a distorted epistemology (Bateson, 1973: 113).

What Bateson has to say above is perhaps still true today nearly thirty years after his words were published: that when Anglo-Saxons think of the emotions they tend to think in terms of quantity or substance rather than about *patterns of relationship*. We tend to believe that our anger, envy, or grief is like an object contained inside us that we can reflect upon and work with. And yet when one thinks about it more analytically, emotions only have sense and meaning in the context of relations to other bodies, both human and non-human. When we get angry it is usually because another person or some group of people have denied us the respect we think we deserve, or because some non-human object is block-ing our goals (like the car that 'stubbornly' refuses to start on a cold winter morning). And when we are envious it is because others have what we cherish and feel that we deserve (Sabini and Silver, 1982). In all these cases, and many others we could think of, our emotions are an active response to a relational context: to other bodies with which we are related and that respond to our actions in particular ways. Indeed, when we feel angry or irritated it is at someone or something, the image of which usually soon appears to us. Even when this is not the case, as with feelings that seem to have no context and can dog us for many years, we often eventually discover they have a relational context after all. An example of this is the case of the author William Styron (1992), who, after suffering a terrible and seemingly inexplicable depression that drove him to a failed attempt at suicide, discovered in a psychiatric ward that his feelings were related to the death of his mother in his youth. During the period of this bereavement, Styron was in the marines and, as he realized later in life, felt unable to grieve properly in that environment where men were not expected to display emotion. So even where there is a long, winding, and obscure route from the relation (or the loss of a relation) to the feelings it inspires, the route is nevertheless there and is traceable. That is, if one is looking for it.

Often, though, this is not the case. Even today, psychologists studying emo-tions tend to search for the neural-chemical element of a feeling—such as high serotonin turnover in people who are highly aggressive—as if the neural-chemical is actually the *cause* of the emotion rather than part of a bodily response to relations. In such an instance we are still searching for substances in the body that correspond to the words we have for emotion. The alternative to this in recent years has been the turn to discourse in both sociology (Jackson, 1993) and discursive psychology (Harré, 1986). The latter has attempted to shift the study of emotions towards a study of the words that different cultures have developed for emotional states. It is these 'emotional vocabularies' that are thought to give the cultural meaning to emotion states and, thus, prescribe what we are to feel in certain cultural contexts. Although this contribution has been highly valuable to the debate on emotion, discursive psychology tends to play down the bodily aspect of emotion, that is, the role of *feeling* as something other than simply a secondary phenomena produced by discourse. Because of this, discourse theory cannot fully explain the ambivalence of human feeling where emotions conflict or are not always the ones prescribed for that particular cul-tural context. Also, it cannot explain the common experience of not being able to put our feelings into words: that is, of knowing we are feeling something, yet not being quite sure exactly what emotion we are experiencing. Feeling and emotion words, then, do not always correspond and this is how we can use irony, wit and sarcasm. What we must do is to outline what I believe to be the complex relationship between feeling and emotion, for the two are not always identical even though they are interrelated.

This means, however, that just as feeling and emotion cannot be reduced to the body, nor can they be explained only in terms of discourse. Here, I want to extend my earlier work on the relational context of emotion (Burkitt, 1997) in which I claimed that emotions are best thought of as complexes. That is, emotions have meaning only in the context of relations, involving active bodily states or feelings and the speech genres through which we attempt to articulate those feelings. Emotions are complexes because they are products of both the body and discourse yet are reducible to neither. Indeed, I will try to show here how language use is itself, in part, a bodily phenomenon based in the utterance. However, this leads to a larger point that I want to make, which is that emotion is composed of *both* the material and the ideal—of both matter and meaning within the context of cultural relations. Because of this, body and mind, emotion and consciousness must also be seen as interrelated phenomena, the one contained within the other.

First, though, I want to elaborate upon the distinction between feeling and emotion in the context of social relations.

Social relations and structures of feelings

Raymond Williams (1977) has talked of 'structures of feeling' to indicate the sense people have of changing social meanings and values as they are actively lived and felt in the present moment. With this concept he does not want to indicate the social in the past tense as already stabilized institutions and ideologies about which people have clearly formed ideas. It is because we always think of the social in this way, in the past tense as already formed 'structures', that we begin to divorce the social from the personal, which is something we regard as being lived in the present moment. By 'structures of feeling' Williams is indicating the sense of changing meanings and values by which people act in the present moment, in a social context that is not ossified but is a continuous and living present. Here, meanings and values are not stable and fixed but are in a constant process of change and modification, so that while people may not have clear ideas about the way these meanings and values are changing they nevertheless 'feel' this in their social relations. As Williams says,

> We are talking about characteristic elements of impulse, restraint, and tone; specifically affective elements of consciousness and relationships: not feeling against thought, but thought as felt and feeling as thought: practical consciousness of a present kind, in a living and interrelating continuity (1977: 132).

Here, Williams is attempting to indicate that consciousness can only ever be disengaged from actual, present social reality in part, as when we look back on the past from a distance in time. In this mode, consciousness is reflective consciousness that can see itself and its society from the distance of time, if only a few moments. With a time lapse, society and self appear as objects: clearly formed substances on which one can reflect. In the present moment, however, consciousness is engaged and practical: it does not have the luxury of the distance of time and is not working with clearly formed ideas of self and society as objective entities. Working in the fluidity of the present where things are changing, practical consciousness is guided more by the feeling of its changing circumstances, *specifically affective elements of consciousness and relationships*. That is, the way the relational context calls out actions marked by impulse or restraint. Clearly, when acting on feeling we are aware of what we are doing, so we cannot say that feeling and thought are two separate elements, hence the reference to thought as felt and feeling as thought. Even though we may not clearly articulate what we are feeling as a specific emotion, we can still think what we feel in the sense of being aware of, and being guided by, a feeling or feelings. Here, feeling is not named as a specific emotion for, instead, we are working in that state which Bateson indicated, where we are aware of the patterns of relationship and their emotional push and pull on us. We are therefore aware of the patterns of relationship as a structure of feeling located by our bodily engagement in the social world.

Williams is not trying to divorce present from past and to say that the conception of society and self as objective is a false idea. He wants to account for the influence of the past in terms of social formation and ideology and the pressures these exert on us in the present. Humans never act as a blank slate, even when we act impulsively, as our actions are always connected in some way to the past. The present moment, too, soon becomes the past, and we make sense of it by connecting it to what we already know, articulating it in relation to some already formed ideology. While that ideology may be changed in the process, past and present are linked in a continuity of practical consciousness and discursive or ideological articulation of the structures of feeling. Nevertheless, the feeling of an open and fluid present is an important moment in the social process.

What this emphasizes is the importance of structures of feeling in guiding actions within the context of social relations. We may be aware of the patterns of relationship more by a common structure of feeling than by ideas and conceptions. In this state such feelings may be taken as private or idiosyncratic because they have not yet received social articulation. Yet when they do, as often happens in literature or other art forms, we can recognize the communality to our structures of feeling. For my purposes here, however, what this shows is that we can sense a structure of feeling before we can consciously articulate this as composed of specific emotions. We could say, then, that feeling is part of practical consciousness and involves the way we can act within our social world through a sense of what has to be done. Emotion, however, belongs to discursive consciousness and involves the way we articulate these feelings through what Harré called emotional vocabularies. Through such vocabularies, we reflect on our feelings and identify some as specific emotions. This makes sense of the claim once made by George Herbert Mead that emotion does not appear in the instant moment of active bodily engagement. For us to identify a feeling as an emotion there has to be a delay between the impulse and the action it calls forth, a space for reflection in which we can identify the impulse or feeling as an emotion. Having said this, feeling and emotion are intimately connected. We could say, paraphrasing Vygotsky's ideas on the relation between thought and words (1987: 250), that feeling is not expressed but completed in the word as emotion. This means that feeling is restructured as it is articulated consciously through words as an emotion. It does not remain the same and is simply expressed in words: the feeling goes through a transformation as it finds utterance in words—it becomes like an object that can be reflected upon. It is at this point that emotion finds its form in words in a seemingly objective or substantial form, rather than as the patterns of relationship. In this sense also, words for emotions may not entirely exhaust feeling, especially in conditions of rapidly changing contexts of practical activity. Here, there may often be the sense that we cannot fully express in official language, or even in the less formal aspects of the emotional vocabulary, what exactly we are feeling. This sense may remain vague and amorphous until a new vocabulary emerges that seems more appropriate.

All this, of course, raises the issue of the relation between discursive thought, feeling, and emotion. Vygotsky (1987) has made a significant contribution to the debate around this issue by claiming that there exists a dynamic, meaningful system of the psyche which constitutes a unity of affective and intellectual process. In this system the affective-volitional sphere is at the base of thought, producing and directing it. Some motive that is directed towards its own realization always stands behind thought (Vygotsky, 1987: 282). For Vygotsky, motive is composed of inclinations, needs, impulses, affect and emotion. A complex understanding of another's thought only emerges when we discover its real affective-volitional basis. This can be discovered like the emotional-volitional subtext of a role in a play, through interpretation of the part a character is playing. Here, Vygotsky draws a parallel with the work of the Russian drama teacher, Stanislavskii, who argued that for an actor fully to realize their part in a play, they must uncover the affective-volitional core that motivates the character they are playing. Vygotsky illustrates how we may interpret the affective-volitional motivation of a person by analysing the feelings that lie behind the verbal expressions of the characters in a play, an excerpt of which is reproduced below. Note how, given what we said earlier, the feelings that lie behind the expression of the three characters in the excerpt below evolve from the patterns of relationship in which they are enmeshed. It seems that in this scene, a young lady and her maid are welcoming the young lady's suitor, about whom she has ambiguous feelings.

Text of the play	*Parallel feelings*
Sophia: Oh Chatskii, I am glad to see you.	Wants to hide her confusion.
Chatskii: You're glad. That's good. Though can one who becomes glad in this way be sincere? It seems to me that in the end, people and horses are shivering, and I have pleased only myself.	Wants to appeal to her conscience through mockery. Aren't you ashamed! Wants to elicit openness.

Liza: But, sir, had you been behind the door, not five minutes ago, you'd have heard us speak of you, Miss, tell him yourself!	Wants to calm Chatskii and to help Sophia in a difficult situation.
Sophia: It is always so—not only now. You cannot reproach me so.	Wants to calm Chatskii. I am guilty of nothing!
Chatskii: Let us assume it is so. Blessed is the one who believes, and warms his life.	Let us cease this conversation.

(Vygotsky, 1987: 282–83).

In this scene, typical of human interactions, not only do the feelings involved emerge from the relations between the characters—a young lady and a male admirer, her servant trying to help her in a difficult situation, while both are trying to calm and placate a man of, perhaps, some importance—, but also the spoken sentiments do not correspond with what the person is actually feeling. The young lady says she is glad to see Chatskii when actually her feelings are, to say the least, ambiguous, if not the opposite of being glad. Chatskii picks this up either through the intonation in the way she speaks her words or through her body language. In other words, her physical demeanour gives away her true feelings. Chatskii responds to this in kind, through sarcasm: 'you're glad, that's good', a statement obviously made with such an intonation that it communicates he has picked up on her confusion. So each character is reading behind the vocal expression of emotion to the feelings communicated in the person's whole way of being: not just their verbal expressions but also their physical being.

As Bakhtin (1986) has pointed out, the words in an emotional vocabulary or 'speech genre' are neutral in terms of the feeling aspect of emotion. Even a word such as 'joy', which carries the meaning of happiness, can be used to the contrary depending on the expressive intonation it is given, as in the phrase 'any joy is now only bitterness to me' (Bakhtin, 1986: 87). Expressive intonation does not, then, have to follow the meaning of the word itself: in fact, it can be juxtaposed against that meaning as in irony, sarcasm or wit. Here we can see how emotion is a complex in which the feeling or expressive intonation with which words or phrases are said is used as a counterpoint to discursive meaning, creating the full spectrum of emotion. Emotion, then, is not found in discourse alone, for there has to be an expressive, feeling element behind the words and thoughts. The emotion vocabulary and the discursive consciousness it creates complete the emotional experience, but do not entirely construct it. And the feelings are expressive of patterns of relations rather than inner causal forces. Again, to take another example from Bakhtin, the expression 'he's dead' exclaims shock at the news of someone's death and can be tinged with sadness or gladness depending on one's relationship with the newly deceased. Here, expressive intonation comes from the feelings that stem from the nature of the relationship, ones that emerge first of all in practical consciousness and are then completed in discursive consciousness.

However, words themselves can also function at the level of practical consciousness. In speech, utterances can be expressions of immediate feelings when language functions in its practical aspect. As Merleau-Ponty (1962: 180) remarked, once we have learnt a language it is enough that we possess its articulatory and acoustic style as one of the modulations, one of the possible uses of our body. Language thus functions as an element of practical as well as discursive consciousness: while it largely constructs discursive consciousness it comes to substitute for the more natural elements involved in practical consciousness, such as an exclamation replacing a cry as an expression of pain. This does not mean that practical consciousness is not fully socialized, only that it is not wholly discursively constructed. There remains about it something of the practically engaged, non-reflexive bodily belonging to the world.

Images and emotions

The idea of Vygotsky and his followers, that emotion is a complex process involving both affective and intellectual elements, can be traced back to the influence on his thinking of the philosopher, Spinoza (1677/1973). He is also important for illustrating how emotion emerges in a relational context. For Spinoza, emotions are understood as modifications of the body by which its power for action is either increased or diminished (Brown and Stenner, 2001: 89; Spinoza, 1677/1973: E.III def. 3). At the same time, emotion also involves the idea of these modifications and how they affect the body. However, such modifications only occur in relation to other bodies, human or non-human, so that 'affects are emergent orderings of the relational field made up in the encounter between manifold finite beings' (Brown and Stenner, 2001: 89). In this way, Spinoza firmly establishes emotions as emergent within relations, encounters and action. This is also tied to power relations in the social field, for Spinoza identifies two basic affects— euphoria and dysphoria. Euphoria is felt whenever the body experiences an increase in its power in an encounter with another body. Here, the modification of the body occurs in such a way as to increase its capacity for action. On the other hand, dysphoria is felt whenever the body experiences a decrease in its power for action in an encounter with another body. So the more positive feelings and emotions such as joy or ecstatic happiness will stem from euphoria, while the more negative ones such as sorrow or sadness will come from dysphoria. Either way, the emotion is part and parcel of the emergent orderings of the relational field (Brown and Stenner, 2001: 89). We will return to the issue of power relations and the emotions in the last section here.

However, Spinoza also includes in the affects of the orderings of the relational field the modifications brought about on the body by the *images* of other bodies (human and non-human), so that emotions are not simply tied to the immediate encounter. They can be stirred just as much by the image of absent bodies, or by fantasized and, thus, imaginary bodies. Through these images the body becomes disposed for acting in a particular way. Thus, Spinoza links '*being affected* (through the image) and the *capacity to affect* (as the result of modifications)' (Brown and Stenner, 2001: 91). We are, then, affected by other people and things, or by their image, and the affectation the encounter stirs also increases or diminishes our powers of action. Like G.H. Mead, Spinoza understands that human interaction involves not only being affected by others and acting on that affect, but that the subsequent action also affects the others in the relation and, in turn, spurs them to further action. Spinoza, though, also takes account of the power of the image in this process and, like Vygotsky, considers the way in which thought—in this case, in the form of a mental image—and emotion are always part of a system. As Brown and Stenner put it,

> All encounters, even those where only the image is actually present, lead to modifications and determinations for action. The euphoria resulting from an encounter with a loved thing, for example, configures the body as a lover disposed to love. All things may now be encountered according to this *sympathetic* disposition (2001: 94).

Roland Barthes (1990) elaborates on this idea in his book on love, in which he refers to the 'image repertoire' and its role in the emotions. Only in Barthes' account the love of which he writes is unrequited, so instead of the image-repertoire in which the loved other is caught up causing the lover euphoria, the images of the loved one bring only pain. The lover is therefore not disposed to love but to loss and abandonment. Barthes shows us how, in love relations, the image-repertoire we all possess, which roughly defines our desire, circulates around actual bodies so that something in the other stirs our amorous feelings. That something may be vague and amorphous, just as the image-repertoire may not be a clearly defined set of images available to consciousness. Yet something about another human body appeals to us, arouses us, so that fragments of the body are assembled into an overall picture that enchants us and seems to bring into clear focus the object of our desire. The body of the other, therefore, is literally idealized through the image-repertoire. Driven by the image-repertoire, which finds expression in other bodies yet itself remains unattainable as a complete abstract picture, we find ourselves at the limit of language because the image-repertoire can never become a concept or tangible image open to linguistic articulation. What we *feel*, then, often remains an enigma for us.

> Herein a great enigma, to which I shall never possess the key: Why is it that I desire So-and-so? Why is it that I desire So-and-so lastingly, longingly? Is it the whole of So-and-so I desire (a silhouette, a shape, a mood)? And in that case, what is it in this loved body which has the vocation of a fetish for me? What perhaps incredulously tenuous portion—what accident? The way a nail is cut, a tooth broken slightly aslant, a lock of hair, a way of spreading the fingers while talking, while smoking? About all these *folds* of the body, I want to say that they are *adorable*. *Adorable* means: this is my desire, insofar as it is unique: 'That's it! That's it exactly (which I love)!' Yet the more I experience the specialty of my desire, the less I can give it a name . . . Of this failure of language, there remains only one trace: the word 'adorable' (Barthes, 1990: 20).

Here we see how fragments of the material body of the other are reassembled through the image-repertoire into an idealized whole that becomes the loved other. We then feel fascination and enchantment with the other and, as literal words fail us, we cast around for the metaphors for love. Usually, we define love and our fascination with the other in terms of magic: we are under someone's spell, entranced. Except, of course, when love is unrequited, as in Barthes' fragments of the lover's discourse, in which case the images that are stirred are ones of abandonment (like the lone figure walking along a windswept, deserted beach) and the feelings are of grief, even suicide. The lover may actually torment himself with the very images that stir jealousy, abandonment, and despair. In this case the love that the lover feels for another disposes them to sorrow rather than joy, so that 'any joy is now only bitterness to me'. Fragments of our own bodies get drawn into these metaphors and feelings, to the extent that the body itself feels the emotion as a physical sensation. The metaphor of giving love is of giving our heart to another and, when our love is unrequited, we feel the gift has been unaccepted, our hearts thrown away or broken. With this comes the sensation of a breaking, aching, or heavy heart. One of the unrequited lovers who surfaces in the fragments of Barthes' text finds himself going on a trip for a few weeks and at the last moment wants to buy a watch. In the shop, 'the clerk simpers at him: "Would you like mine? You would have been a little boy when they cost what this one did," etc.; she doesn't know that *my heart is heavy within me*' (Barthes, 1990: 53).

However, whether love is requited or unrequited it is nevertheless the same manifestation, only the dispositions, actions, and sentiments are different depending on whether the other reciprocates. Even if the loved one is won over, they and our love for them remain an enigma. As Barthes says, we can *reflect* on the images provoked by the love relation, but this never turns into *reflexivity*. When we are 'in' love, our reflection is immediately absorbed in the mulling over of images, but these never turn into a concept of love through which we could try to analyse and understand the image-repertoire or what fuels it. 'Hence, discourse on love though I may for years at a time, I cannot hope to seize the concept of it except "by the tail": by flashes, formulas, surprises of expression, scattered through the great stream of the Image-repertoire' (Barthes, 1990: 59). However, not only can we not discover love and desire 'in' ourselves, we cannot discover it 'in' the body of the other.

> I am searching the other's body, as if the mechanical cause of my desire were in the adverse body (I am like those children who take a clock apart in order to find out what time it is) (Barthes, 1990: 71).

It is as mistaken to look for our desire in the body of the other as it is to look for time inside a clock because, like all emotions and feelings, love and desire are not 'in' the body of self or other: they stem from the relations between two or more people and are reflected in the feelings, metaphors and images those relationships provoke. What we need to explain now are how relations are expressed in images. We also need to examine what Barthes insinuates but never explains: the 'force' that compels the lover's action and discourse. Maybe that force is in the relation with the loved one, yet we still need to think about the way in which an image-repertoire develops and how it becomes charged with erotic energy.

Feeling, metaphor, image

What I am arguing so far is that feeling and emotion only appear in the pattern of relations us humans establish between ourselves, and also in the relation between us (as a social group) and our world. In these webs of relationships human and non-human bodies interact and modify one another. These modifications are the feelings we have about our connections to other people and things in our world and how they affect us. Within our cultures we develop different emotion vocabularies to name these different feelings. Yet the emotion we verbally express is not necessarily what we 'feel' and it is also possible to have a clash of feelings, an ambiguity that is hard to express verbally. In addition, as established patterns of social relations change, we may have a feeling or sense of how the social world is changing that we cannot exactly put into words and it is left to artists, political groups, or social scientists, to give expression and cultural form to these feelings. Words and images can then come to express or represent (in the sense of 'stand for' rather than exactly replicate the nature of) these feelings. But now the question is, how can humans—whether they be artists, members of political groups, social scientists, or everyday actors—turn their feelings about relationships into images that seem to express something of those relations? And how does the body figure in this, so that we can actually feel what takes form in images and words as bodily sensations associated with the emotion?

First of all, in any relation between humans or, for that matter, between humans and other animals, there always occurs some form of communication that expresses or, as Bateson (1963) puts it, seeks to 'define the contingencies of that relationship'. Bateson seems to be using the term 'contingency' here in the sense that each relationship, although containing elements that we can all recognize, is uniquely contingent upon time, probability, the actions of the related participants in the encounter, and other peculiar orderings of that encounter. In these encounters the bodies of the various related persons are affected by the actions of the others and these affects are communicated as what psychologists have traditionally called 'signals of state'. However, Bateson chooses to refer to these signals as 'definitions of the contingencies of relationship' (1963: 233). That is because the body-state, which serves as a signal to others in the relationship, is not just a response to the encounter, as behavioural psychology would have it: it is also a way of defining the relationship and thus eliciting certain appropriate actions from others. Bateson illustrates this with an example of the interaction between a cat and its owner.

When I open the refrigerator door, the cat comes and rubs against my leg stating some variant of the proposition 'meow'. To say that she is asking for milk may be correct, but it is not a literal translation from her language into ours. I suggest that more literally we should translate her message as 'be mamma'. She is trying to define the contingencies of relationship. She is inviting me to accept those contingencies and to act in accordance with them. She may step down somewhat from this high abstract level by indicating urgency—'be mamma now'; or she may achieve a certain correctness by ostensive communication 'be mamma now in regard to that jug'; but, in its primary structure, her communication is archaic and highly abstract in the sense that its prime subject matter is always relationship (1963: 233).

For Bateson, the metaphoric language of dreams is intermediate between the relational language of the cat and the objective language we use consciously to complete our feelings and thoughts (thought, of course, being motivated by feeling and so constantly interrelated with it). In dreams, for example, we define relationships with an utter disregard for the relata. In this case, the communication of feelings can be metaphorical, which explains how some feelings can remain unconscious or beyond consciousness: they may not be expressible in words or there may be resistance to their verbal, conscious articulation. This was the case with Sophia, the character in the play quoted previously, who felt unable to express her feelings of unease or ambiguity at the appearance of Chatskii, a would-be suitor.

Yet how is the human body capable of such metaphoric communication, in which relations are felt as physical sensations in the body, which can be transposed into images and language, or hidden therein? And how can it be, as Bateson indicated in the quotation that opened this essay, that the words which express patterns of relationship are experienced as referring to things in themselves—substances or forces?

Again, all this is due to the power of metaphor and the central role of the human body in producing metaphoric understanding and meaning. As Mark Johnson (1987) argues, human meaning is originally non-propositional and preconceptual, which is to say that meaning is not a primary product of any of the discourses of human cultures. While our discourses obviously create meaning they do not contain within them the *possibility* of meaning, of humans creating meaning out of our active relations to one other and to the world in which we are embedded. Indeed, Johnson argues that a more primary form of meaning can be found in what he calls the 'image-schematic structures' through which it is possible for humans to have coherent experiences that we can understand. Discursive meaning is therefore only one level or one dimension of meaning in the broader sense, rather than the primary aspect of meaning it is often taken to be in the social sciences today. Instead, discursive meaning is an elaboration of embodied human potentials that make possible and give depth and resonance to human meaning in all its different dimensions. These embodied potentials are realized first of all as image-schemata, which are not pictures of the world (although as Merleau-Ponty (1968) understood, vision may well be a primary aspect of human perception, along with the other senses, that contain within them the structures of thought), but are instead patterns of embodied motor activities that give a meaningful structure to physical experience. Here, I would say that such 'images' are felt rather than consciously reflected upon, just as we may know our way around a city by the feel of where we are located and the direction we need to take to reach our destination, rather than by a consciously visualized map 'in our heads'.

One of the key aspects of the image-schemata that reflects the way in which we, as humans, interrelate with our world, is the impression of force. As Johnson says,

> Take the concept of *physical force* as it operates in the 'physical appearance is a physical force' metaphor. Though we forget it so easily, the meaning of 'physical force' depends on publicly shared meaning structures that emerge from our *bodily experience* of force. We begin to grasp the meaning of physical force from the day we are born (or even before). We have bodies that are acted upon by 'external' and 'internal' forces such as gravity, light, heat, wind, bodily processes, and the obtrusion of other physical objects. Such interactions constitute our first encounters with forces, and they reveal patterned recurring relations between ourselves and our environment. Such patterns develop as meaning structures through which our world begins to exhibit a measure of coherence, regularity, and intelligibility (1987: 13).

Soon we realize that we, too, can be sources of force on our own bodies and on other objects. We can manipulate objects in a way that feels as though we are centres of force and develop patterns for interacting forcefully with our world.

> We encounter obstacles that exert force on us, and we find that we can exert force in going around, over, or through those objects that resist us. Sometimes we are frustrated, defeated, and impotent in our forceful action. Other times we are powerful and successful. In each of these motor activities there are repeatable patterns that come to identify that particular forceful action (Johnson, 1987: 13).

We can then employ this sense, this feeling of being in the world in an active and interrelated way, to other relations that do not have forceful origins. We can talk about sexual relations as driven by a force, so that we are propelled along by an 'inner drive' or attracted by a desired other by a compulsion so powerful it is experienced as a 'force'. Johnson examines the explanations offered by men who have raped women and finds this metaphor constantly at work in their explanations:[1] that the appearance of the woman was a 'force' so powerful they were compelled in their actions. Thus he talks of the idea of 'physical appearance as a physical force'. What Johnson is showing so clearly is how the body is modified in its interrelations and interactions with other people and objects, creating a basis for an understanding of the world. This image-schemata is a felt, embodied understanding of the world which is open to re-articulation in images and words. But this process operates metaphorically where one symbol, an image or a word, stands for something other—a feeling or bodily understanding; an 'image' in another sense of that word. So our sense of bodily modification, of being affected by and affecting other people and things, can give meaning to the concept of force. As Johnson (1987: 14) remarks, the 'feeling' of what force means could be described as its 'emotive meaning'. So, as regards the notion of sexuality as a force, 'we are not talking about an emotional overlay on, or response to, some core concept of sexuality but rather about bodily and imaginative structures of attitude, rhythm, pattern of interaction, sense of pressure, and so forth, that are constitutive of sexual force' (Johnson, 1987: 14). Thus, the bodily understanding of force, its feeling, infuses the discursive meanings of a culture and informs our emotive understandings of a range of experiences; from sexuality as force or drive, compelled by 'internal' or 'external' forces, to the sense of 'I can' which gives emotional meaning to most of our verbs. Similarly, notions of forces or pressures being 'internal' or 'external' is central to the human embodied experience of the skin around the skeletal-muscular structure as a barrier or container, but also as the sensitive membrane that connects us through touch to everything 'outside' of us. The experience of being inside and outside various structures and containers also extends this image-schemata.

This all points to what Johnson has highlighted above; that schemata are recurrent relations between humans, or between humans and their environment, which structures our ongoing ordering activities and creates the possibility of making these relations meaningful. At base, these structures are not clear pictures or linguistic propositions but the ordering relations which are experienced primarily as feelings. Some of the names referring to feelings also refer as clearly to the recurring relations, such as dependency, hostility and trust. Others refer more specifically to what the relation makes us feel, defining them as emotions such as love, jealousy, fear or anger. And many metaphors refer to the bodily feelings associated with the emotion, such as 'bursting' with love, 'insane' with jealousy, 'struck down' or 'paralysed' with fear, and 'boiling' with anger.

However, what is also interesting about this idea is that for the image-schemata to become truly meaningful, they must be based on *recurring patterns of relations* between us as humans and our world. In this sense they are like the habits as described by Dewey (1922/1983) or the concept of *habitus* as developed by Mauss (1935/1973) and Bourdieu (1977; 1990). They are the structuring structures that make it possible for the world to be intelligible to us while, at the same time, configuring our bodies as disposed to certain feelings and actions. These feelings themselves may become habitual so that it is possible for certain people to produce patterns of responses to situations that tend to characterize them. So some people may be regarded as quick to anger, while others are seen as generally 'laid-back'; some may be regarded as disposed to jealousy, whereas others are more aloof. As Buddhists often point out, such emotions can begin to dominate our thoughts, locking them into habitual ways of perceiving the world that prevent more open perceptions of our present encounters and contexts. However, what is important to note is that emotional dispositions are not automatic: as Dewey says with respect to habits, each person has many different habits and dispositions, some more latent than others, and any number can be called out in a particular encounter. Thus, different habits can clash, making it so that although each one of us may be characterized by certain dispositions to action, it is impossible to predict with certainty how we will respond in any context. And thought is always called upon in such instances to interpret both the situation and our contradictory feelings about it. Again, thought and emotion cannot be separated, as they work together in the interpretation of our social situation and our world.

Patterned recurring relations, then, develop as meaning structures through which we understand the world. These are perceptible primarily as a bodily sense of being in the world through movement, touch, vision, and all the other senses. These bodily structures are *felt* through patterns of action largely shaped by the customs and habits of the social group, and interpreted in a symbolic way through metaphor; by deploying the symbols and signs of the group to form images that can 'stand for' or represent the bodily senses. Emotion is a complex formed from these different elements, in which bodily feelings take on more consciously articulated form as specific emotions.

However, what is left out in this explanation is how our relations to others and to the world are marked by power. It is rare to find a relation that does not have some element of power in it, whether it is our claims about the 'mastery' of nature, of harnessing her powers, or understanding the formation of the universe, or whether it is the attempts of a state to alter the behaviour patterns of its citizens, or the struggles and compromises of two people living as a couple. In all relations we find some element of power and so, if my thesis here is correct, we will find power as a key aspect of emotion. The question now is how can we see power at work in feelings and emotions, as well as in the symbols and metaphors used to represent them?

Relations of power and the emotions

I think that one of the clearest examples we have of power working as patterned relations that structure action is in the later works of Foucault (1979; 1982). He has described power as:

> a total structure of actions brought to bear upon possible actions: it incites, it induces, it seduces, it makes easier or more difficult: in the extreme it constrains or forbids absolutely; it is nevertheless always a way of acting upon an acting subject or acting subjects by virtue of their acting or being capable of action. A set of actions upon other actions (Foucault, 1982: 220).

So power is not an action that imposes itself directly on another person by the very force of imposition: it works more subtly through social relations as a structure of actions that aims to *affect* a field of possible actions. What is also of interest to us here is that none of this would be possible without the emotions. As Spinoza noted, emotion is tied to the emergent ordering of the relational field in which one is likely to experience euphoria if the power of action of the body is increased or dysphoria if it is not. Looking at how Foucault describes the way power works as the affects of a structure of actions, it is said these incite, induce, or seduce. However, incitement, induction, or seduction would not be possible without the fact that human relations are always charged with emotion. In order to be incited one must be angered or provoked by the strategic action of others into a counter-attack or retaliation, an opposing strategy that seeks to counter the opponent's move. To be seduced, the structure of actions must lock into one's image-repertoire, producing feelings of desire for other persons, objects, or objectives. And to induce, the structure of action must inspire us or motivate us in some way, calling out a certain style of conduct from us. Thus Foucault argues that 'power is less a confrontation between two adversaries or the linking of one to the other than a question of government . . . it designate[s] the way in which the conduct of individuals or of groups might be directed' (1982: 221). Violence or struggle does not define power; instead its defining element is the modes or strategies of action that structure the possible field of action of others.

However, this can also work on a micro scale as well as on the macro scale. In our interactions, we can act with strategic affect towards the field of actions of others so that power relations are always to some extent reciprocal. As Bateson put it, we seek a definition of the contingencies of the relationship, in that through our actions and communications with others we seek to define the relation in the context of the encounter. We seek to define its parameters, its nature, and, in the process, the type of conduct we want to elicit from the other. Like the cat whose actions signalled 'play mamma', we are always engaged in processes of mutual incitement, inducement and seduction. As Foucault says, 'the exercise of power consists in guiding the possibility of conduct and putting in order the possible outcome' (Foucault, 1982: 221). This can apply as much on an interpersonal level as it can on an institutional or governmental level, although Foucault of course concentrated mainly on the latter. However, institutions are composed of human relations and governmental structures attempt to plug into them in order to shape conduct.

The way we understand these social relations of power and the way we feel they are affecting us is largely determined by the image-schemata that seem to make sense of our feelings and give them meaning. Thus, relations of power are often described as 'forces' working on us like the affects of a physical force such as gravity. This is a useful metaphor because power, as a relation, is unseen, just like gravity, yet both elements structure our possible actions. They enable and constrain our actions and movements in socio-physical space. Yet by working on the possible field of social action, power also seeks to influence our gestures and utterances, our feelings and thoughts. While the metaphor of 'force' may not be useful in understanding the relational origins of power, it does make meaningful and tangible its affects upon us. In an earlier publication, Foucault himself cannot help but make constant reference to 'force' when talking of power relations: thus, power needs to be understood 'as the multiplicity of force relations immanent in the sphere in which they operate and which constitute their own organization' (1979: 92–93): and power is to be located in 'a moving substrate of force relations' (1979: 93). While this view may have been modified somewhat in the later works, it shows how humans find meaning in bodily metaphors that help to make sense of both physical and social affects working upon us. This is the way in which we make sense of the structures of feelings about the ever-changing social formations in which we live, through the metaphors that come to represent these feelings and make possible their social articulation.

If emotions are complexes that express our whole way of being—our physical and discursive life, our material and ideal presences and absences—then it is hardly surprising that power relations and emotions are also inimical. But this opens up a whole new research area for sociologists—the emotional dynamics of power relations.

Notes

1 Tim Beneke (1982) *Men On Rape.* New York: St. Martins Press.

References

Bakhtin, Mikhail M. (1986) *Speech Genres and Other Late Essays.* Tr. V.W. McGee. Austin: University of Texas Press.
Barthes, Roland (1990) *A Lover's Discourse: Fragments.* London: Penguin.
Bateson, Gregory (1963) 'A Social Scientist Views the Emotions', in P. Knapp (ed.), *Expression of the Emotions in Man.* New York: International University Press.
Bateson, Gregory (1973) *Steps to an Ecology of Mind: Collected Essays in Anthropology, Psychiatry, Evolution and Epistemology.* St. Albans: Paladin.
Bourdieu, Pierre (1977) *Outline of a Theory of Practice.* Cambridge: Cambridge University Press.
Bourdieu, Pierre (1990) *The Logic of Practice.* Cambridge: Polity Press.
Brown, S.D. and Stenner, P. (2001) 'Being Affected: Spinoza and the Psychology of Emotion', *International Journal of Group Tensions*, Vol. 30, No. 1, 81–105.
Butkitt, Ian (1997) 'Social Relationships and Emotions', *Sociology*, Vol. 31, No. 1, 37–55.
Dewey, John (1922/1983) *Human Nature and Conduct.* Illinois: Southern Illinois University Press.
Foucault, Michel (1979) *The History of Sexuality*, Volume One. London: Penguin.
Foucault, Michel (1982) 'The Subject and Power', in H.L. Dreyfus and P. Rabinow, *Michel Foucault: Beyond Structuralism and Hermeneutics.* Brighton: Harvester.
Harré, Rom (ed.) (1987) *The Social Construction of Emotions.* Oxford: Blackwell.
Jackson, Stevi (1993) 'Even Sociologists Fall in Love: An Exploration of the Sociology of Emotions', *Sociology*, Vol. 27, 210–20.
Johnson, Mark (1987) *The Body in the Mind: The Bodily Basis of Meaning, Imagination, and Reason.* Chicago: Chicago University Press.
Mauss, Marcel (1935/1973) 'Techniques of the Body', *Economy and Society*, Vol. 2, No. 1, 71–88.
Merleau-Ponty, Maurice (1962) *Phenomenology of Perception.* Tr. C. Smith. London: Routledge.
Merleau-Ponty, Maurice (1968) *The Visible and the Invisible.* Evanston: Northwestern University Press.
Sabini, J. and Silver, M. (1982) *Moralities of Everyday Life.* Oxford: Oxford University Press.

Spinoza, B. (1677/1993) *Ethics and Treatise on the Correction of the Intellect*. (Trans. A. Boyle). London: J.M. Dent.

Styron, William (1992) *Darkness Visible: A Memoir of Madness*. New York: Random House.

Vygotsky, Lev S. (1987) 'Thinking and Speech', in R.W. Rieber and A.S. Carton (eds), *The Collected Works of L.S. Vygotsky: Volume 1. Problems of General Psychology*. New York: Plenum Press.

Williams, Raymond (1977) *Marxism and Literature*. Oxford: Oxford University Press.

Notes on contributors

Jack Barbalet is an Australian sociologist, currently Professor of Sociology at the University of Leicester, where he is Head of Department. He has written extensively on political sociology, sociological theory, and the sociology of emotions. His most recent book is *Emotion, Social Theory, and Social Structure: A Macrosociological Approach* (Cambridge University Press, 2001). He is editor of the *Journal of Classical Sociology*.

Mabel Berezin is Associate Professor of Sociology at Cornell University. She is a comparative historical sociologist whose work explores the intersection of political and cultural institutions with an emphasis on modern and contemporary Europe. She is the author of *Making the Fascist Self: The Political Culture of Inter-war Italy* (1997) as well as numerous articles, review essays and contributions to edited volumes. She has edited two collaborative volumes: *Democratic Culture: Ethnos and Demos in Global Perspective* and *Re-mapping Europe: Territory, Membership and Identity in a Transnational Age* (forthcoming, Johns Hopkins University Press). She is working on a project, When Democracy Produces Its Opposite: A Comparative Study of European Populist Politics, that aims to explore how security as a political emotion contributes to a disjuncture between democratic practices and sentiments.

Charlotte Bloch is Associate Professor of Cultural Sociology at the Department of Sociology, University of Copenhagen. She has researched and published in a number of areas of sociology, including education and social class, the problematics of everyday life, unemployment and the life course, quality of life, emotions of everyday life, and emotions and the emotional culture of Academia. Her most recent book, in Danish, is *Flow og Stress* (2001); its subtitle translates in English as 'Moods and the Culture of Feelings in Everyday Life'. Her research is presently focussed on the sociology of emotions.

Ian Burkitt is a Senior Lecturer in Sociology and Social Psychology at the University of Bradford. His research interests include the social context of self-identity, embodiment, and emotion. He has previously published an article on the subject of emotion (Social Relationships and Emotions,

Sociology, Vol. 31, No. 1, 1997) and is the author of the books *Social Selves: Theories of the Social Formation of Personality* (Sage, 1991) and *Bodies of Thought: Embodiment Identity and Modernity* (Sage, 1999).

Helena Flam received her Fil.Kand from the University of Lund, Sweden, and her Ph.D. from Columbia University, New York. She was a co-founding researcher at the Swedish Collegium for Advanced Study in the Social Sciences, fellow at the Max Planck Institute in Köln and assistant professor at the University of Konstanz. Since 1993 she has been Professor of Sociology at the University of Leipzig. Among her publications are *Mosaic of Fear: Poland and East Germany before 1989* (Columbia University Press, 1998). Her early contributions to the sociology of emotions were collected in *The Emotional 'Man' and the Problem of Collective Action* (Peter Lang, 2000). Universitätsverlag Konstanz will publish her introductory text on the sociology of emotions this year.

Theodore D. Kemper has worked for more than 30 years in the sociology of emotions, contributing the first book-length treatment in the field, *A Social Interactional Theory of Emotions* (Wiley, 1978) and numerous articles on the subject. The central thesis of his work is that most human emotions result from outcomes of social relations, understood as occurring in two main dimensions, namely power and status. He has also examined social relations as both precursors and successors of testosterone secretion in both males and females in *Social Structure and Testosterone: Explorations of the Socio-Bio-Social Chain* (Rutgers University Press, 1990). He is currently Professor of Sociology (Ret.) at St. John's University, New York.

Jocelyn Pixley is a Senior Lecturer in the School of Sociology, University of New South Wales, Sydney. Her major publications are in economic sociology; they include *Citizenship and Employment: Investigating Post-Industrial Options* (Cambridge University Press, 1993) and, with Michael Bittman, *The Double Life of the Family* (Allen & Unwin, 1997), as well as numerous articles on social and economic policy. She is presently writing a book on her research on emotions in finance, to be published by Cambridge University Press.

Chris Shilling is Professor of Sociology at the University of Portsmouth. He has published extensively in the areas of social theory and the body, and in sociological theory, and his work has been translated widely. His recent books include *The Body and Social Theory* (Sage/TCS, 1993), *Re-forming the Body: Religion, Community and Modernity* (Sage/TCS, 1997, with Philip A. Mellor), and *The Sociological Ambition: Elementary Forms of Social and Moral Life* (Sage/TCS, 2001, with Philip A. Mellor). He is currently writing a book entitled *The Body in Culture, Technology and Society* with Sage Press.

Index